CREA

YOUR OWN

FLORIDA
FOOD
FOREST

CREATE
YOUR OWN
FLORIDA
FOOD
FOREST

Massively Revised, Super Expanded,
and *Lavishly Illustrated*
2nd Edition

DAVID
The GOOD

GOOD
BOOKS

Create Your Own Florida Food Forest
Florida Gardening Nature's Way
Massively Revised, Super Expanded, and Lavishly Illustrated 2nd Edition
David The Good

Good Books Publishing
goodbookspub.com

ISBN: 978-1-955289-09-2

Contents

Dedicated to my parents, Bill and Jenni.
See what you two started?

PREFACE
TO THE
2ND EDITION

Just over six years ago I wrote the first edition of *Create Your Own Florida Food Forest*. It was the first book I ever published, and was little more than an inspiring booklet that clocked in at less than 15,000 words total, yet it has sold over 6,000 copies, plus I gave away almost 2,000 copies and received many positive reviews from gardeners who were inspired by my ideas. It also contained the "Florida Gardening Cheatsheet" in the appendix, which ranked a wide range of edible plant species on a five-part scale ranging from "Totally Stupid Easy" to "Forget It." This appendix and the research it represented was later expanded into my exceptionally popular book *Totally Crazy Easy Florida Gardening*.

When I wrote the first edition of *Create Your Own Florida Food Forest*, my two Florida food forest projects in the north and south of the state were only a few years old. Now the North Florida food forest project is eleven years old and the South Florida food forest project is almost a decade old. Both have proven their worth and paid for themselves many times over, despite being grown on less-than-ideal soil with minimum care. At this point, I have an even better idea of what works and what doesn't, as well as how much neglect a Florida food forest can take and still be productive. This revised and expanded version takes a popular small booklet about the wonder of Florida food forests and expands it into a full, illustrated book on creating a food forest in Florida, no matter where you live in the state. You'll learn more about species, planning, tropical fruit tree options and how to grow more food for less work. I'll also cover ways to turn Florida sand into soil, as well as how to propagate and grow some of the most wonderful trees in the world.

On a personal note, since the publication of the first edition, my Dad, Bill Perry, passed away in a car accident while returning from visiting family and sharing the Gospel at a camp in Virginia. He was the co-creator of the Great South Florida Food Forest Project as well as my spiritual and writing mentor. I miss him greatly. As we built the food forest together, I got to see him shift from a landscape and lawn normie to a true forest gardener, enjoying the process of removing ornamentals and replacing them with fruit trees. Now his grandchildren are still enjoying the fruit from the trees we planted together, though we all miss Dad terribly. He died in the saddle, doing what he loved, and I know we will meet again in the perfect garden on the other side. The Great South Florida Food Forest Project is now tended by my mother Jennifer and my sisters Christi and Jessica, along with my sister Linda and her husband and children who send me regular updates on blooms and fruits along with pictures of my beautiful nieces and nephews picking mulberries.

In 2016 I sold my North Florida Food Forest Project to a fellow gardener and it is still growing in abundance, year after year. Then we moved to the island of Grenada and grew a wide variety of tropical crops, bought our own land and planted two tropical food forest projects. After the island was locked down and became less safe due to the Great Corona Crisis of 2020, we put our land up for sale and left in August, fully intending to move back to Florida. Instead, due to a long string of Providential appointments, we ended up just a few miles over the Florida border in the state of Alabama where we are now happily gardening on a few acres of awful, dead, grit. And yes—a food forest has already been started!

—As my food forest knowledge and experience has grown, it is time for this book to grow as well. Thanks to the help of Matt King, my production editor, as well as a talented collection of volunteer artists and the organizational work of my sister Christi, you now hold in your hands a complete illustrated manual for the creation and maintenance of food forests in Florida. This new edition expands on the ideas on the first edition and gives a much deeper look into the intricacies of a food forest while filling in the gaps of the first edition.

I am indebted to the work of other forest gardeners, such as Toby Hemenway, Geoff Lawton, Martin Crawford, Bill Mollison, David Holmgren and Robert Hart, as well as to the work and encouragement of my fellow Florida gardening friends including Curtiss Besley, the Singleton family, Mart Hale, Josh Jamison, Andi Houston, Craig Hepworth, Green Deane, Joshua Adler, Joe Pierce, Jo Leyte-Vidal, Kelly Carvallis and the Gainesville Gardening and Preparedness crew, Farah Chaffin, David Harold, Spyke's Grove Farm and Nursery, Carolyn Smith, the Stanley family, Blue Star Nursery, Eric Moulton, Chestnut Hill Tree Farm, Bill Hall, Dave and Guda Taylor, Oliver Moore, Grower Jim, Karen Hill, Allan Dovico, Cathy Bowers, the late John Starnes, and of course, all the Good Gardeners who continue to support my work. Julia Morton's books have also been a great help—I've collected them all in my library. Wish we could have met.

This new book is over five times the size of the original booklet. It now contains in-depth profiles on Florida food forest plants as well as my notes on how the ones I planted performed in my various projects.

Another exciting addition is the artwork. Thanks to the work of 52 artists from Florida and around the world, this book is not just a gardening book, it's a book of original art. Though I often do my own pen and ink illustrations, as in my book *Florida Survival Gardening* (in which I also had the assistance of my artistically minded children) it was fun to include outside illustrators and make it a gallery of creativity.

In the first edition I was more focused on the northern half of the state. Since then, I have done more work in South Florida as well as spent four years gardening in the equatorial tropics. This revised version reflects that experience and covers the more tropical half of Florida in depth as well as greatly expanding my previous writing on the northern half of the state.

May this new edition be a useful edition to your Florida gardening library.

INTRODUCTION

Imagine transforming your yard into a Garden of Eden. Fruit trees sway overhead, berries and flowers burst forth from the shade, and alongside soft paths sweet potato vines intertwine with passionfruit and native wildflowers. Through the air, bees and butterflies buzz and flutter, spreading pollen and beauty in their cheerful wake.

You can make this happen in a startlingly short period of time. You don't need to over-plan or over-think. Spacing isn't super important. You can start with seeds, cuttings or potted trees. You can even plant a decent food forest just by visiting your local international market and collecting seeds and roots to grow.

Your limitation is your imagination. Florida wants to grow forests. Before development and clearing, our region was a verdant jungle—a land of lush foliage and beautiful flowers. We can create that flowering jungle again and tailor it to serve us by growing plants and trees that provide food, beauty, wildlife habitat, building materials and fuel.

In a food forest your garden stretches into the sky. No more fighting with infertile sand and nematode-knotted tomato roots in a sandy patch of sun-burned ground that eats compost like a sinkhole eats houses. Instead, your garden is the forest.

In Florida our abundant rainfall and warm climate allows for the rapid growth of trees and plants, provided you choose the right species.

Thus far I've planted two personal food forest projects in Florida; one a little south of Gainesville in zone 8/9, the other in tropical urban Fort Lauderdale. The first food forest began in 2010—the second in 2012. Both are now thriving, beautiful ecosystems with food literally falling on the ground all over the place, and both continue to grow in complexity and productivity as the years pass. Beyond those projects, I have assisted with many other projects through consultation, planning, providing plants, and sometimes digging!

In the northern half of the state, we can grow pecans, peaches, pears, apples, blueberries, grapes and cherries, along with many other temperate species. It is also warm enough in winter to grow sub-tropical to tropical species like loquats, Japanese persimmons and bananas. If you're in South Florida where it only freezes once in a blue moon, you may not have luck with pears and blueberries—but rejoice!—the great bounty of the tropics is open for your plunder. Rather than maybe fifty or so fruit tree species, you can literally grow a thousand species, along with a plethora of exotic spices and perennial vegetables. In this book you will discover many exciting edible plants for both the northern and southern half of the state.

I don't get why so many folks living in a tropical paradise like Florida spend hours on their boring lawns and toxic landscape plants instead of bringing forth an abundance of excellent food from the earth. Many fruit trees and shrubs don't even require watering once they get established, yet people slave along, mowing and fertilizing their worthless lawns.

Is that you? I hope you'll quit. Plant something edible, then plant another, and another, and another. Soon you'll be reaping the sweet bounty and having plenty to share. You can grow a food forest in Florida. It's easier than you think. I did it, and so can you.

May this book provide you with encouragement, information and inspiration.

—David The Good

Part I

The System

WHY A FOOD FOREST?

Did you ever leave your yard alone for a few weeks? Or a few months? Or a few years? When I was a kid, Mom and Dad once took our entire family—five girls and two boys—on a road trip up the Eastern Seaboard to visit family and see sights we'd never seen. We made it all the way up into Canada, driving over the border and back, just so Dad could say we'd visited another country, then worked our way back down, visiting my Great-Grandparents, aunts and uncles, cousins and friends. We even got to eat fresh apples from a Revolutionary War-era orchard in the mountains of North Carolina. The trip lasted an entire month. When we got home, we were amazed to see how tall our front lawn had grown! It was almost up to my knees, green, thick and wild. Weeds had appeared and everything looked strange and abandoned. In normal years Dad never let the yard get out of control, but with just a month of Florida summer rain and no care, the place looked like a foreclosure home. In fact, taking a look at foreclosures gives us some insight into what happens to a lawn long-term when folks lose their over-mortgaged "pride of ownership" and leave their underwater houses for friendlier shores.

First, the grass grows long and sends up seed heads. Opportunistic weeds start to appear. Vines grow over the fence. Buried acorns sprout. Black cherry and wild plum pits dropped by powerline-straddling birds germinate amidst the un-raked leaves. I have a friend who picked loads of berries from his local "blackberry patch"—which just so happened to be the front yard of an abandoned house in his subdivision.

As soon as our management ends, complex biological webs begin their assault on imposed order and HOA regulations. A grass lawn is a very low-level ecological system. Nothing stands still for very long in nature. If you take a look outside the neighborhoods at what wild areas are left, you'll see mature tree-filled ecosystems. Oaks, pines, mangroves, hickories, sumacs, mulberries, bays and dozens or even hundreds of other tree species fill empty lots and roadsides across Florida. And between them grow a host of other species, like beautyberries, mimosas, shepherd's needles, wild grapes, coral beans, blueberries, smilax, wild coffee and more.

Can you say the same about your yard?

Only if you leave it alone!

Yet if you let nature plant it without help, sometimes the results aren't pretty for a long, long time, and they're not going to feed you very well.

Dog fennel and Brazilian pepper, anyone?

Maintaining grass or an annual garden is tough. You'll almost never see trees naturally growing alone in a field of grass, except in the African savannah. And there they have frequent wildfires and grazing animals that keep forests from forming. Here we have lawnmowers and string trimmers. You have to slave at your yard work or your patch of corn because you're restraining an ecosystem that doesn't want to stay as it is.

There is an opportunity here, if you choose to run with it.

What if you created a forest ecosystem piece by piece? But rather than letting birds and squirrels and wind-blown seeds start it—you plant it. The more species you add, the more ecological niches you create. Different plants attract different insects, birds and other friendly creatures. And with a wide variety of organisms, it is hard for pests or diseases to destroy your system. Predators have hiding places and species-specific pests like aphids can't jump plant to plant as easily.

Chinch bugs can wipe out a lawn. A late frost can wreck a citrus grove or strip the blooms off your peaches. Drought can ruin a wheat field. But if you're growing dozens or even hundreds of different species, the chances of the system failing completely are practically nil. Every year, you will harvest something! A bad year for the peaches may not be a bad year for the yams, and a bad freeze might harm the key lime but give you a bumper crop of pears. All your eggs are scattered across many baskets.

What you want to do is create an ecological web rather than a monoculture of grass or mass planting of a single ground cover.

English horticulturist Robert Hart is the pioneer of modern food forestry in the West. He took a tiny orchard and filled it with edible perennial species, stacking herbs, vegetables and berries into every corner until the system matured into an amazing food-creating machine. His work has since been improved upon and expanded by permaculturists such as Bill Mollison, Geoff Lawton, Toby Hemenway, Eric Toensmeier, Stefan Sobkowiak and Martin Crawford. Additional work has been done in the study of agroforestry—particularly traditional systems—as typified by the work presented by Dr. Craig Elevitch in his excellent Agroforestry Journal and also shared by ECHO in Ft. Myers and in the highly productive Syntropic Agriculture system of Ernst Götsch in Brazil.

Before plantation agriculture came to the islands of the South Pacific, many homes had tree gardens around them, bearing abundantly whatever the weather. In Indonesia, there is a great tradition of food forests. In the Caribbean and Central America, you will find semi-cultivated forest gardens here and there among the sugar cane, corn and pigeon peas. Villages in Africa often had useful species and trees around them, sometimes tended by the community. These systems are not new, but they are less common in temperate climates. In warm, wet areas, making a jungle of food is easy and it produces a lot faster than up north.

Unfortunately, most Floridians do not work with the climate and instead work against it, focusing on raised beds of tomatoes and lettuces rather than tropical and subtropical trees and shrubs, herbs, palms and vines. This is not a temperate climate—why put in the hard work to grow touchy Northern veggies when you can instead plant a super-productive long-term perennial system?

In terms of effort, forest gardening beats annual beds hands down. Think about how much work it takes to weed, hoe, till, plant, spray, and harvest a garden.

Talk about labor!

Now think about how easy it is to pick up grapefruit, pears, mangoes, starfruit or pecans from beneath a mature tree. When a tree gets big enough to take care of itself, it becomes a long-term producer of food without all the murderous work. Sure, you may have to do some pruning and some chopping of bindweed every once in a while, but that's easy compared to digging a new garden bed and babying a crop of annuals.

Healthy forests are self-feeding, self-mulching, self-watering and self-perpetuating. Ever dig into a forest floor? It's usually covered, beneath the leaves, in rich compost. That's compost *you* didn't have to make.

The work is in the establishment more than in the maintenance. Getting the sand to turn into soil is key, as is keeping young trees alive until they can fend for themselves. Once you have that down, you're set.

Food forests are long-term, beautiful, shady escapes from hard work and the stresses of life. It's time to take a long vacation from your lawn... and never come back.

THE LAYERS OF
A FOOD FOREST

Before we go any further, we need to take a look at food forest design. Robert Hart's ground-breaking food forest orchard contained seven layers, much like a wild forest. This was adopted by others, then tweaked with the addition of nitrogen-fixers, palms and other elements.

Let's look at this basic design and then start dreaming about how we can apply it here in Florida.

NOTE: The species I mention in the following explanation are just here to give you a small idea of what's possible. In later chapters we'll cover a much larger list of edibles in depth.

1: The Canopy Layer

The canopy layer consists of your tallest trees. This can vary according to the size of your land. If you have lots of space, you might plant very tall trees. In a small backyard, your canopy layer might be no taller than an orange or a dwarf (or regularly pruned) mango tree. In North Florida, large canopy trees could be pecans and chestnuts. In South Florida, your canopy layer might be tamarinds, mangoes, lychees and cinnamon.

2: The Sub-Canopy Layer

Beneath your tallest trees is a "low-tree" or "sub-canopy" layer of fruits, nuts and other edible species. These are shorter trees that can be tucked around the big guys. In North Florida this layer could consist of oranges, mulberries, apples, pears and other delights. In South Florida you might plant starfruit, grumichama, jabuticaba, acerola cherry, limes and other tropical fruit.

3: The Shrub Layer

Here's where you'll pop in edible and useful shrubs, smaller nitrogen-fixers, pollinator attractors, and berries. In North Florida, you might plant blueberries, dwarf mulberries, goumi berries, wild roses (for hips), tea and edible hibiscus shrubs. In South Florida, you might add miracle fruit, cassava, Surinam cherry, edible hibiscus shrubs and coffee.

4: The Herbaceous Layer

This is a layer of perennial vegetables and herbs. You can really pack these guys in around the trees and shrubs, using whatever space is available. In North Florida, you could plant chaya, rosemary, sage, gingers, cannas and basil. In South Florida you could also add longevity spinach, Surinam purslane, malanga, monstera and plenty of other perennials.

5: The Rhizosphere

This is a fancy way of saying "a root layer." This layer overlaps with your herbaceous and shrub layers, along with the yet-to-be announced vine and ground cover layers. It might contain gingers, yams, arrowroot, taro, cassava, yacon, sweet potatoes and more.

6: The Ground Cover Layer

In North Florida, the ground cover layer may be somewhat seasonal since the frost often takes it out, but in both halves of the state you can plant sweet potatoes, oregano, mint and other plants that creep along and also produce food. Pumpkins are another good ground cover, though they are very aggressive. Your main ground cover in some instances might just be thick mulch to keep the sand from being too infertile. The edges of a food forest system can also host annuals such as okra, beans, peas, lettuces and other traditional garden crops.

7: The Vertical Layer

The vertical layer, also known as the vine layer, consists of vines and creepers that use your other trees and shrubs as support.

In North Florida, this layer could be yams, grapes, hardy kiwi and native passionfruit (maypops). In South Florida, it could also host yams and grapes along with black pepper, tropical passionfruit, betel leaf, Malabar spinach, passionfruit and dragonfruit.

Along with these seven layers, a "palm layer" for the tropics has also been proposed by Geoff Lawton and Bill Mollison, since many palms will happily grow up through a tropical forest canopy without casting too much shade beneath. A palm layer in South Florida could be coconuts, and in North Florida, pindo palms or native cabbage palm. Others have proposed a "mycorhizzal layer" for mushrooms, or an "aquatic layer" for pond plants added to the mix—but you don't have to overthink things. Just start with the basic seven-layer framework and things will plan themselves out easily enough.

Now you may be looking at your grass and saying "where in the world would I start?"

Glad you asked. We should start with the soil—but first, a brief intermission is required to help along those of you who aren't quite ready to leave the lawn behind.

"BUT... WAIT! IF I PLANT A FOOD FOREST, WHERE WILL MY KIDS PLAY?"

"I can't plant a food forest! I have kids! They need a lawn to play on!"

Have you ever had that thought? Though it seems like a strange excuse to some of us mad scientists, I've heard it multiple times.

There's this idea that the lawn is sacred and that it's just The Place for Kids to Play. But what if you live in the forest? Would kids not be able to play? I think Christopher Robin would disagree with that conjecture.

Sure, a lawn is good for "kill the man with the ball," soccer, slip n' slides and wrestling... but the forest has its own appeal. Secret hideouts, climbing trees, hide and seek, tree forts; heck, even paintball is better in the woods.

Just because you have forest instead of lawn, it certainly doesn't mean your kids will have no place to play. In fact, they may have more fun playing than they would in a bare yard.

Let's take a look at a few of the amazing perks of involving children in your food forest project.

Benefit #1: Your Kids Get To Play In The Woods

When I began The Great South Florida Food Forest Project in my amazing parents' backyard, my mom, always thinking of children and grandchildren, told me she didn't want to take up so much yard that there wasn't a play area.

Unfortunately for mom, I have a rebellious streak and my dad was also a free thinker, so piece by piece, we filled up a lot of the former play area with plants. Cassavas, an avocado, naranjillas, cannas, a mulberry tree... the list kept growing as the "lawn" shrank.

Later I made some proper paths through the rapidly growing forest area.

A week or so after I installed them and went home, my mom called me.

"I was watching the _____ kids for their mom the other day... they really love those paths! They were running and skipping through the food forest and bumping into each other... hiding back there and having a good old time."

Sometimes some fun, winding paths can make all the difference. It's nice to be able to walk safely through a forest. It doesn't have to be a dark and inaccessible jungle.

When you build a food forest, you're building a managed forest ecosystem. No big bad wolves or witches with gingerbread houses—which is good, because gingerbread can't compare to fresh fruit and nuts.

Just ask your local dietician.

Benefit #2: Your Kids Get To Pick and Eat Real Food

Speaking of diet, you might not be able to get your baby to eat healthy and delicious limburger cheese (I've tried but the baby just won't. I think he thinks it's some kind of carrion), but I haven't met many kids that hate fruit.

In my North Florida yard I planted a huge variety of edible berries and fruit, many of which I planted with children in mind. Jamaican cherries, blueberries, mulberries, strawberries, Surinam cherries, figs, kumquats, Simpson stoppers, beauty berries—the list just keeps going!

As a kid we had a grapefruit tree in the backyard. We ate them, threw fruit at the neighbor girl (sorry, Aimee—you know we love you), built a tree fort in the branches and generally adored that old tree. When I was ten and my (now wife) Rachel was eight, she took me and my brother down her road to see a "blackberry tree" that a neighbor was growing. It was a mulberry, though we didn't know that at the time, and we loved eating that fruit. (I later named and propagated the variety, but you'll hear more about that in the mulberry tree profile in a later chapter).

Think of how much fun it is to eat fresh fruit! Persimmons beat the living daylights out of grass. As do starfruit. And any fruit beats the living daylights out of Nesquik, donuts, Cheez Doodles and other trashy children's "food."

When you plant food, you're making an investment in your children's health. Of course, they won't know it is a nefarious plot to give them nutrition—they'll just think you're great for planting those delicious things.

Benefit #3: Your Kids Get To Enjoy Nature

I really feel for families who have to live in apartments. Apartment complexes are usually grim places. Parking lots, grass, a few trees and if you're lucky, you get a fake lake with a fountain, along with your own flock of surly Muscovy ducks.

Suburbia isn't much better. It's like an apartment complex except without the fake lake. There's plenty of talk about "food deserts", but there's really no need for any place in Florida to lack food. We can grow a vast variety of fruit and nut trees. We're only stopped by our strange desire to plant grass and oleanders instead of sweet potato vines and loquats. I don't get it. The opportunities are endless. Grab them!

As kids we had some places in the neighborhood to play (there were great big ficus trees in the park), but we really, really loved going on vacation in the country where there were real woods.

Though a food forest can't replace true wilderness, it does provide a child with a lot more nature than a standard lawn. His chances to catch bugs, watch birds and butterflies, flip over snail-concealing logs and hunt for lizards are greatly increased. These are important things, though they seem trite to the adult mind.

We're all part of an ecosystem. Children get to see a lot more of nature's interaction in a little patch of forest than they will in a huge patch of ChemLawn.

Seriously: hide and seek, fresh fruit and mayonnaise jar terrariums containing lizards and weird beetles? How can you beat that?

If my mom came around, so can you. It's more fun than you—or your children—can imagine.

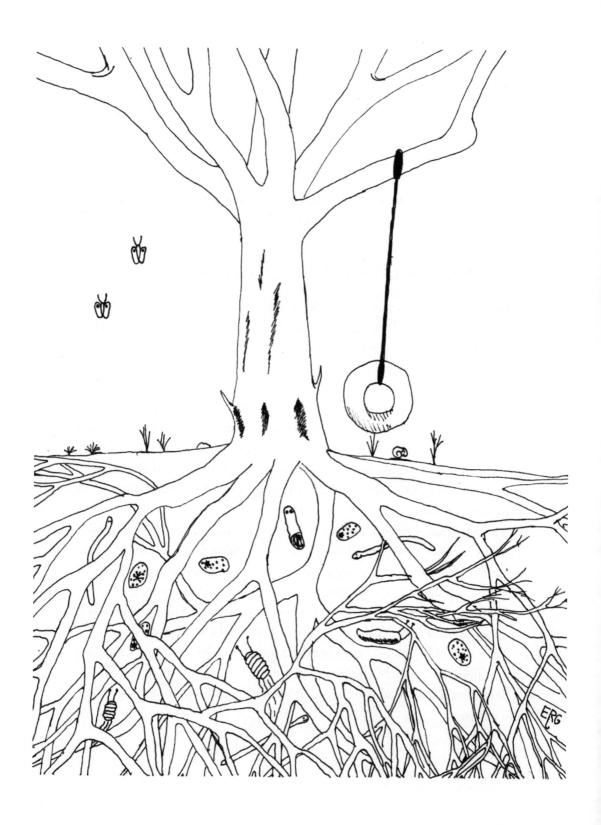

BUILDING YOUR FOUNDATION

Ah, the soil. Where life begins.

What soil? I can hear you asking. Florida doesn't have soil! Heck, it would be generous to call it dirt! It's just sand, sand, sand!

Unless you live in a place with clay or muck, or worse, limerock "soil," you probably have sand in Florida. There is sand everywhere. Some of it is better quality sand with more organic matter and tilth in it, but it's still sand. In North Florida I had grey sandy loam soil in my backyard and a harder, yellowy-gray sand in the front yard. In South Florida, we dealt with "sugar sand," which was a dirty white sand with almost nothing in it. Dig a little beneath the surface and you got pure white construction sand.

Though the first thing you'll want to do is to start planting trees, something has to be done about the "soil" conditions. I have made the mistake of planting some fruit trees right in the sand and trying to keep them happy. They weren't. Once a forest gets established, a lot of leaves drop to the ground and keep the sand covered, allowing it to stay cool and moist and build up some humus and a good microbiology. But when you start with a grass lawn or patch of weeds over sand, getting your first trees going is a pain. I spent way too many days dragging a hose around before I got smart about building the soil.

The best thing you can do to save yourself a lot of trouble is to create a layer of deep mulch right at the beginning of your food forest project, and at the same time, plant a bunch of plants that can be chopped and dropped as mulch as the system grows.

Mulch Bandits

"I'm going to grab all the yard waste the neighbors are chucking," I said. "Think that's legal?"

"I don't know," Dad said. "Probably not, but I don't think anyone will really care."

"Good," I said, then headed off down the street to start dragging green trash bins back to my parents' place.

We had a patch of really lousy sand to deal with and there was one way I knew how to deal with it: drop tons of organic matter on the ground! In Ft. Lauderdale, the city gives you bins to load up with your yard "waste," then takes it away to be processed separately from household garbage. This meant that on our road there were about eight 80-gallon rolling bins waiting by the side of the road for the trash truck to arrive. Perfect.

I rolled them back to my parents' yard one after the other, dumping loads of brown leaves, grass clippings, elephant ear leaves, chopped palm fronds, weeds, vines, fern leaves, croton prunings, schefflera branches and the other debris from perfect little yards filled with grass and ornamental plants. Dad had already gathered a load of cardboard from the recycling bins and we were ready to sheet mulch.

A year or so before, we had started the food forest with a few fruit trees planted in the sand and patchy grass and weeds behind the house. They were not particularly happy and we wanted to plant more and build the soil up so they would thrive. For years Dad had attempted to grow grass in the backyard without much success unless he watered, fed and mowed it all the time. Now we were going to make a forest, so we had to improve the ground and get it to hold some water and nutrients. Neither of us wanted to work to keep this system going—it needed to live without too much time being expended. I lived almost five hours north and my Dad was a busy man, writing books and teaching as well as pastoring a small church.

Earlier in the day we had planted a few new fruit trees. We watered the entire area around the planned food forest very well, deep soaking the sand. Then we laid down sheets of cardboard over the weeds and grass. Now it was time to stack up our pilfered yard waste.

I dumped bin after bin on top of the cardboard, eventually stacking a pile over two feet tall, spreading it almost up to the trunk of each tree in the system.

After returning the bins, Dad and I looked at our handiwork.

It looked terrible. It was a big, ugly brush pile with some little trees sticking out of it.

Our neighbor looked over the back fence.

"What is this mess?" he said, taking a drag on his cigarette.

"This will rot down and make the trees happy," I replied. "We're building up the soil."

"We have good soil in Cuba," he said. "This is not soil here."

"I've heard about your soil," I said. "Great cigars in Cuba—they say the tobacco tastes better than it does anywhere else."

"Everything grows good. Good red soil," he said. "Not like this."

"We'll work on it," I said.

He shook his head, unconvinced, then left us.

A few months later, we met again at the fence—but I'll share that story in a minute.

Mulching Materials

Some Floridians have been able to catch tree company trucks as they clear the power lines and get a big pile of chipped trees dropped in their yard. We did this in North Florida and I got plenty of material in a hurry. Others, though, have not had much luck. It depends on the company and if their mulch is predestined for somewhere else than your yard. You cannot fight the mulch's ultimate destiny.

Some cities, like Ft. Lauderdale, have bins for yard waste that can be looted. Obviously, don't do this if it is illegal, especially if a cop is watching you. Neighbors will often dump their trimmings and leaves in your yard if you ask them.

Some cities shred trees and pile up the mulch where it is free for the taking. We got a load of mulch from the City of Plantation one year and it was good stuff.

Be cautious of city composting programs. The compost may contain biosolids which include toxins and heavy metals. Even worse, it may contain rotten hay or manure that is laced with long-term herbicides that will kill your food forest. Do not trust hay, straw or manure. Look up "aminopyralid" herbicide and you'll see why. I lost a lot of good plants due to that stuff. It's being sprayed on fields across the state, then coming through in hay, straw and manure, which sometimes ends up in compost.

Most yard waste is safe to use. Grass clippings may not be, especially if your neighbor is paying for Better Grass Through Chemistry, i.e., lawn services that spray

weed-and-feed and other toxins to keep grass monocultures looking vibrant and weed-free. Prunings from shrubs, fallen palm branches, coconut husks, leaves, etc. should be fine, though.

Starting with a big old pile of yard waste kicked the South Florida food forest into high gear from the start. I've got it down to a science now. It's a whole new branch called *Throwingthingsonthegroundology*.

Unlike other branches of science, this branch of science uses branches *FOR* science! Whoooooooooaaaaaaaaaaa!

Building a Forest Floor in Five Steps with the Esoteric Science of Throwingthingsonthegroundology

1. Pick your space
2. If the weeds, grass or shrubs are taller than a few inches, chop them to the ground
3. Water the area deeply to fill the ground with moisture
4. Lay down a double layer of cardboard or a thick layer of newspapers for weed block and soak it all with the hose
5. Stack a whole bunch of organic material on top of the weed block, then water again to soak everything

A forest floor is not covered in grass. Instead, it is a mix of decayed material, covered with still decaying material with regular new additions of leaves and twigs and fruit and other debris on top. The whole forest floor is like a compost pile. It doesn't get tilled and it replenishes itself over time as material falls from the trees. Yet a forest may only drop a few inches of material in a year and takes its time to build up the soil layers. We don't have to wait that long when we gather lots and lots of stuff and dump it on the ground all at once to start our forest. This gets things kicking FAST!

Annual gardeners have used this method of stacking up organic matter in their vegetable gardens. Most of us are familiar with Ruth Stout (*Gardening Without Work*), Patricia Lanza (*Lasagna Gardening*) and Paul Gautschi (of the *Back to Eden* film) and their deep mulch gardening methods. Personally, I find that deep mulching annual garden beds in Florida is a huge amount of work and hard to maintain due to how fast our soil eats organic matter—yet I find it very, very useful in perennial systems. Bare soil around trees and shrubs is hard on them, especially when the soil is just sand. Trees like to have a nice, cool, forest floor environment around their roots and that's what we're creating right at the beginning. Since we don't have a forest already, we literally build it from the ground up.

Wetting the ground at the beginning is important. If you mulch on top of dry soil water can hardly get through to the tree roots. It takes a long, long time to get that sand wet under the mulch. But if you soak the ground at the beginning, then mulch over the top, the moisture stays in the sand beneath and helps the mulch above rot down into soil.

Covering up the existing weeds and grass with cardboard or another weed block starves them of light, making them rot down into the soil, creating humus while attracting worms and a host of other beneficial organisms.

We wet the cardboard after laying it down to make it stay in place and to make it easier for subsequent rains to soak through. If you do not have cardboard or are worried about potential contaminants in it or in newspapers, no worries. Banana leaves, palm fronds, heliconia leaves, or other big leaves act as a decent weed block. Just put a lot of them down as they aren't as thick or long-lasting as cardboard.

After you have your weed block layer in place, chuck a bunch of biomass on top of it. We're talking logs and prunings and grass clippings and raked leaves. You can also throw some seaweed down if you live near the beach. That adds extra nutrients to the system. If you have compost, throw some of that there too. Anything that adds nutrients and feeds the plants is great. Feel free to throw in paper plates, coffee grounds, shredded paper and kitchen scraps to your pile of yard waste. If it looks too ugly, smash it all down and throw some nice, purchased mulch over the top. I got away with some really ugly sheet composting that way. No one even knew there were chicken bones and rotten potatoes hiding under there but they fed the trees quite nicely.

What Our Neighbor Learned

A few months after the big yard waste drop, I came back to check on the food forest. The yard waste mountain had already shrunk quite a bit, settling onto the ground, browning and rotting.

I dug around beneath it and found something I had rarely saw in that backyard when I was a kid. Life!

Worms and beetles and millipedes. There was a lot of tiny life beneath that pile of rotting material, and not only that, a forest floor was starting to develop.

I pulled up a good handful of crumbly, black, sandy humus. It looked nothing like the soil we started with, except for the grains of sand mixed into it. It smelled alive, like fresh mushrooms, and was the best soil I had ever seen in that yard.

"Welcome back," the neighbor said from behind the fence.

"Good to see you," I said. "Look at this!"

I brought a good handful of new soil to the fence. "See? This came from all the yard waste we dropped."

He looked at my handful of black, living humusy soil.

"Well," he said after a moment. "I never saw this before." He looked closer and shook his head. "I learned something new today."

I know how he felt. It seems like magic to me as well. The first time I sheet mulched on top of rocky clay soil in Tennessee, the resulting rich loam a year later was a wonderful surprise. In Florida, the breakdown process happens much faster.

You can turn Florida sand into good stuff. It's not easy, and it doesn't last if you don't renew it regularly, but if you create a food forest with lots of mulch at the beginning, then grow plants you can keep dropping to the ground to build the forest floor, you can indeed turn sugar sand into good, healthy ground.

At the beginning of your Florida food forest, an easy option is to start with a load of mulching material from outside, then start producing your own mulch right in your food forest.

Producing your own mulch? Like—with a chipper?

No—no need for a chipper. Just grow various plants that you can chop into pieces and throw on the ground. Many plants can be cut again and again to serve as mulch, and they'll keep coming back. When I was a kid there was an *Albizia lebbeck* tree that kept growing in the hedge just on the neighbor's side of the fence. My dad cut that thing down again and again, trying to get rid of it—and it kept coming back. I know now that the tree was a nitrogen-fixing, fast-growing pioneer species that would have been great as a chop-and-drop tree for a food forest, but back then we just thought it was a pain in the neck. There's a good chance that right now you have something growing in your yard that is similar. Instead of trying to kill it, why not turn it into a compost factory? Cut the top off, throw it around a tree you want to feed, then let it grow back again. When it grows back good and strong, cut it again.

And plant more trees like it, which leads us into the next chapter.

OVERPLANT OR
GO HOME!

Getting enough mulch isn't always easy and the less you can bring in from outside, the better. Healthy forests don't require the addition of mulch and your growing food forest won't either if you plan it right. You also dodge the risk of importing pests, pesticides and who-knows-what-else.

Right from the beginning of your food forest project, stop throwing away leaves, twigs and grass clippings. Drop them right around your plants as they become available. Even hunks of logs are great. They'll make nice seats or borders in the short term, then rot down slowly over time, feeding fungi and worms while turning into rich, moist humus. Dad and I put log chunks everywhere when we first built the food forest. They are all part of the soil now.

If you have thorny material, like bougainvillea branches, chop them up and put them in places where they won't wound bare feet. They are NOT nice to step on, but they will rot down into good compost. Some people have asked me about using poisonous species in mulch, like castor bean, oleander, Brazilian pepper or even poison ivy. In the case of poison ivy, I just throw it someplace in the sun to dry out completely so it doesn't re-root, then throw it next to the base of a tree and mulch over it. In the case of the other plants, just chop them up and use them for mulch. As they rot down, the soil ecology will de-toxify them. Remember, poisonous leaves are falling on the ground all the time and it isn't killing nature or animals. Direct consumption of something toxic will hurt you, but the soil is really good at breaking things down into safe humus.

Some of Florida's worst invasive plants are excellent food forest mulch. If you live near a waterway infested with water hyacinth, throw it on your food forest to rot down. It waters and feeds the soil at the same time. The mimosa trees of North Florida can be chopped repeatedly and re-grown for a never-ending source of nitrogen-rich mulch. The dreaded Brazilian pepper (sometimes called Florida holly) is really hard to kill. If you have one in your yard, you can cut it again and again for mulching material. Since it wants to grow, let it grow—then take all its hard work and feed it to the soil. The common paper-podded *Albizia lebbeck* that shows up in weedy lots across the southern half of the state (the one my Dad hated so much!) is another plant you can cut again and again to feed to your forest floor. Even meleleuca bark is good mulch.

The time to think about mulch-producing plants is right at the beginning of your system. Planting trees specifically as chop-and-drop to feed the food forest makes a lot of sense, yet it's a step many people skip, instead moving right on into planting fruit trees. I've seen too many food forests that are more like orchards than self-sustaining forests. Orchards are great, but they aren't food forests.

Buying mulch and constantly scavenging is a waste of money and time. It is easier to grow your mulch right in the system.

Whereas nature drops leaves now and again through the year and builds soil slowly, we are going to plant a bunch of fast-growing plants and chop and drop them again and again to grow soil in fast-forward and give our Florida food forest a serious kick-start. With a little human management, we can do in a few years what it would take nature decades to accomplish.

There are two main groups of plants I like to use as mulch: biomass plants and nitrogen-fixing plants. These overlap quite a bit, as some nitrogen-fixers make a lot of biomass, but it's a general idea. If you're familiar with how compost piles are traditionally built, you know that there is a ratio of carbon to nitrogen that leads to a fast-burning pile and rapid generation of humus. We want both carbon and nitrogen in our mulch layer. Many bagged mulches are almost all carbon, such as cypress and pine bark nuggets. Landscapers love these because they break down very slowly, meaning that a single application lasts a long time.

You don't want that. You want to build soil. Mixing up lots of "green" and "brown" material leads to the faster breakdown of material and much better nutrition for the roots in your food forest. The ideal way to build your food forest is to make it self-feeding via the regular addition of new layers of plant material to the forest floor. If you plant it right, all you need to keep it fed and mulched is a machete.

An excellent biomass-producer that acts as a fertilizer and mulch is *Tithonia diversifolia*, also known as "tree marigold" or "Mexican sunflower." Don't mix it up with its cousin, the other "Mexican sunflower" (*Tithonia rotundifolia*), which is an annual of little use as a chop-and-drop. *T. diversifolia* grows to a height of 16–20' and produces lovely blooms. It grows very rapidly and can be chopped and dropped around fruit trees multiple times a year.

The woody stems root easily and can be chopped into 12–18" long pieces and stuck half-way in the ground wherever you want to plant more of them. Just know that once you plant them, they get big and bushy and like to spread by falling over and rooting, so be merciless with your machete. This rank and vigorous growth habit is your ally in building soil. You can easily get four chop-and-drop harvests per year and the leaves rot rapidly into the ground, providing plants with phosphorus, nitrogen and other nutrients. If you cut mature canes, make sure you lay them on top of dry mulch or each other so they dry out and don't re-root right next to your trees. Or chop them up small. If any pieces do root, just yank them up and toss them in the sun to die, then throw them wherever you like.

Another tree that makes a great chop-and-drop is moringa. Moringa has many uses, as it is edible, medicinal and anti-fungal. It's also very good at growing on marginal soil and bringing up lots of micronutrients with its vigorous root system. The trunks are very weak and easy to chop and the tree regrows quickly when pruned. Allegedly, the leaves also contain growth-boosting compounds that increase the vigor of other plants when used as fertilizer. Some people have expressed dismay that I use such a valuable tree as a chop-and-drop but why not? They grow like weeds in Florida. You can have plenty of moringa for medicine and food as well as for compost.

If you can find trees and shrubs that are nitrogen-fixers, plant those in between your other plants. What does "nitrogen-fixing" mean? It's the process by which certain bacteria form relationships with certain plant roots to take atmospheric nitrogen from the air and turn it into a form the host plant—and its neighbors—can use.

Remember how George Washington Carver planted peanuts to restore ground made infertile by years of cotton growing? Peanuts add nitrogen back into the ground and many other plants can do the same. Cassias, poincianas, *Leucaena*, pigeon peas... there are a wide variety of trees and shrubs that will improve your soil. Plant them densely and cut or prune them back as they grow, throwing their trimmings around your fruit trees and shrubs just like you do with grass clippings. As you do, they'll drop nitrogen nodules from their roots in response to the pruning, feeding the ground from beneath, even as their tops feed the ground from above by rotting into humus. The common silverthorn hedge is a great nitrogen-fixer that can be cut again and again to feed other plants. I grew my citrus right next to a big hedge of them and fed the prunings to them over and over again—and grew some great oranges, lemons and grapefruit!

You may already have some nitrogen-fixers in your yard. Maybe even a tree you've tried to eliminate. Let's just say it's a mimosa. That's a great tree.

At this point, you might be thinking "But M.C. Davy G., WHAT? Mimosas? They're INVASIVE!" Everyone hates mimosa trees these days. It's fashionable,

I suppose, though they were first brought to the states and became a popular ornamental tree. Now people say things like "They're an invasive!" or "They keep growing back when you cut them down!" or "They grow SO fast!!!" or "I CAN'T KILL THEM!"

It's true: mimosa trees are an invasive species that keeps growing back when you cut them, and yes, they grow fast. That's because mimosas were designed to fill a specific environmental niche: they are what botanists call a "pioneer species."

According to Infogalactic.com: "Pioneer species are hardy species which are the first to colonize previously disrupted or damaged ecosystems, beginning a chain of ecological succession that ultimately leads to a more biodiverse steady-state ecosystem."

Did you get that? Mimosa (more properly known as *Albizia julibrissin*) is a species that shows up in poor soils and disturbed areas. It grows quickly, seeds prolifically, fixes nitrogen in the soil—which improves the area—and eventually dies and rots after years of dropping humus-creating leaves and branches. There's a reason you see mimosa trees growing around junkyards, roadsides and construction sites. They're there to fix things. The problem is, they're not a native, so they fill a niche that would normally be filled by something local.

Yet we can use them for good in a food forest. If you have mimosa trees, put them to work. Instead of trying to completely kill an invasive mimosa tree, use it as "chop and drop" mulch instead.

I had a mimosa tree growing next to a Chinese chestnut tree in my front yard food forest in North Florida. Every time the mimosa got taller than the chestnut, I cut the mimosa back to 4' or so with my machete, then roughly chopped up the leaves and branches and dropped them in a rough ring around the chestnut. I did this over and over again, mulching that chestnut. As I cut back that mimosa and used it for mulch on top of the ground, I was also feeding the chestnut from beneath with the roots and nodules it was losing beneath the ground. How cool is that?

Sometimes problems can be solutions. We have a problem: an invasive tree that keeps growing back. But we have another problem: poor, sandy, nutrient-deficient soil. The second problem can be solved by the first. Let that mimosa tree grow a bit and gather up nutrition from the soil to feed its growing leaves and branches. Then take its hard work and give it to something else!

I used to hate invasive trees that would keep coming back—until I realized I could use them for better things. Instead of seeing these persistent plants as a problem, I now see them as a source of food for the trees I love. It is satisfying to chop down an invasive tree and feed to something edible.

It's not just invasive trees you can use for chop and drop, either. You can also use sweet gum and oak, sumacs or just the weeds that grow in your yard or in the empty lot across the street. Chop them down and use them for mulch around trees you want to feed. Some people don't like the look of rough branches and weeds as mulch. These people are sissies. Don't be a sissy. Chop and drop everything and let the ground eat it. Just chill a little. Trim the mimosas, drink a mimosa, and watch your food forest grow.

Trees like mimosa show up because they're designed to restore a forest environment. Work with them to improve the soil. Keep them cut so they won't go to seed and use those trimmings to feed something else.

It's important to get lots of material growing that you can drop on the ground. A wide range of species is best, as different plants excel at accumulating different minerals. Let patches of weeds grow a few feet tall, then chop them down and throw them at the base of a tree you want to mulch/feed. Easy! Unless you live under an HOA, that is.

Overplant! Plant stuff everywhere and let nature sort it out. Hack paths, scythe the weeds, feed the ground.

Why is it that we find wandering through a lush woodland a wonderful thing, yet fight against lush growth on our own properties? In our yards we have disconnected ourselves from natural ecosystems. They're scary I suppose. I mean, what would the neighbors think? Our gardening efforts are feeble and contrived. We clear and cut and till and plant at extension-approved intervals and spacings. Forests are much more exciting and don't have to be carefully planned.

Yes, sometimes you might plant things too close and end up with a tree (or three) that's too shaded or too strangled (CHAINSAW TIME!) but you might be surprised how tight your spacing can get before a tree becomes completely unproductive. Beyond just the trees, packing in a lot of biomass by adding a large number of plant species builds soil and creates a lush and resilient ecosystem.

I have seen multiple food forest projects that miss the benefits of density. They've made the transition from standard annual gardening to a more permaculture approach; yet they look more like an orchard without straight lines than a species-rich forest edge. It's fine to start by planting trees and mulching away the grass around them—but once you've got those trees as scaffolding, don't quit! Build density and you'll get more food and have less work in the long run.

You can prune trees to let in light. Density doesn't have to create complete shade. In fact, you should go out and chop things down now and again. It increases the productivity of the system by letting in some light and encouraging the understory to take off.

Larger trees can also be good shelters for less cold-tolerant species. Along with pineapples, I also grew guavas and other tropicals around the trunks of some large oak trees in my North Florida Food Forest Project. Despite winter temperatures dropping into the teens on some nights, they didn't freeze to death. The overlapping density of the system allows them to grow where they normally could not.

Some trees can also support climbing species. I grew yam vines up a sweet gum seedling that popped up in my food forest. The tree grew rapidly and I considered cutting it down to replace with something edible, then realized I should just take advantage of its quick growth and strength as a support. I wouldn't grow yams over my *Hachiya* persimmon tree, but on a sweet gum? Who cares!

If you add nitrogen-fixers, nutrient accumulators and pollinator-attracting plants around your fruit trees, you can support those trees better than you can with just mulch. I also like to plant herbs, leaf crops, sweet potatoes and wildflowers. I cannot stress enough the value of building a forest floor with lots of chop and drop, then planting thick, dense swaths of plants that require a machete to get through.

Seriously—if you have to weed with a machete, you're doing it right. Large amounts of plants build soil quickly and hold in water and nutrients. They'll also feed you.

Well-known permaculture teacher Geoff Lawton teaches people to install food forests in his film *Establishing a Food Forest the Permaculture Way*. In it he recommends dedicating 90% of the mass of a new food forest to support species that get chopped and dropped to build the forest soil. Over time, you'll take those trees out of commission and your fruit trees will take their place. Again, according to Geoff, only 10% at the beginning of the system should be dedicated to your fruit/nut/productive trees.

At the climax of the system, the ratio is reversed. The support species are down to 10% or so and the productive trees comprise 90% of the forest.

That is Geoff Lawton's approach and I think it is quite sound. If you simply decide to plant an orchard and haul in a bunch of mulch, you are missing using nature's approach of pioneer species leading to permanent species and you have to do a ton more work than if you just planted a bunch of mulching species at the beginning to use to feed your long-term trees.

Grow plants in place. Chop them down. Build the forest soil in fast-forward. As you do, chop down weeds for mulch and throw kitchen scraps around trees. Take mulch when you can get it. Grab some seaweed and throw it in there if you like. And by all means, rob the yard waste bins.

Add Life Fast

Throwing seeds around is a Good Gardener Best Practice (GGBP) and allows you to add life to your food forest in record time. Did weevils get into some of your dried beans? Don't throw them away—throw them in the food forest! The resulting bean plants—if any sprout—will feed the soil, even if you never harvest them. If they don't sprout, they'll still rot down and feed the soil. I once gave my children a bunch of old beans and told them to go have a bean fight in the front yard. Not only did they have fun, they scattered nitrogen-fixers everywhere!

I can never remember what the heck I've planted so I'm often surprised by what pops up. Every day is Christmas.

But don't stop with just beans. Throw around lots of other seeds as well. Good species include mustard, black-eyed peas, grains, lentils, chick peas, peanuts, all sorts of tree seeds (especially from nitrogen-fixers), old vegetable seeds, wildflower mixes, buckwheat, amaranth, bird seed mixes, mung beans, etc. You're just shooting to get a bunch of life on the ground with a good bit of nitrogen and carbon growing in place. Throwing seeds around lets nature pick and choose what works and what doesn't. Depending on what species you throw around, sometimes you'll have seeds coming up a year or more after you threw them.

Just make a big old mix of everything you can find, then throw it over an area, then scatter compost or sand over the surface or lightly rake or crumble the seeds into the ground. If you have them, scatter some grass clippings to keep the sand protected and moist. Keep it thin, though, because you want the seeds to come up through it. Run a sprinkler to get it all going. In two weeks, you will have a carpet of green.

If you are in the Central to Northern parts of Florida, it makes sense to divide these mixes into batches of cold and warm-season seeds. In the fall and winter, tailor your mixes a bit towards cold-season annuals. Brassicas like mustard, collards, rapeseed,

turnips, kale, etc. are good, as are lentils, chick peas, fava beans, winter wheat and grain rye. These can take the occasional frost. In the spring, go for black-eyes peas, mung and other beans, marigolds, peanuts, etc. But even if you just make a seed mix of whatever you find, nature will select for you.

One of the best places to get cheap seeds are the bulk bins at the local supermarket. Many of them germinate just fine and you can get a lot of seeds for a few bucks. I've also bought bags of the wildlife mix sold at the hardware store and thrown it around. And I've bought out all the old seeds at the local Dollar store when they are marked down, then ripped open the packets and added them in. It's a nice way to practice some gardening anarchy and see what happens. Almost anything is better than sandy ground.

If you have tree seeds, like *Leucaena* and moringa in the mix, watch for them to come up and try not to knock them down. They'll become long-term chop-and-drop trees for your system. When I lived in Grenada, I took a long hike with one of my sons and we picked seed pods off every nitrogen-fixing tree we could find and made a big seed mix to plant in our food forest project. *Leucaena, Inga, Erythrina, Cassia...* we had all kinds of luck in the jungle. Quality time plus free seeds!

I also stick cuttings in the ground and start a bunch of tree seeds in pots to plant out later. We'll talk more about propagation and setting up a home nursery in chapter seven.

There are a lot of trees used as ornamentals in Florida which make good chop-and-drop nitrogen-fixing additions to a food forest. *Bauhinia* (orchid-tree), royal poinciana, dwarf poinciana, cassias, etc. Once you recognize the pods and blooms of some nitrogen-fixing species, you start to see them everywhere. We also gathered the bright red beans of native coral bean and planted them by the base of our fruit trees to add nitrogen. As a bonus, they brought us beautiful blooms.

Get lots of life going quickly to build the soil and your fruit trees will thrive.

And speaking of fruit trees, isn't it about time we started planting the fun stuff? I can't believe it took us five chapters to get here. Who is writing this thing, anyhow?

AT LAST!
FRUIT TREES!

When I ran my Florida Food Forests plant nursery, I once helped someone obtain a big load of fruit and nut trees for a food forest she was starting near Ocala. Instead of planting a bunch of support species, she instead planted a winding orchard of edible trees and mulched them with truckload after truckload of mulch. This works and it will bring her a yield, but it also requires repeated mulch drops sourced from outside their property.

As she built the system, she added irrigation and flagged down trucks to get chips dropped—and there never seemed to be enough mulch. It took a lot of effort to grow those trees, as she was taking a piece of lawn and going directly to forest without using nature's natural method of plant succession. The woman came from a landscaping background and it was just too hard for her to wrap her mind around the idea of succession and some creative anarchy. Mulch is great, but it does not add much nitrogen or feed the life beneath the soil like your support species will. Like I said in the last chapter—go big!

Remember how I talked about foreclosure properties and how they start with weeds, then pioneer plants, then eventually grow into forest? If you fast-forward that process by putting in lots and lots of biomass plants and nitrogen fixers right up front, you are growing your own mulch in place. You also reduce the need for irrigation and fertilizer. In fact, you can often eliminate both. I can't overstate the need to give your plants lots of friends they can eat as they grow.

Another good trick I learned from Geoff Lawton's food forest projects is how to time the cutting of materials to feed the ground. When it is dry and hot, don't chop-and-drop trees. Wait until "precipitation is higher than evaporation," as Geoff puts it. The shade of your support species will help keep the ground cool when it is hot and dry, as it usually is during the spring. When the summer rains start falling and all the trees start soaking up the water and springing for the sky, you can start chopping down biomass to drop on the ground as mulch. This also opens up the canopy so sunlight reaches your young fruit trees. When the ground is hot and dry, don't mulch unless you water heavily first. Just as mulch holds water in moist soil, it also keeps the soil dry if you add a layer when there is little moisture in the ground. Work with the seasons. We usually did a few good chop-and-drop sessions in the summer, then let things go through the dry winter and spring.

Okay—enough—I could talk about chopping and dropping for an entire book. It's my favorite thing to do! But this chapter is about getting fruit trees started, not how I take out my anger issues on innocent leguminous trees with my razor-sharp machete, so we'd better get planting.

The "Island Method" of Planting a Food Forest

Though you can start an entire food forest all at once, you may not give it the care it needs. We've found that working with highly improved islands of ground works better than planting a field and trying to keep it all happy. As much as I wish we would all get a great, happy mix of support species growing first, most of us aren't good at it. In my first two food forests, I never had quite enough support species at the very beginning so I still had to haul some mulch and amendments and a hose around from here to there to keep young fruit trees happy.

Do as I say—not as I do!

I'm sure you feel the same way about fruit and nut trees as I do. Sometimes they just jump into your shopping cart. They cry out to you as you pass them at nurseries, promising you wonderful harvests if you just buy them right now and take them home. And they're much more fun to imagine in your yard than a big mess of support species. So, like me, you sometimes plant big fruit trees right in a big bare spot of ground... and then you have to baby them like an orphaned lamb.

It works better to use what I call "the island approach." Others might call this creating "plant guilds," but I'm not all that organized about it. I've just found that it's easier to manage a small oasis than it is to try and keep fifty fruit trees happy without irrigation and tons of mulch.

If you don't have a bunch of good support species all over your new food forest space, just start small—but not too small. Get yourself a fruit tree or three and some edible shrubs and perennials. Tear out some grass and plant a little informal grouping of trees. Then surround those with shrubs—and surround the shrubs with small perennials. Mulch and water heavily and try to keep the grass out until the shade does the job for you. As you plant, stick in some nitrogen-fixers and *T. diversifolia* cuttings, or pigeon peas, or whatever you have that can be chopped and dropped. If you can gather chopped materials from the edge of your yard, or grass clippings, or rotten produce from a road-side stand, coffee grounds, water hyacinth or whatever, and sheet mulch that space right at the beginning, it is way easier than weeding. That island will then thrive and create its own little living ecology.

I once made a super fertile island in the middle of my front yard by dumping about a ton of rotten produce on the ground, then heavily mulching over it. The worms and soil life had a bonanza under there! And as a bonus, I got some interesting volunteer plants, including chestnut seedlings.

Once your first island is happy and/or a few more fruit trees have somehow shown up at your house, do the same thing again.

This method also keeps you from having to tear out an entire lawn and go through the "bad haircut" phase of a food forest system. If you deal with HOAs or annoying neighbors or code enforcement, you can treat your growing food forest like little sections of landscaping, mulching to the edges and then mowing around them. Over time, just add more islands until eventually you have an entire forest. You can build an island every weekend or two and make great progress.

The "Plant It All At Once" Method

Some gardeners wish to get the whole system planted right away, rather than starting in pieces. If that's you, go for it. It's harder, though, unless you have access to tons of mulch or an already wooded or shrubby area that can be chopped down to feed the ground when you start.

Whether you decide to use a plan or just wing it by planting things willy-nilly (like nature does, that crazy gal), I highly recommend you do not skip out on the nitrogen-fixers and biomass plants.

For each fruit tree you plant out, plant lots of beans and pigeon peas and *Tithonias* and rye and whatever else you have that can be used for mulching. If you already have seedling trees growing, like oaks, sumacs, sweet gums, or even camphors and other invasive species, chop their tops off at head-height and use the branches for mulch rather than getting rid of them completely. You'll appreciate all the free fertility, trust me! This practice is called "pollarding." When the trees are cut like that, they do not fight vigorously with your new fruit trees and will act as "nurse" trees, providing shade in the dry times and mulch in the wet times.

Let me tell you about another food forest project that ended much worse than the one that needed constant mulch inputs.

There was a person living out in the sticks of Central Florida in a newly renovated trailer on a few acres of scrubland. The surrounding terrain was very sandy and dry, with a patchy mix of palmettos, hawthorns, smilax and pines. The owner of the land was a prepper and liked the food forest concept, though he wasn't really a gardener. Instead of attacking the food forest himself in pieces, he hired me to source the plants and turn his entire front yard into a food forest all at once.

I came over and took a look at the land and realized that it would need a lot of mulch and regular irrigation just to get started. He told me not to worry about it and to just get him a big mix of plants and start planting and he would keep it going.

I gathered a big collection of trees and plants and came back with a couple of my kids a few weeks later to plant the food forest. In my van and trailer I had a bunch of great stuff, including persimmons and loquats, soap nuts, mulberries, cassava and chaya, pecans and chestnuts, pears, peaches, plums, *Tithonia* cuttings and a big old bag of seed mix filled with beans, moringa, peanuts, buckwheat, wildflowers, nitrogen-fixing trees and a crazy mix of other species. In a great stroke of luck, there was a tree company clearing the lines in his neighborhood so we flagged them down so they could drop some chips on his yard. Then we got planting. It was hot, dry work and I worried about those trees as we put them in. If you've ever gardened in the sugar sand of Central Florida scrubland, you know how hard it is on plants. These guys were going to need a lot of care to get growing in that dead, yellow-white sand, and yet here we were planting a whole quarter acre or more with a bunch of nursery-grown trees.

"You have to mulch it deeply," I said. "You'll also have to water this multiple times a week."

"I will," he said, pulling out a lawn sprinkler and starting it up. "We'll just keep this moving around."

"Great," I said. He paid me for the trees and kindly gave my kids a few bucks for helping.

A few months later, I visited again. The system was growing. The trees were mostly alive, though some of them were sunburned. Mulch was spread around a good bit of the system, and various wildflowers were blooming here and there. It didn't look great, but it was definitely not dead. If it could get through that first year, I figured it would pull together as a system and survive into the future.

Then I didn't hear from the owner for a long time. More than a year, if I remember correctly. I finally got in a touch again and asked how the food forest looked.

"It's pretty much dead," he said.

"What?" I replied. "Are you serious?"

"Yeah," he said. "I'm sorry."

"What happened?" I said. "Did you not water it?"

"Not for some months," he said.

As the conversation went on, I found out that he had to deal with a personal situation out of state and had left his food forest to the ravages of a scrubland summer without care. As there was no mature forest floor with deep, cool mulch, and little shade around the young trees and plants, Florida rejected the food forest and replaced it with scrappy weeds and scrub plants. He was upset by it, but it couldn't be helped in his case unless he had been able to get someone to come way out into the sticks and care for it.

Just a few miles away, I had other friends who planted a food forest around the same time, this time on a field in the middle of dying citrus groves. They were a delightful married couple. She was a cheerful extrovert with a wide smile and he was a tough and sarcastic entrepreneur with steel in his spine. A true alpha type who was not scared of anyone and who took great care of his friends, including his beautiful wife. Their yard was sandy and hot, with lots and lots of sun and dry breezes that evaporated all the moisture from their sugar sand yard. Yet they were able to get their support species going, plant a large food forest and keep it mulched, watered and growing for the first couple of years until it "stuck" and became a thriving, cool, productive ecosystem. Unlike my other client, they didn't have to leave their food forest during the critical establishment phase.

If you can't take care of a big food forest in the first years, don't start big. Start with the island method and get a small area strong and fertile and established before you go big. Going big may just lead to disappointment and dead or stunted trees, so take bite-sized pieces if you are afraid you won't be able to care for a large space. Also, do not overestimate your time and capabilities. Some of us are super-enthusiastic about starting projects, but not as enthusiastic about maintaining them.

On the other hand, some people are too timid and fail to get much of anything going. It's important to avoid that end of the spectrum as well.

I knew a person who asked me about starting a food forest back when I was only a year or so into my North Florida Food Forest Project. He was very interested in creating a system but also wanted to make sure all the planning was done properly so he could perhaps later use one piece of the land for chickens and another piece for a field for kids to play in, and another section just for food forest, but with spaces for future garden beds, maybe, and...

...so what happened was, he was really cautious about planting. Only a few trees went in here and there and others were left in pots. Instead of jumping in and at least starting a few islands of food forest, he scattered trees here and there, afraid to make big commitments. Now, nine years later, there still isn't much of a food forest there. There are a few fruit trees without many support plants. The occasional patch of ginger or cassava. And lots of plants that have grown right through their pots into the ground where they were placed while the owner struggled to figure out his master plan.

Unlike most permaculture practitioners, I don't like to do much planning. Drawing site plans and doing exact spacing is boring. Instead, I collect and plant lots and

lots of plants, then see what interactions arise naturally. If trees get too big or end up in the way, I prune them or just chop them down to feed to other trees. As a result, I have two excellent food forest projects growing in Florida with lots and lots of species and an order to them that has evolved over time into rich, interlocking ecologies. Some of the original plants are gone, just as in a natural forest. Making mistakes is part of the process. Fear of failure or overplanning is paralyzing. Don't worry about it.

Here is a fine and true saying for you to print out and hang on the wall above your potting shed:

> *Most of life's problems can be fixed with a chainsaw.*
>
> —David The Good

Planting Trees

Enough philosophy. Here's how to plant trees.

Dig a hole that is a few times larger than the size of the root ball of each tree you're planting, then plant it at the same depth it was growing at in the pot. Though I don't recommend amending the soil in the planting hole as a general rule, I will sometimes bury a dead animal or fish guts or meat scraps a little ways under the new tree to give it some extra fertility. It's a good way to recycle dead pets, as the song relates:

Buried my rabbit neath the cherry tree
One fine afternoon
Some day I know we'll meet again
On a fruit salad spoon

Laid my hamster to rest last night
Beneath a pumpkin vine
Some day I know we'll meet again
In a Thanksgiving pie

If it dies when it's at my house
It'll end up in the soil
My trees are all fed by pets
Shuffling off this mortal coil

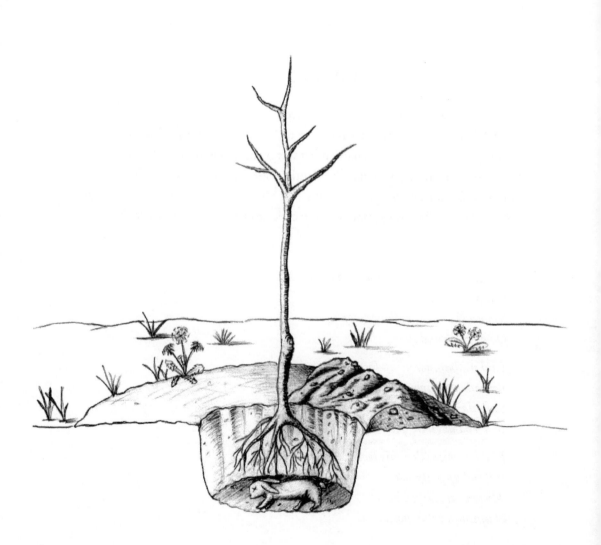

The most recent theory I've heard on growing trees is that amending the planting hole with compost, or manure or caffeine extract or whatever, encourages the young tree to keep its roots in that area of high fertility, rather than spreading out into the native soil and building a strong root system. On the other hand, my friend Eddy dug a huge hole for a seedling avocado and filled it with tons of fertile soil and lots of MiracleGro crystals. It grew like crazy and fruited in its fourth year. Of course, he also threatened to kill it if it didn't bloom, so maybe it was more fear than MiracleGro that brought it into an early adulthood.

I once planted a mulberry on top of a bucketful of raw manure and another one in just native sand. The one on top of the manure turned dark green and made big leaves yet the other tree ultimately grew faster and is still bigger some years later. Obviously, experimentation is in order, but for now I recommend just planting your tree in a nice, loose hole made from native soil, then feeding from the top down as nature does.

Once you have your tree in the ground either on top of a deceased rabbit or not on top of a deceased rabbit, water it very well, being sure to flood the entire hole so the roots can settle in and air pockets are reduced. Then remove the weeds in a 4' circle around the tree. If you have some compost, throw it down now. At the same time, a few handfuls of wood ashes, chicken manure, cottonseed meal, alfalfa pellets or even dog food can also give the tree some fertility it will find later as well as feeding the soil life.

Over that layer, put down some cardboard, chopped branches, hunks of wood, piles of weeds, grass clippings and mulch of all kinds to pin down the weed-blocking cardboard. If you want things to grow fast, you can put up some standpipes, set out a sprinkler, or just drag a hose around to keep the trees watered in their first year. When it's not raining during the warm season, give them a deep soak once a week, or twice a week if they look sad.

The best time to plant trees in North Florida is in fall or late winter/early spring so they can get established when it isn't hot. Bare-root trees work quite well when planted this way. In South Florida, the best time to plant fruit trees is any time from fall through into early spring. Transplanting trees in the summer heat or in the dry spring is hard on them and they take more care and water to get established, but if that's the time you must plant, by all means plant—just make sure they stay watered!

Though many people will tell you to take great care in getting your tree spacing correct by calculating the final size of each tree, this isn't strictly necessary. I know, you've seen mature mangoes and said, "my goodness, that would never fit in my yard!" And you're right. But those trees aren't pruned. You can head off insane levels of growth through regular pruning, then use the prunings to feed your forest floor. Even the largest mango cultivar can be kept to 8' in height if you prune. If you like pruning and think you'll stay on top of it, you can plant a lot in a small space. If you have more space and would rather live and let live, then space your trees with their eventual height in mind.

Remember also that if you put a bunch of trees together and never cut them, they need to be spaced wide enough that the sub-canopy trees and shrubs do not get completely shaded out by the canopy trees. I planted a trio of Japanese persimmons in my North Florida food forest. Two of them were in full sun and bore fruit. The last was in two-thirds shade under an oak tree and never bore a thing. Some trees really like the sunshine and need that solar energy to produce fruit. Others can take some shade. Oranges and pawpaws will still make fruit in partial shade beneath larger trees. Peaches and persimmons and loquats usually don't. Sometimes, even the canopy trees quit being all that productive if they are too close and don't get enough sunlight through to their lower branches.

There is an abandoned mango orchard near my old house in Grenada where all the trees have grown large and crowded into each other. Though the original spacing wasn't bad, they have stopped making fruit on most branches because there just isn't enough sun. Almost all the mangoes are now being produced at the very tops of the trees where they get full sun. If I owned the land, I would chop all the centers out of the trees and prune back the branches sprawling sideways so much more light gets in. In a year or two, they would produce many tons of fruit rather than a smattering here and there.

If you buy expensive trees for your food forest, you'll certainly want to keep them all alive and as productive as possible.

My approach differs, as I always keep a little nursery of plants going at my house and most of my trees cost little or nothing to produce. Instead of fiddling around with trying to get all my spacings perfect, I walk around and plant trees closely, figuring I can always chop some of them back—or remove them—if they get too crowded. Remember, *most of life's problems can be fixed with a chainsaw*. If you don't have a chainsaw, an axe, machete or pruning saw stand in quite nicely. We are playing survival of the fittest, rather than trying to baby everything.

I do have my favorites, of course, those being rare species and trees that cost me a bit of money to purchase. Those I keep spaced and protected. But all the seedling soursops and moringas and mangoes and pomegranates? We'll just see which ones do great and then keep those, or, if I am feeling sentimental and not violent enough to murder the poky ones, I will prune them back to let light in.

We often think of fruit trees as being "needy." Some trees warrant this preconception. Planting a grafted nursery-grown plum or peach tree in rough sugar sand usually leads to disappointment. They aren't as scrappy as a mimosa or a chinaberry tree, that's for sure. Hence the reason chinaberries and mimosas are classified as invasive— and show up everywhere—whereas cultivated plums and peaches very rarely self-seed in the wild or have any ability to compete with native vegetation, let alone invasive trees and vines.

If you want to grow fruit trees without a lot of work, it's very important to pick tougher varieties and put them in a situation where they are not forced to compete heavily for resources. In my backyard in Grenada, I had a starfruit tree. Three years ago, it was overshadowed by large trees and covered in vines. Unable to reach the sun, it sat in the shade, thin-leafed and barren of fruit. Once we chain-sawed down the competition and brought it sunlight along with water and fertilization, it rewarded us by bursting into bloom and bearing multiple large crops of sweet fruit. Starfruit are tough and quite easy to grow but they still cannot compete with choking vines and overshadowing pioneer species.

In a food forest system, you need to manage the system well enough that your fruit trees can become the canopy and suppress other species. As they're highly bred and touchier than wild trees, this requires a little extra work but once they are well-established, you have very little left to do. The important thing is to really give them every advantage when they're young so they reach a healthy maturity. Grow trees that fit your climate and make sure they get lots of water, compost and mulch when young. That's really the two-part key to having happy fruit trees.

Triangular spacings are better than square spacings since they allow you to put in more trees and give the system a natural feel. Unless you are planting your food forest for commercial production, in which case you may want to plant trees in defined alleys as Stefan Sobkowiak does in Quebec or Ernst Goetsch does in Brazil. For the last few years, I've been working on an similar organized food forest system I call Grocery Row Gardening, which puts all the layers of a food forest into 4' wide beds with 3' wide pathways. In it, I combine vegetable and small fruit production with an orchard, spaced carefully and regularly pruned. In the summer of 2021, I released a short book on this experimental system titled, simply enough, *Grocery Row Gardening*. If you're interested in trying a highly organized food forest system like that, you might enjoy that book. It's a bit different from the food forest system we're covering in this book but may work even better in a small yard. However, unlike a traditional food forest, there is more maintenance involved as the trees must be contained due to the tighter spacing.

But you don't need rows or grids or anything to plant a food forest. Trees do not care about geometry and will happily grow even if you plant them in bizarre patterns. I usually just plant a tree, then walk a few paces and plant another, then plant a third at a roughly equidistant point to finish the triangle.

However you start, your food forest should eventually become a little chunk of half-open woods. If you have more space, start with some great big trees in the middle; pecans or full-sized mangos, for example. Then surround those with location-appropriate trees from the lists of species later in this book—or from whatever you find and love.

It makes sense to start with the canopy layer and hang the rest of the system on it. If you have three pecan trees at the points of a 60' x 60' x 60' triangle, you can start filling in the inside of the space with tons of chop-and-drop species, smaller trees, then shrubs, groundcovers, etc.

The canopy and sub-canopy trees take a good bit of time to get going. For the shrubs, think of things like Surinam cherries, pigeon peas (they're edible and fix nitrogen), dwarf bananas, katuk, curry leaf, edible hibiscus, and prickly pears.

NOTE: after reading this portion, my proofreader Amy wrote:

Surely you didn't mean to recommend planting those darn cacti on purpose. That's like saying "Toss sand spurs into the wind." But, hey, you're the plant master so I reckon you know what you're doing. I pay kids $10 a bucket to get rid of those things. I let them live along fence lines though... especially my sister-in-law's fence line.

I laughed. There are less annoying prickly pears, but point taken.

Then around those, add in cassava, herbs, passionfruit, yams, sweet potatoes, chaya and other herbaceous edibles and vines. At the beginning of a food forest system, you have a lot of light coming in so there's plenty of space to plant annuals and short-term perennials that provide you with quick food as you wait for your trees to grow.

We experimented with a lot of mixed plantings. Most of them worked well, but some did not. The worst one was interplanting blueberries and sweet potatoes. The sweet potatoes took off and produced well in the mulch around the young blueberry bushes, but the blueberries were not happy at all. They seemed to hate the root disturbance. Another time, I planted a very tall cassava variety with sweet potatoes. The cassava grew marvelously and shaded out the potatoes, giving us a yield of cassava but not much in the way of sweet potatoes. This same system might have worked well if we had spaced the cassava farther apart. Florida sun is very hot and you can often grow "full sun" crops in part shade without issue. I had a nice jalapeno bush growing at the bottom of a fruit tree one year, no problem.

We also had luck growing pineapples around the trunks of large oak trees which protected the pineapples from winter frosts. Despite the pineapple plants being a "full sun" crop, they still bore, which was great as growing them in the open would have killed them. The fruit was a little small but it was better than no pineapples at all.

You can grow a ton of food between your trees at the beginning. Seminole pumpkins, melons, sweet potatoes and other sun-loving ramblers bring you yields in months as you wait for your trees to bear. We got great sweet potato yields early on

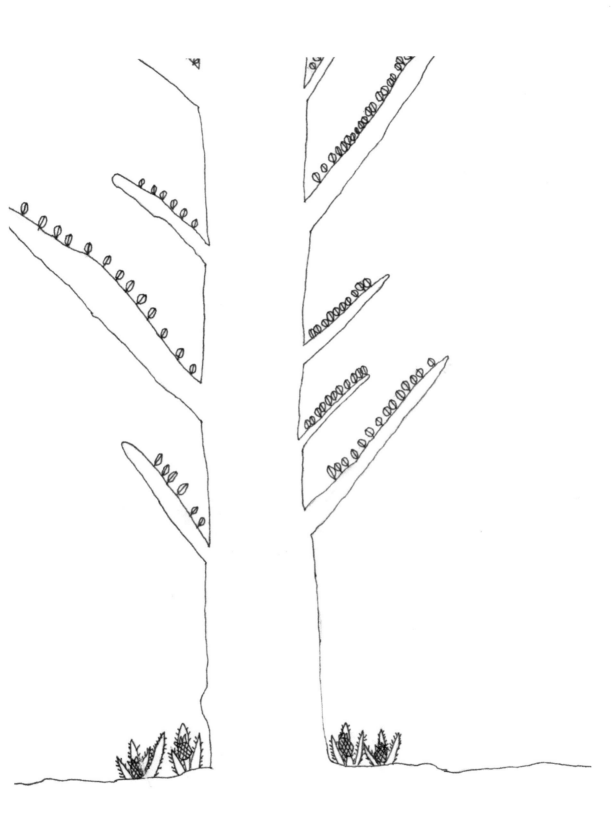

Pineapples Around an Oak

in our North Florida food forest. In the South Florida food forest project, my mom grew a bunch of kale one year at the base of a coconut palm surrounded by katuk and other long-term edible shrubs. Before they filled in, there was plenty of space for annuals. In my tropical food forest system, I grew pigeon peas, corn, cassava and pumpkins between my young trees and one of my sons had a good watermelon patch beneath a coconut palm.

In North Florida one of my neighbors nicknamed me "Jungle Jim" thanks to my densely planted front yard food forest. I didn't mind as I was rather proud of my crazy jungle. It was still young and weedy then, with rambling pumpkins and sweet potatoes in areas that are now shaded by persimmons, mulberries and chestnuts. Over time, the composition of the space changes and new yields emerge as the old ones decline.

Strolling through that food forest is like taking a botanical tour. Weeds are happy alongside rare perennial vegetables and butterflies drift past in a constant dance shared with bees, dragonflies, beetles and wasps. Along one path is a loquat tree next to a fig. Below the fig are edible elephant ears; behind it is a root beer plant at the base of a young queen palm. Beyond that are shampoo gingers, blackberries, native pawpaws, bananas, Singapore daisies, an orange tree, more figs, Jerusalem artichokes, black-eyed Susans, watermelon vines, yacon, a magnolia tree, cassava, Confederate rose, pears, a bottlebrush tree buzzing with bees, dwarf mulberries, a honey locust, Mexican sunflowers, Christmas cassia, sumacs, St. Christopher lilies, a Key limequat, rambling sweet potatoes, turmeric, firespike, African blue basil, apples, wild plums and other species. And that's only one quarter of the food forest project... just a slice along a single path!

Your focus should be on that long-term goal of creating a self-sustaining forest that requires very little work and contains a wide range of food and life. It will be a beautiful, shady, wonderful place of fruits and nuts and butterflies, with rich soil and mushrooms and birds. The first few years are the hardest. It requires some watering, feeding, trimming and weeding. Some plants won't survive. But then, magic happens. The forest begins to take over and soon you have a garden you can pass onto your children's children—which isn't something you can say for the weedy patch left after summer's sweet corn harvest.

There's no time like the present to get your hands in the dirt and start learning. You won't screw this up. Whether you start in islands or plan the thing meticulously, or just plant like an anarchist, if you keep your trees alive for the first year or two, they just start to take care of themselves and get all they need from the rain and the natural fall of leaves.

Walk around in the woods and look at how trees and plants interact. Start spotting the different layers of a forest and see how all the spots are filled. Then come home and do the same thing in your yard.

If you don't have much time, just do a little when you can. Even a few minutes a day adds up. It takes seconds to pop a seed in the ground. It takes a few minutes to start some cuttings. It takes an hour to plant a half-dozen fruit trees.

It's not long at all. Don't be paralyzed. Take bite-sized pieces when you can and it will happen.

GROWING YOUR OWN PLANTS FROM (ALMOST) SCRATCH

A successful businessman once told me, "Time is money and money is time. If you don't have time to do something, spend money. If you do have time, spend that to make money."

That advice works if you're building a business—but it also works if you're growing your own food.

Trees, shrubs and even veggie transplants are expensive. If you're broke, like many of us—fear not; you don't have to spend a fortune to plant a food forest. Learning a few simple propagation tips will save you big.

Are you ready?

We'll start with the most basic of basics: seeds.

Growing From Seed

In the spring, many gardeners go down to the local nursery or home improvement store and load up their carts with nursery-grown plants. You can buy transplants for everything, including corn and melons.

This is rather ridiculous.

First, a lot of plants don't transplant well—and the ones that do often grow just as well from seeding in place, if not better. Buying lots of transplants is a waste of money, particularly when you're adding plants to a good-sized food forest.

If you grow seeds in the ground where they're planted, the roots expand rapidly through and down into the soil, rather than being bunched up in a pot. They also don't have to deal with radically different growing conditions as they go from a nursery and into your terrifyingly sandy Florida yard. Nursery plants are grown in perfect conditions, in perfect soil, then sit in variable light conditions until sold, wrapping their roots around and around in a small space. When you direct-seed plants, they acclimate to the sun and soil right away and start jumping immediately, without a rough transition from pot to earth.

Yet the trick is keeping them from death as they grow. It's easy for small seedlings to get trampled, eaten, or choked out by weeds and lost.

All that to say, there are benefits to direct seeding and to growing in pots. I do both in my food forest projects.

Jackfruit do not seem to like transplanting at all, so I start them from fresh seed right in the ground, planting a half-dozen or more seeds an inch or two deep in a loosened and weed-free spot of soil. Then I water and watch for them to come up in a month or so. At that point, I water regularly until they reach a height of a foot or so, then cut all but two or three of them. When those reach about 2' tall, I pick the best-looking one and chop the other one to the ground. Now I have a seedling jackfruit with a great root system growing right into the native soil. I use the same method with papayas.

Many other trees, however, I grow in my nursery area first. To start tree seeds, just make some cheap planting flats from 18" pieces of 1" x 6" lumber, then fill them with soil and plant seeds in them, watering regularly. When they sprout and grow a little, transplant them into individual pots. Or just start seeds in pots right from the beginning.

Getting seeds is fun. Even a trip to the supermarket is a chance to add species to your food forest.

Pomegranate seeds germinate readily, as do citrus seeds. Mango pits grow wonderfully. Apples, pears and stone fruit sprout after some chilling in the fridge first. Put them in a baggie of moist soil and wait until they start growing roots, then plant them out in pots. The best option for ensuring these seedlings are suited to Florida

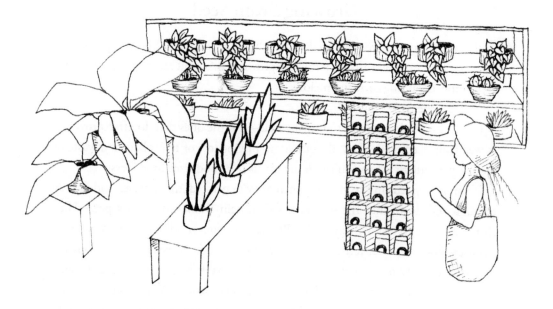

conditions is to plant seeds from fruit already growing in Florida, but I will plant every seed I can find just to see what happens.

Many herbs take a while to get going from seed, but you can plant quite a few for a paltry sum. Some shrubs, like Surinam cherry, are easy to start from seed and don't take all that long to grow up. Often tropical plants have seeds that do not keep well and need to be planted fast without being allowed to dry out and sit around. Jackfruit, citrus, canistel, loquat, wax apples, lychees and many others are this way.

Another fun way to have a constant supply of trees and shrubs is to create a special garden bed dedicated to starting long-term perennials from seed. Put this bed someplace where you'll pay attention to it, like in your annual gardens. A 4' x 8' bed filled with good soil and watered a few times a week can produce a lot of young seedlings. You can plant carefully and label your plants or just stuff in random seeds every time you eat a good passionfruit or wild plum and grow whatever comes up, trusting that they're probably edible. Personally, I like the latter method. Randomness is exciting. Plus, I'm terrible at labelling.

I remember walking through my yard with Rachel one spring and saying, "whoa, sweetheart, look at all these little trees coming up. They look like persimmons!"

"You planted them," she said. "Last fall, remember? You were wandering around eating persimmons and shoving the seeds into the ground when we were talking."

"Oh yeah..."

Which brings us to another thing which must be discussed. At this point, some readers may be experiencing cognitive dissonance trying to reconcile my advice to grow fruit trees from seed with the Official Serious and Very Sad Facts Which Boring Gardening Experts Share.

Trees from seed get a bad rap.

"It takes forever," some BGEs say. Others say, "You'll just get bad fruit!"

No on both. Just no.

First, it doesn't take forever to grow fruit trees from seed, but it does take time. I planted two seedling peach trees in my North Florida back yard. At one year old—from a germinated pit!—they were 5' tall and had 1" thick trunks. At three years old they were 15' tall and were loaded with peaches.

To grow them, I cracked open some peach pits, removed the kernels, soaked them overnight then put them in the refrigerator in a baggie of moist potting soil. When roots started growing a few months later, I planted them in pots, then transplanted them when they were about a foot tall into a nice holes I dug 2' deep and filled with manure, compost and surrounding soil (ignoring my own advice on using just native soil). A little watering and they were off to the races. At a year old they were a lot healthier than the 6' grafted trees I had planted two years before. Tap roots are key to many trees' growth: by letting them get going from their infancy where they're going to spend their lives, you give them a big jump.

Some trees take a long time to reach maturity from seed, of course. Citrus may take 8–10 years before they bear, as will pecans and some other fruit and nuts. That means plant them NOW! How much money are you out? None. Just do it. If you get tired of waiting, learn to graft. That allows you to take some wood from a producing tree and add it to your seedlings, getting you fruit quickly.

Heck, if you want fruit fast, get yourself a papaya from the store and scoop out the seeds. Don't let them dry out or anything—there's no need. Just plant them, jelly and all, in a good-sized pot or flat and start watering. Put that pot in a warm spot. In a few weeks, little papaya trees will start emerging. Let them grow a little, then thin them out to leave 10 or so good ones in the pot. When those reach 6–12" tall, transplant them to individual pots or put them right into your food forest. Or follow the station method mentioned above, growing them like jackfruit seedings in the ground. If you're in a frost-free region and keep them watered, they can produce prodigious quantities of fruit within a year or two.

Starfruit are also easy to grow from seed. Just plant some in a pot, water, then transplant later. In a few years you'll have fruit. There was a bilimbi in my tropical food forest that bloomed for the first time in 2020. I started it from seed four years previous.

The second argument against growing trees from seed (with the exception of those seedlings you intend to graft later on) is that you don't know what you're going to get. You might not get something good, Boring Gardening Experts will say.

They are wrong. Most of the time you get good or great fruit. You're maintaining genetic diversity and, even more interestingly, you could potentially end up with something better than the parent.

There's a seedling June plum in my tropical food forest with variegated foliage. I've never seen another like it. Growing from seed opens up very interesting possibilities for new varieties with very little downside. So plant trees from seed—and if you really aren't happy with the fruit, graft on them or cut them down and feed them to another tree. Or use the wood in your smoker. Fruit wood is good for that!

Growing from Cuttings

Cuttings root easily from some plants and poorly from others. Look up your plant on the 'net first or in my book *Free Plants for Everyone*, then decide if taking cuttings is the way to go. Or just try it.

Figs, pomegranates, roses (look for ones with large hips—those are good for food forests!), lemons, blackberries, blueberries, grapes, rosemary and a wide variety of other edibles are pretty darn easy to start from cuttings.

Get a sharp knife and take hardwood or softwood cuttings, depending on the species. Don't take huge cuttings—just 5–8" or so is usually good.

Then dip the bottom ends in rooting hormone. You can get rooting hormone at any garden center. It's cheap and well-worth the money. Then stick a few cuttings in a pot of decent well-draining potting mix, or vermiculite, or sand and peat or basically whatever you have lying around.

Water well, then put a plastic bag over the top of the pot to retain moisture and rubber band it in place. I call this the "mini-greenhouse" method of plant propagation.

Make sure they don't dry out and in a month or two, they should start rooting. When they start putting on new growth, give one a little tug and see if it's rooted. Be gentle, take the bag off, wait a little longer, then pot them up. I rooted blueberries and lemon trees on my windowsill in the kitchen in about two months this way. I've even used white plastic grocery bags over tin-can pots and rooted acerola cherries under my potting bench. In fact, I forgot all about them for months and months, then came back to find well-rooted little trees.

Some plants root from freshly cut branches simply jammed in the ground. Figs, gumbo limbo, some mulberries, cassava, chaya and moringa are known to do this with varying levels of success.

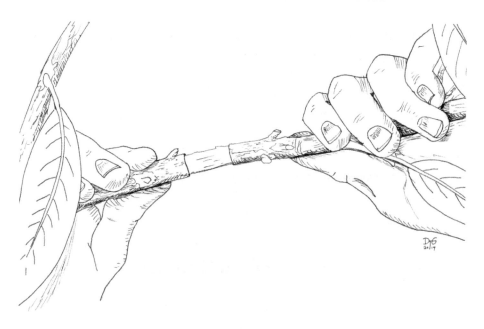

Other Methods

Air layering is a fail-safe method for many shrubs and trees, plus you get a decent-sized plant in the end.

The benefit of air-layering is that the original plant supports the baby plant as it grows, meaning you don't have to bother with bags and pots and such. You do have to use a sharp knife and get a hold of some sphagnum moss or potting soil and plastic wrap. If you can handle that, you can air layer.

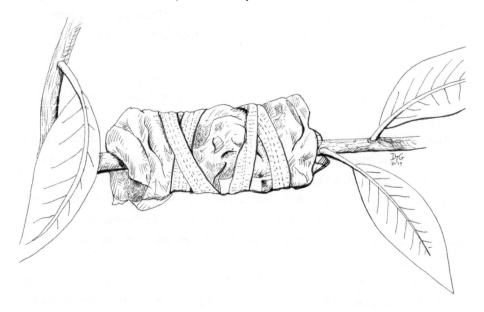

First, pick a small branch the tree can afford to sacrifice. Remove a 1" strip of bark all the way around the branch where you'd like new roots to grow. Everything from that point up will eventually be your new tree. Once you've made this cut, dust it with rooting hormone, then wrap the wound with a fistful of moist sphagnum moss (if you have it—if not, potting soil works fine). Then wrap that up like a hard candy with some plastic wrap or tie the ends with string, rubber bands or flagging tape.

A few months later, look through the plastic to see if there are roots forming inside. Usually it takes quite a while, sometimes up to a year. When the plastic is filled with roots, carefully cut the branch below the air-layered portion and pot up your new tree. Water it well until established and don't leave it in full sun to dry out.

Tip-layering is a method that works well on cane fruits such as blackberries and Mysore raspberries. When you see a nice, sprawling branch growing, bend the tip of it down and bury it in the ground. I started a little thicket of blackberries this way. The tip will put down roots and the old branch often withers away and leaves a new baby plant behind. Simple!

Setting Up A Nursery Area

If you have a half-shady area near a faucet, plus pots and dirt, you can grow up a bunch of your plants for later transplanting to the garden or your yard.

When I prune, I often save some of the clippings and start them in pots on my back porch for later planting out. Having a convenient location really helps with this. Some cuttings take, some don't. It takes a few minutes, and timing makes a difference: I once tried rooting mulberries during the fruiting season and had a complete failure of all fifteen cuttings. It happens. All you're out is a little time.

Try, try again.

When you consider that pomegranate trees sell for $20 apiece... figs in one-gallon pots are often $10.00 each... and other trees and shrubs all bear price tags of their own, you can save a lot of money really fast. It takes an hour to make yourself a couple hundred bucks worth of baby plants. Time well spent.

Plus, if you manage to grow more than you need, you can give away the extra or even sell and barter plants here and there. I did this for years and eventually opened my own little plant nursery to sell what I grew.

Win!

Sources of Plant Material

When you start out as a gardener, you might be pretty short on plants. This is the time to go meet other gardeners. They'll often share cuttings and seeds with you.

Gardeners are some of the nicest people on earth and most of them genuinely love sharing what they have.

Compliment someone's canna lilies and you might get a root pressed into your hands. Ask about someone's fallen mangos and they'll usually give you a basket. Tell someone you're just getting started and they may give you more seeds, bulbs and cuttings than you can handle. Just remember these folks when you have something extra of your own and pass it on.

Another way to find propagative material is to hit botanical gardens or Master Gardener program at the local extension. Sometimes cuttings and seeds can be had for the asking. I also recommend scouring the net for permaculture enthusiasts in your areas, rare fruit clubs, plant geeks that run small nurseries, community gardens and plant-related non-profits. Don't steal cuttings and seeds—I know the temptation is real—but it isn't good for your soul, and it doesn't allow you to meet up with cool people. Instead, you're sneaking around. It's so much better to make friends and share. That said, if a plant is at a public park or hanging over the sidewalk, I don't really see the harm in taking a fruit or a small cutting to propagate. We pay taxes for public spaces and you're helping that tree reproduce itself.

But it's more fun to meet gardeners, be friendly, bring some seeds to share and start trading. I enjoy taking potted trees and plants and just giving them to strangers with gardens. If I see a pretty garden in someone's front yard, I'll sometimes stop and give them a plant and tell them I love what they're doing. Instant friendship!

And of course, if you can't find what you need that way, there's always the seed rack, plus plenty of great seed companies that sell online. I've also had luck getting rare edibles on etsy and ebay, though there are also tons of scammers on there, especially outside the US.

And don't forget: Oriental or International markets are also excellent places to find seeds, roots, sugarcane stems and more.

When you're limited on funds and need to grow food, quit giving all your money away to nurseries. Start looking around for likely cutting and seed sources and get propagating. It's a great feeling to see your little babies grow into productive adults—try it and see.

Again, when you spend $25.00 on a tree, you don't really want to jam it into a shady corner and hope it survives. I think economics are part of the reason some of the food forests I see are so regimented. The spacing, the watering systems, the perfect mulch circles—they make sense when you're protecting an expensive investment, but they don't make sense time and resource-wise.

I used to worry a lot about my trees. Now that I maintain a nursery and do a lot of propagation, I don't worry as much.

When you start your plants from seeds and cuttings they're more expendable. You just don't have that much money out there. It costs pocket change for decent dirt and old coffee cans. Even old pans and milk jugs can be pressed into service as pots. And you can even make your own potting soil.

Buy a couple of healthy plants from nurseries, then start a lot of babies from those initial purchases. Plant your peach pits. Chop-and-stick Mexican sunflowers. Divide clumps of chives and tuck them in around your apple trees. Save seeds from nitrogen-fixing cassia trees growing in your local park. Propagation makes food forests accessible to anyone. I enjoy plant propagation so much I wrote a whole book on the topic—if you don't own Free Plants for Everyone, I think you'll enjoy it. And if you don't want to buy another book, I've also posted lots of articles and videos on plant propagation. I want every gardener to save money by growing their own trees and plants. It really is like printing money.

Now that you know how to build soil, plant trees and start your own plants, what about space? What if you really, really want a food forest but you don't have a big yard?

Read on!

FOOD FORESTS
IN SMALL SPACES

Do you wish you could grow a fruit tree—or a dozen—in your backyard, but think you just don't have the space?

It's time to rethink that assumption.

I realized years ago that the supposed maximum size of trees isn't a set thing. If you stay on top of pruning, you can do some amazing things with your fruit trees. While visiting the farm of a man who had formerly worked for the University of Florida, I saw peach trees that were kept at an easily pickable 8' height via aggressive pruning when they were young. On Grenada I saw a fruit-laden tamarind tree that had been repeatedly cut by a local electric company—at only about 6' in height! The branches stuck out sideways low to the ground and bore pods after the center was cut down. Instead of harvesting fruit with a long pole from branches 40' in the air, the owners (and local schoolkids) could just pick by hand.

A full-size tamarind tree can easily shade most or all of a typical backyard. A full-size apple can almost do the same. Yet the answer we are often given to this issue is to "plant dwarf trees." Dwarf trees are deliberately grafted onto rootstocks that restrict the growth of the tree. Unfortunately, this also leads to weaker trees that die much younger than standard fruit trees.

What if you could just plant a full-size tree and keep it under control? After all, isn't that what Bonsai growers do?

It's more possible than you might think. You can fit a dozen or more fruit trees in a little backyard with less work than you would expect. What about planting a hedge of plums or lemons? Or a three-trunked apple tree that your children can pick without a ladder?

A few years ago, I discovered a marvelous book by Ann Ralph titled *Grow a Little Fruit Tree,* which really put together a lot of the thoughts I'd been having about smaller fruit trees as well as provided simple instructions for making it happen.

As she writes:

You don't need to buy dwarfs or ultra-dwarfs if you want small trees. Europeans have used pruning to keep ordinary fruit trees small for centuries. Take a visit to a historic garden in the United States, and you will discover that our own Founding Fathers often kept their fruit trees small. Once you understand the simple logic of pruning, keeping a fruit tree appropriately scaled is easy enough to do. In fact, regular pruning is the best way to control the size of a fruit tree.... Any type of deciduous fruit tree responds to the keep-it-small pruning treatment—the oldest heirloom or the most recent introduction. Choose whatever variety of apricot, apple, cherry, fig, quince, persimmon, plum or pluot—a plum-apricot cross—is most ideal for your palate and your climate. Keep it small. Put away the ladder. You can plant more trees than you planned to, either singly around the garden, or in a hedgerow along a sunny fence, or even three little trees closely spaced and pruned to grow apart from one another (three fruit trees together where you thought you only had room for one). You can work fruit trees into an existing landscape. You can accommodate favorite fruits that need another tree for pollination. Within attention to ripening times, you can harvest fresh fruit in reasonable quantities from your garden from late spring well into winter. Factor in citrus if you live in a citrus-friendly climate and you can harvest fresh fruit from your garden year-round.

—*Grow a Little Fruit Tree*, Ann Ralph

I'm sold.

In the book she shares simple techniques for keeping fruit trees small, including when to prune and how to prune. I was already experimenting with keeping tropical trees at smaller sizes, then I came across *Grow a Little Fruit Tree* and found it to be a great guide on the topic.

If you've ever seen piles of smashed fruit wasted beneath a towering tree, the idea of a small, pickable tree that bears you perfect fruit you can harvest by hand becomes quite appealing.

I've had to pick a poorly maintained orchard before and it's a pain to climb for fruit or knock them down with poles in order to gather them from the ground. Of course, even without tending, we still got fruit.

If a gardener spends his time reading Ag extension guides to growing trees, he'll start to think you need huge spaces between individual specimens in order to get production. Yet forests don't work that way. Trees are packed in here and there in a crazy quilt of life. When you look at your backyard and compare it to commercial tree spacings, you might get the idea that it's impossible to grow much of anything.

Nope. You can chop and chop and chop and chop and chop and keep things under control—plus the prunings feed the soil. There are also other techniques that are quite fun. You can get crazier than you think.

Dave Wilson Nursery has posted videos on YouTube showing trees planted three to a single hole—just 18" apart! As they grow, they're naturally dwarfed—yet there are three types of fruit growing in the space where one tree would normally be. Branches growing towards the center are pruned, making the mature trees look like a three-trunked fruit shrub.

We are experimenting with that method right now, planting plums, chestnuts and even pecans with multiple trees in a hole. Now: imagine you planted sweet potatoes around those trees, or green onions, or yacon. Then grow passion vines up through the middle. Your production from the space has just jumped higher.

Better yet, plant a row of trees this way and tuck in berry bushes and other perennials along the front and back of that row, with various herbs mixed in to repel pests and provide you with culinary delights. Whether or not you plant more than one tree in a hole, you can easily manage rows of pruned trees. Just prune in summer to reduce the vigor and control tree heights. By planting a row of trees— and perennial shrubs, if you like—you can create a long, edible fruiting hedge. A "fedge," as it's called. Or go further and try my Grocery Row Gardening method of mixing heavily pruned fruit trees right into your garden beds.

If you're gardening in a small space you don't have to give up on tree crops. You just need to do things differently.

Don't be afraid to experiment. Life is more resilient than you might think. There are ways to prune, pollard, bend or dwarf trees that will make them manageable.

In my front yard food forest, I planted more trees long after I had "too many" for the space. Again, as trees are expensive, just start your own. If you do that, a failure won't break the bank.

Fear not and plant a lot. And chop chop chop!

You can also redirect trees to grow in horizontal space, rather than vertical. Some trees, like mulberries, can be heavily chopped or even coppiced to keep their fruit close to you and their tops from towering overhead and eating all your yard's sunshine. They'll grow back and fruit the next year even after being chainsawed to the ground.

Others can be trained against walls or even sent along wires like grape vines. That process is called "espaliering." It's a serious way to save space, though it's fiddly and labor-intensive compared to just jamming things together and pruning.

This chapter wouldn't be complete without raising some of the objections I get from prospective food forest builders and other gardeners who think I'm nuts for planting roughly 100 fruit trees on a half-acre.

Let's do it in my patented Imaginary Gardening Conversation Laid Out Like The Dialog Of a Play(TM) method:

DAVID THE GOOD: ...and see, I jam in all kinds of stuff into a tiny space and let it fight. That way I'll have lots and lots and lots and lots of food.

COMMON-SENSE GARDENER: But what about when they get big? Won't they shade everything out?

DAVID THE GOOD: No... I won't let them.

COMMON-SENSE GARDENER: How will you stop them? I learned that life finds a way. That it breaks free.

DAVID THE GOOD: I want them to break free. I want them to all fight together. I want dinosaurs to show up.

COMMON-SENSE GARDENER: That won't happen. What about the problem of shade. What will you do?

DAVID THE GOOD: It MIGHT happen. Haven't you heard of Mokele-mbembe?

COMMON-SENSE GARDENER: Oh for goodness sake, you irritating–

DAVID THE GOOD: Machete. And bow saw.

COMMON-SENSE GARDENER: What?

DAVID THE GOOD: That's how I'll add in light. I'll take out limbs here and there and add them to the forest floor.

COMMON-SENSE GARDENER: Do you think that will be enough?

DAVID THE GOOD: Probably not.

COMMON-SENSE GARDENER: So what else will you do?

DAVID THE GOOD: Bait. I'll add lots of bait. Wonder where I can get a mammoth carcass... maybe from Siberia? That would bring 'em in.

COMMON-SENSE GARDENER: The trees???

DAVID THE GOOD: Oh yeah, lots of dinosaurs are herbivores, I think. I would need trees they like. Hmm...

COMMON-SENSE GARDENER: ...

You know, people just don't have any sense of adventure.

When you take a small space and think in all directions, growing up—growing against walls—tucking things into small spaces—pruning like a madman—turning trees into shrubs or treating them like vines, man, you can do a lot more than you think!

Get out there, get thinking about what you can do creatively to maximize your space, then get planting.

And if any dinosaurs show up, please call me.

A Potted Food Forest

Before we end this chapter, it's worth addressing the idea of growing a food forest in pots. Though it sounds a bit crazy, it's more than possible to make a portable food forest. Sometimes we don't own the land we garden, or aren't sure if we'll have to move soon, yet we'd love to have a food forest. Or perhaps we only have a little back porch area or a condo patio, yet the idea of a food forest is such a wonderful idea that we can't stand it. I understand! In Grenada I had to rent for a few years but I didn't want to give up on growing trees and perennials. Instead, I grew lots of trees and herbs in pots.

It can be done, though it takes a little more effort than planting in the ground. You have to get containers and you need to keep them watered, plus you have to make sure the weeds don't grow all around the pots and into them, choking out your plants. Unlike a regular food forest where you can run around with a scythe or a string trimmer, you have to hand-weed your potted plants. If you put your pots on top of nursery grade weed fabric or a hard surface, like a driveway or brick patio, weeding is much easier. Otherwise, you have to move your pots around and cut the grass growing up between them. That takes some work, especially when you are growing larger specimens in pots.

Another benefit of putting your pots on a hard surface is that the plants won't root through into the ground. If you put a potted tree on bare ground and leave it long enough, some of the roots are going to escape through the drainage holes and dig their way into the native soil. If you let this continue for a year or more, those roots will become the tree's primary source of food and water, getting thicker and and growing deep into the ground. Eventually, the pot will bust apart and the tree will have effectively planted itself there.

I've seen this happen many times. If you later want to try and move a tree that's rooted heavily into the ground, you'll have to chop the roots and that causes great stress on the tree. To prevent this from happening with trees sitting on top of the ground, move them around occasionally to break the young root connections before the roots become huge and immobile.

If I were to arrange a potted patio food forest, I would make smaller trees the canopy layer. Acerola cherries, black Surinam cherries, jabuticaba, guava, starfruit and other shorter trees are easier to keep growing in pots. However, I have kept a seedling mango growing in a 50-gallon pot and even got it to fruit. That tree had 60' potential, but I pruned it aggressively to keep it under control and it worked. I did the same with a lychee and got fruit.

That said, trees that are naturally short and make small fruit are easier. The root constraints of a pot also restricts growth. Sometimes the roots end up filling the entire pot and twirling about so much that the tree wilts repeatedly and never seems to be happy. When this happens, I un-pot the tree and hack off the edges and bottom of the root ball, slicing through the circling roots and removing handfuls of small, tangled roots. At the same time, I prune off a third or more of the top of the tree. After this process, I re-pot it in a larger sized pot—if it needs that—or I just put it back in the same pot with some new potting soil around the root ball, provided I feel the current pot is as large as I want to go.

There are great big black nursery pots that work well for trees. Sometimes you can buy them from local nurseries. Local landscapers may even give you pots for free. I've also gotten pots online from Greenhousemegastore.com. We've also used old refrigerators, barrels, bathtubs and other improvised containers for growing perennials. It looks kind of trashy, but it works.

You can arrange a container food forest similarly to an in-ground food forest. Put a few bigger potted trees in the center, then put rings of smaller potted perennials and berries around them. In the larger pots you can also plant herbs and vegetables as groundcovers beneath the trees. If you don't want to buy as much soil, I've found that filling the bottom of pots with rotten wood, leaves, grass clippings, shredded paper and even some kitchen scraps will fill up the space and feed the trees over time. Top off with decent soil and plant! You can buy potting soil in bulk from landscape suppliers and save a lot of money over getting it in bags. It's usually sold by the cubic yard.

Feeding and watering trees in pots takes more effort than a food forest in the ground. If you don't water your trees regularly, the soil may turn "hydrophobic" and refuse to get wet when watered. If trees are wilting regularly even when you water them, pick up the entire potted tree and see how heavy the dirt feels. If it's lighter than expected, it's probably shedding the water instead of soaking it up. A quick fix for this is to stick the entire pot of soil, tree and all, in a big container of water, like a half-barrel or a kiddie pool. That will re-hydrate the soil.

To feed potted trees I often use slow-release fertilizer granules. They aren't organic, but the entire process of growing in pots is not particularly natural anyhow and I've not had great luck keeping trees lush and green in pots without adding a little bit of fertilizer. If you want to work harder, you can make compost and give it to the trees, or feed them with compost teas, but 90-day slow-release fertilizers are much easier when you have a lot of trees to care for. I don't think the trees mind either way. In a regular food forest it's not necessary, but pot-grown trees can't reach their roots out to grab what they need beyond the tiny space of their pot.

One final benefit of a potted food forest is that you can move the tender trees into a building during a frost event. In North Florida we would haul our potted lemons, mango, coffee, jabuticaba, guava and starfruit trees into the house during freezes. Though it wasn't as ideal as growing these trees in the ground, our climate wasn't ideal either and having them in pots gave us the chance to grow truly tropical plants that wouldn't have survived in our main front-yard food forest.

If you have a small space, you can still make a food forest. Pruning, training, pots—whatever it takes. Don't give up on your food forest dream!

WILDLIFE AND FOOD FOREST SYSTEMS

A food forest yields fruits and nuts, wood and more—but that's still not the full extent of its benefits. It also brings a great amount of life to your land. A multi-species forest teems with wonderful life beyond just the trees and plants. Butterflies and bees, lizards and armadillos, beetles and frogs, birds and dragonflies—you may have planted a food forest in order to feed yourself, but you also have made a place for nature to colonize. The colonization process is one that greatly excites me and is something my children have also loved. It doesn't start right away, but as your system grows in plant interactions, animal life finds it and makes itself at home.

Oceans of ink have been spilled on the value of incorporating animal life on the homestead, with great ideas on "mob grazing" and chicken tractors and cut-and-carry systems for goats, as well as the value of bees and guinea fowl, ducks and even worm farming. These are all good things if you love taking care of livestock, but if you're more of a low-maintenance gardener, you don't have to feel bad about skipping domesticated animals altogether. God will provide many useful species for your food forest and they won't require feeding, watering or de-worming.

I have put chickens to work in my food forest and vegetable gardens. Yet chickens are also high maintenance and almost always require supplementary feed unless you make careful (and extensive) plans to feed them completely off your land. Over the years my view on chickens has changed. At first, I viewed them as essential to a small homestead. This was years ago when I had stars in my eyes about home-raised eggs and meat, with chickens free-ranging around a farmyard and kids carrying fluffy hens about. We learned later that chickens aren't quite as perfect as they appear in magazine articles. Free range birds decorate your porch with droppings and tear up anything you mulch or plant. They also get eaten by predators, often in gruesome and terrifying ways. As I looked at the cost of feed and housing and my monthly budget, I grew less and less enamored with my flock and ended up selling it. Later, we tried again in the tropics but our half-wild yard fowl had a propensity to run away and not return.

When I got back to the States in 2020, I resisted the idea of getting chickens again, until I saw empty shelves in the local grocery store and realized that the supply line really might shut down at some point. I was also pushed to get chickens by my friend Carolyn Smith, who sent me multiple superchats on YouTube for a "chicken fund."

Eventually I gave in at the beginning of 2021 and am glad I did. We are raising them with much more success here in the Alabama countryside than we had in our previous locations. Part of this is due to having more land and resources and the other part of it is due to our past experiences informing our current methods. The issue of getting enough chicken food still exists, but we are trying various experiments again to see if we can balance buying food and free ranging with tractors and home-raised grains.

There is a good argument to be made that the cost of chickens and their eggs should be less of a consideration compared to the superior quality and nutrition afforded by home-raised eggs and meat. Incorporating them is a worthy endeavor, but it may not be possible for those with limited time or severe budget constraints. There is also a learning curve, and keeping animals—even just a few hens—does tie you down much more than does a food forest.

Over the years we experimented with goats, rabbits, ducks, guinea fowl and velociraptors. Most of them were more trouble than they were worth to us in yields. Especially when the velociraptors figured out how to get into the emergency ice cream stockpile in the chest freezer.

In an urban environment, domesticated animals are even harder to keep in a food forest—and some pets that are often added to yards, such as dogs and cats, can be destructive in a food forest system. Dogs will dig and trample and sometimes even eat your plants. Cats happily murder birds, lizards and other beneficial species. If you keep pets, it's important to make sure they don't damage all your hard work or make it impossible to get a system going. I knew a man in North Florida who told me he couldn't grow gardens in his backyard because his two huge dogs destroyed everything. Ouch.

Instead of having a garden that could feed his family, he had to feed two large animals that also kept him from growing food. Gardens are generally assets, whereas pets, even adorable little Poofykins, may be liabilities. If you have pets, figuring out how to keep them from wrecking your hard work should be at the top of your priority list. When your food forest system grows in maturity, the pets won't be as big an issue. Dogs and cats may even become assets as they chase away deer and squirrels. I certainly understand the value of animal companionship—just don't let your pets keep you from growing food. It's worth figuring out how to balance both pets and gardens.

But pets and domesticated animals aside, this chapter is on bringing wild nature into your system. There are a lot of wild creatures that do plenty of work behind

the scenes. Many of them aren't usually recognized as our partners in food growing. Some are considered little more than nuisances to be fought with—and you may have to fight with them as the system grows—but overall, the benefits provided by wild animals are usually greater than the damage. In the case of deer, exclusion is a good plan, whether through large fences or via putting in tough hedges that redirect their browsing activity. In some places you will find establishing a food forest impossible unless you can exclude deer and/or hogs. It's a serious issue, and investing in a fence or a good farm dog or two may be your only option.

In the case of two-legged animals seeking to steal fruit or break into your house, tough and thorny hedges are a very good idea, especially when paired with a fence. In the northern half of the state, a silverthorn or pyracantha hedge is an excellent deterrent. In the southern half of the state, it's hard to beat the stopping power of bougainvillea, though I also remember my grandpa's under-window planting of super-thorny bromeliads with razor-sharp hook-edged leaves. Yikes they were mean, especially when you tried to retrieve a football from back against the wall behind them. There was no way to escape un-bloodied!

Eventually I intend to spend some serious time writing about the value and installation of Death Hedges, but they're beyond the scope of this book. Physical barriers, either living or non-living, will exclude the worst problems from your food forest, but there is a lot of nature you can't exclude—and many of those visitors are quite beneficial, even if they're don't appear so at first glance. Or sting, as in the case of our first good guy.

Wasps

Nobody likes getting stung. Some people can even die when they get stung, thanks to allergies. If you don't fall into that camp, it's a really good idea to invite wasps to take up residence on your property.

Why? Because a lot of wasps are voracious insectivores. They hunt down and kill caterpillars and other insects, then bring them home and feed chunks to their babies. Fortunately, it isn't hard to attract them to your yard—they'll come on their own. It's more a matter of holding back your urge to bust out the bug spray as soon as you see a nest.

I wasn't always part of the Wasp Fan Club. For years I fought them, throwing rocks at nests and spraying every colony they built around my house. Then one day I was reading permies.com and came across a video where Paul Wheaton was filming a gal named Christy Nieto who was standing near a big hornet nest. She said something along the lines of "this gooseberry hedge behind me was always completely defoliated by caterpillars and never gave us a thing until that hornet nest showed up. Now the caterpillars are gone and we're getting harvests."

You can find the video on Paul Wheaton's channel. It's titled "The value of the paper wasp in permaculture."

After seeing that video, I went outside and started watching the wasps in my garden. They would often hang around on the edge of the beds like they were waiting for me to show up so they could sting me. That's what I had assumed, but I was wrong. As I watched wasps, I saw one wrestling a caterpillar around on the ground, stinging it and tearing out chunks of green, gooey flesh.

Those wasps weren't waiting to ambush me. They were there to ambush caterpillars! I had been so blind!

Suddenly, my entire Theology of Wasps was turned on its head. Instead of seeing them as an enemy sent by Satan to torment man after the fall and ensure we could no longer wander around as naked fruitarians, I saw them as God's Lethal Enforcers, bringing law and order to the cabbage patch.

Obviously, it was time to stop killing them so they could kill my greater enemies—the enemies of my food supply.

The next spring a colony of wasps made a nest over my front door, right in one corner of the door frame—and I left the nest alone. We walked under them every day—carefully—and no one ever got stung. Multiple visitors freaked out about them and looked dubious when I explained that they were my gardening subcontractors.

Some people keep pit bulls or fighting cocks. I keep wasps.

Wasps used to regularly try to start nests in my front mailbox, which gave me an idea. Why not put mailboxes over the gardens? I got a half-dozen battered old mailboxes from a friend who had extras of everything and nailed them to the tops of the fence posts. The wasps moved in over time and our caterpillar problem fell to zero.

In a food forest, wasps manage pests and help pollinate your trees. If you're not allergic, I recommend just leaving them alone.

Wasps will show up in a food forest whether you want them or not. Declare a truce and let them kill off pest insects and you may be surprised by how much easier your gardening becomes.

Bees

Bees are better loved than wasps because most of us have a sweet tooth. If wasps made sugar, we'd love them too. If they made rum, that would be even better, but hey, we're not in heaven yet. Beyond making honey, honeybees are very important for plant pollination.

Many of us know that honeybees are in decline across the United States. I had three colonies die on me in two years. Because of this sad state of affairs, it makes sense to direct our attention to honeybees' lesser-known cousins the "solitary bees." Though they aren't honey-makers, they still pollinate plants and some of them even kill bad insects. This group includes mason bees, carpenter bees and a broad range of often sting-less species that usually nest in holes. Some of them pick up insects to feed to their babies, much like wasps.

Years ago an insectivorous bee built a home for her babies inside a wind chime on my back porch. I had a good time watching her stuff paralyzed stinkbugs in there. She was a total klutz about it, trying to wrestle her burden up into the copper piping, thumping herself against it again and again, then trying yet again until she finally made it. A persistent klutz is to be commended.

After seeing this and having done quite a bit of reading on the topic of pollinators and insectivorous bees and wasps, I built my first solitary bee and wasp hotel one winter by drilling lots of holes into blocks of dry wood and stuffing them into an old wine box with a piece of aluminum on top to keep out the rain. The holes ranged from 1/4" to 5/8" in diameter and were roughly 5" deep. After construction, I screwed the box to the fence over my annual garden. By summer, it was almost completely colonized with good guys.

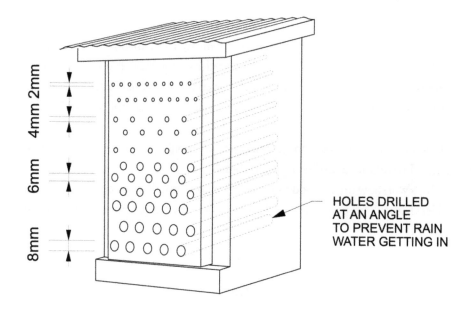

HOLES DRILLED
AT AN ANGLE
TO PREVENT RAIN
WATER GETTING IN

The biggest benefit to having bees around is the increase in fruit you'll get. Pollinators make a huge difference. You can get 30–40% more from a fruit tree when bees are present. For that much yield, taking the time to make some nests is a pretty good trade. Just avoiding pesticides makes a big difference. For a really simple way to attract these species, just set up a dry wood post somewhere and drill a bunch of holes of varying sizes in it. If you build it, buzz will get out and you'll have plenty of tenants in no time.

Lizards

My sister Jessica is not a fan of lizards. When she was a kid, my brother once built her a cool playhouse out of reclaimed fence boards that had been thrown down by a hurricane. After the first week, however, she didn't want to go into it any more because "there are lizards in there."

After this sad event, I painted her a little painting titled "We Miss You."

In it, two lizards have sat down to a meal of insects. Both are sad because my sister—whose portrait they've hung on the wall of the playhouse—is no longer visiting them. They wait in vain for her to take a seat at the table, yet she never does.

I should have become an artist instead of a writer. There really is some deep pathos in this scene. Ruskin would have loved it.

Even if, like Jess, you do not like lizards, they do eat a lot of insects and also fit into a complete food web. Making some habitat for them doesn't have to be a big deal.

You certainly don't have to build and then abandon a nice playhouse.

Though they'll live in trees and bushes, you'll gain a wider variety of species by leaving some brush around, piling some rocks or logs, or letting your grass get tall here and there. Depending on your location, the variety of lizards and their habitats will vary. Some like open sandy patches and others like piles of flowerpots behind a shed. Just see where you witness the most of them and try to recreate those conditions in your food forest.

In South Florida you're going to be invaded by iguanas whatever you do. In that case, I recommend buying some curry powder and a pellet gun. They are delicious. Pow pow.

Snakes

Snakes are greatly underappreciated. I understand that one of their forefathers screwed things up for us by pulling a fast one on Eve, but still—they do add a lot to the natural environment.

Snakes consume lots of rodents that would otherwise wreak havoc. Some also devour cockroaches, bird eggs and even other snakes. If you lived in a region with a lot of poisonous species,  adding space for slithering death monsters might not be a good idea, but in Florida the most poisonous snake we have is the coral snake—and they're quite non-aggressive. Call me crazy, but I don't mind coral snakes.

Much like lizards, snakes like wood and rock piles. They also like chicken coops. We had a couple of huge yellow rat snakes show up and eat eggs now and again. I let them. It's a good trade for the services they provide. I'd rather have snakes than rats or mice.

If you've been killing snakes, I would stop—unless you're shooting water moccasins or rattlers. That's always okay. If you kill harmless varieties, you're just adding to the rodent population. Consider how fast mice and rats and squirrels breed, then consider how many mommy and daddy rodents a snake eats in a year. One snake could potentially eliminate 200+ rodents and potential rodents in one year. Snakes are an important control on runaway vermin populations. Our various rat snakes are good company in a food forest, and black racers are always on the hunt.

Birds

Wild birds feed forests. They'll bring a lot of fertility into your system by consuming seeds and insects from all over your neighborhood, then dropping the resulting manure beneath their perches in your food forest.

Birds grab and deliver nutrients your trees can't reach on their own, acting almost like the arms of the forest, reaching far and wide and gathering nutrients and bringing them back in a form easy for trees to use. Birds will also eat some of your fruit, sure, but they also eat a lot of insects through the year. Overall, they are a net positive to the system, plus they're fun to watch. I've seen a bird sit on a power line, beating and chewing a locust to death. Feels good, man.

To attract more birds, I put up feeders and birdhouses as well as birdbaths. As a bonus, we get to see new species almost every year as the food forest grows.

Bats

Bats are awesome.

When I was a kid, my brother and I caught one in a cave and then released it in my cousin Danny's basement. During the night, it managed to get upstairs into my aunt's bedroom and die while clinging to her window screen. The discovery of its corpse scared the living daylights out of her and got us quite a scolding.

Obviously, letting bats go in a relative's house isn't the way to get them to work on your behalf, but adding a bat house to your food forest isn't a half-bad idea.

Why add bats?

Because by doing so, you get a second shift of insect eating activity. They'll clean up mosquitoes all night while the birds are asleep, plus, if you have a big enough bat house, you can provide your garden or compost pile with a steady supply of nice, hot, nutrient-rich guano.

Finally, bats are also delicious in soup, especially when paired with pangolin.

Various Insects

Butterflies, praying mantises, ladybugs, moths, beetles—there is so much insect life in Florida it's a marvel to behold. As our food forest grew, so did the variety of insects we found, much to the delight of my children. Relatively rare species such as the Luna moth and the "big-eyed elater" beetle came to visit, along with a profusion of butterflies. A wide range of insects is a good thing, as it provides checks and balances on pest species. Having more insects is better than having less insects.

Armadillos

I walked out to my plant nursery one morning and discovered multiple plant pots had been overturned. At first, I thought my children must have run through while playing tag—or that perhaps our two-year-old was digging in the pots. I asked, however, and no one knew what had happened.

I repotted the poor plants and watered them, then thought no more on the topic until the next morning when I walked out to find more pots upset.

What in the world? What was going on?

It must be some sort of animal in the night, I thought. Something was turning over my pots.

I spilled out the soil in an empty pot to re-pot some of the plants and then found a few white grubs curled up in the bottom.

Suddenly, I put two and two together. A creature was hunting in the pots for white grubs. That could only mean one thing. I was being visited by an armadillo.

Armadillos eat snails, slugs and grubs and love to wander around at night, looking weird and eating creepy-crawlies. They're fun to watch, and after we built the food forest, we occasionally saw them in the evening. I had to re-pot plants now and again but at least they were eating the grubs in the plant roots!

Gopher Tortoises

We had a gopher tortoise in our North Florida food forest. He lived up in the front yard and usually stuck around there. Every week or so he would wander around the yard then head back to his burrow. One day he showed up at my back door and scratched at the glass. I let him in and he wandered through the house to the front door, which I opened for him, and he headed back up to his burrow. That blew my mind. Had he been wandering through the yard before the house was built? With their exceptional lifespan, it was quite possible. I planted lettuce in a little patch near his burrow and he enjoyed grazing on the leaves. He'd also eat fruit right from my hand. What a cool tortoise he was—and how interesting to know that he might outlive me.

A permaculture garden or forest can go a lot deeper than just being a bunch of plants or trees you like. When you nurture and protect the animal kingdom, you'll have a healthier food production system and a healthier ecosystem.

Just remember to duck under the wasp nest when you come in the front door.

FIGURING OUT WHAT GROWS IN YOUR YARD

I once taught a three-hour workshop on food forests. My class and I stood beside a chunk of North Florida woods and tried to figure out which plants served which roles and how those roles could be taken up by edible tree and plant varieties. At the end of the class, a fellow stuck around to ask a few questions. One of them was "How do I establish a food forest in arid Texas?"

I get this a lot, though the location varies. Fortunately, I learned some tricks long ago from reading a book called *Gaia's Garden*, by the late Toby Hemenway. If you don't own it, I highly recommend it. I put his ideas into practice and added some ideas of my own with great success.

The advice I gave to the Texan also applies to Florida. Assuming you live someplace in the state where forests already grow or have grown before development took them out—which would be most of the state, I'm going to give you a few tips on how you can figure out what will thrive and produce in your region. Let's start by taking a walk in the woods.

North Florida

Step 1: Analyze the Native Forest

First take a look at what is already growing in the region. Hickories? Oaks? Persimmons? Wild plums? Azaleas? Pay attention to where these plants are growing in the forest and which ones are next to each other.

Once you've done that, look at those plants online and find their close relatives or species known to like the same conditions. For instance, pecans usually grow well in the same region as hickories; chestnuts basically like the same conditions as oaks, Japanese or improved American varieties of persimmon might be good choices where you find wild persimmons, named plum cultivars could fill the niche filled by wild plums and blueberries often grow excellently in the same acid conditions azaleas prefer. Look for edible native vines and plants to fill in the gaps, observe which nitrogen-fixers are in the system, figure out what plants like dry soil, which like bogs, etc.

See how neat that is? You're basically letting the native forest—or even neighbors' thriving landscapes—guide you as you plan your own forest garden. Many native species are good additions. In my food forest, I added wild black cherries (*Prunus serotina*) and plums, along with native persimmons (*Diospyros virginiana*). I also had beautyberries (*Callicarpa americana*) volunteer here and there, along with rampant local muscadines (*Vitis rotundifolia*) along my fence lines.

Step 2: Check Out Commercial Agricultural Operations

Are farmers growing edible trees of any type in your area? Are there blueberry farms? Peaches? Pecans? Grape U-picks? Look around and see.

Call or visit your local agricultural extension and ask them what's being grown locally. If peaches are popular with farmers, ask what varieties, then add those to your plans. You might also add other stone fruit as well. If there is a blueberry farm next door to you, you probably have acid soil that is good for blueberries. Plant a range of them! If the soil is letting folks make money off a particular crop, it's probably a good idea to add it to your food forest.

Now let's try another climate: the tropical tip of the state.

Tropical Florida

Step 1: Analyze the Native Forest

The forest—if you can find any—might contain a range of nitrogen-fixing or useful trees, as well as wild and feral versions of cultivated crops. You might find coconuts, gumbo limbo, hog plums, sea grape, mangos, etc. There's plenty of water here, though coastal areas may have raised salinity that can limit traditional fruit trees.

Step 2: Check Out Commercial Agricultural Operations

There's an abundance of mango growers in the southern end of the state, plus lots of exotic fruit and ornamental nurseries. Landscaping around office buildings often includes palms and philodendrons. Jamaican immigrants are growing ackee and jackfruit; Puerto Ricans are growing plantains, yams, passionfruit and cassava. Commercial operations may be thin due to the lack of available land—but neighborhood gardeners will tell you what you need to know.

WILD MUSCADINE GRAPES

It's too easy when you have a climate this nice. You are in a paradise climate: make use of it. Even the philodendrons at the office park have a relative with edible fruit, the *Monstera deliciosa*.

What About Food Forests in Florida Scrub?

Can you even grow fruit trees in this fast-draining bad, bad, bad sand?

If you have lousy soil or white sand in your yard, you may think you'll never have happy fruit trees... yet all is not lost, even under rough conditions. Fortunately for you, God long ago planned ahead for "bad" dirt and created a variety of edibles that will handle conditions that would be miserable for many of our common fruit trees.

My friend Jeff (Democritus Xenophon III) and I were on our way to deliver a few fruit trees on a spring day when I had to stop the car because I saw something amazing in an empty, scrubby, rough, white-sand lot by the side of the road.

It was a native Florida pawpaw in full bloom... and it wasn't alone.

Across this lot we found at least three different species of pawpaws. There were probably a hundred or so individuals altogether. At that time of year they were in bloom and thus easy to spot.

In Florida, pawpaws tend to be shrubs, not trees. After they bloom, pawpaws tend to blend into the prairies and forest edges. Unfortunately, they won't transplant from the wild until you're a total pro, so don't even bother. The tap root is ridiculous and breaking it will probably kill the plant.

Now—back to my theme of growing fruit trees in scrubland. We now know pawpaws will handle it but the natives don't usually bear abundant crops. So what else might grow?

Well, after seeing the pawpaws, I stepped a little further into the lot and started poking around. To my delight I found a native persimmon tree—and like the pawpaws, it wasn't alone.

There were at least fifty of them along the forest edge, with more seedlings scattered here and there.

Now we have two edible fruit trees that grow in "bad" soil. But we're not done yet. The next plants I discovered aren't trees... but they are wonderful fruit:

Native Florida blueberries!

Some of the plants were completely covered in berries. Our native blueberry plants don't have the large berries of cultivated varieties—but they make up for their tiny size by packing an incredible burst of blueberry flavor you have to taste to believe. In this one lot, there were hundreds of blueberry bushes.

Pawpaw

Florida Blueberries

Beyond the fruit, I also found multiple other useful and edible species, including spurge nettle (edible root), prickly pear (edible pads and fruit), sumac (edible fruit) and *Yucca filamentosa* (a species useful for crafters due to its fibers).

Along with these directly useful plants, there was also a large population of poison oak, a couple of pines, scrub and turkey oaks, various aster family members, smilax and a couple of beautiful milkweed species.

Now, to answer the question, "can you grow a food forest in Florida scrub?"

YES!

Basically, this entire vacant lot is a wild food forest containing a healthy community of plants interacting and producing food with no help at all from humans.

This is why you need to look around at nature constantly and quit trying to force things. You might have a harder time growing apples, peaches, bananas and pears on a lot like that, but you'd probably do great by getting "improved" relatives of the plants that are already there.

If I was going to grow a food forest on land like this, I'd plant Japanese persimmons, rabbiteye blueberries, nopale cactus, hawthorn (and then graft pears onto it), cassava and chaya (relatives of spurge nettle), and of course, some pawpaws. At the same time, I would experiment with deep mulching and biochar to see if I could start to push higher maintenance plants into growing. Starting with the easy stuff is key, though.

You can grow fruit trees everywhere in Florida if you let nature be your guide.

What About Gardening in the Swamp?

What? Scrubland wasn't tough enough?

Some locations are tough—and some are really tough.

One of the least attractive places for gardening is in swampy areas. I've had people tell me they'd love to garden but "can't" since they're subject to long stretches of muck and flooding thanks to their location next to—or in—a swamp.

Fortunately, even if you live in a swamp, there's hope. Let's take a look at how you can quit fussing over what you DON'T have and start using what you DO have.

Swamps Are for Swamp Plants

If you live in the swamp or in a low-lying area that stays damp, you're likely to have bad luck with typical fruit trees and vegetables. A lot of our common crops just don't like waterlogged soil.

Fortunately, there are plenty of edible plants that don't mind wet feet. A few of my favorites include duck potatoes, water spinach, rice, sugarcane, Chinese water chestnuts, water celery, cattails, watercress, canna lilies, malanga, bananas, taro, ground nut (*Apios americana*) and water lotus. You can also grow tupelo trees in the northern half of the state and pond apple trees in the far southern portion. Some pond apples taste pretty good and others are quite bland.

Some useful and edible trees can also take swampy conditions, such as elderberries, pawpaws, chokeberries (*Aronia spp.*), honey locust and willows.

Right there you have plenty of plants you can use to start your own swampy food forest. (Food swamp?)

Take a local foraging class when you get a chance and see if there are any edible wild plants worth adding to your swamp. The Everglades is filled with inspiration!

Swampy Areas Don't Need Irrigation

It's a no-brainer to say so, but swamps don't need irrigation. That right there makes them attractive. Any gardening area you don't have to water is fine by me.

If you look at your wet areas as self-watering gardens it changes your whole outlook. You might try making larger mounds in a swampy area—or hugelkultur beds—and seeing how they do. If they flood as well, build them higher!

I did a horticultural analysis and wild plant ID report for a couple who owned a homestead on the edge of the swamp. The sheer abundance of elderberries along the edge of the mucky area was something to behold. Rather than viewing it as a pain-in-the-neck area with lots of brush that needed occasional clearing, they now view it as their highly productive elderberry patch. They were also able to clear an area and dig a pond alongside the swamp that let them develop an edible water garden. That's good thinking!

Swamps Are Rich in Organic Matter

Another benefit of swampy areas is their ability to hold on to organic matter. Years and years of rotting vegetation combine into thick layers of black muck. If you view that muck as an asset, it makes it less annoying to slog through when you're out frog-gigging.

In his book *Farmers of Forty Centuries*, F. H. King relates how rice paddy farmers used the canals in between their rice plantings as sources of soil fertility. All of their weeds and spent plants were thrown into the canals; then later, the canals were dredged and the rich muck was spread out on the fields. You can do the same if you have a swampy area.

When I was a kid and such things were still legal, companies used to pick up truckloads of muck from the Everglades and sell them to homeowners for their garden and landscape plantings. It worked like magic, adding a massive dose of fertility to the sun-baked sand of South Florida.

Additionally, if you have invasive aquatic species such as water hyacinth, you can scoop them up and throw them in piles in drier areas and they'll rot into fine compost all on their own. Water hyacinth will reproduce at a prodigious rate so if you avoid harvesting all of it, you can grow your own compost without any work.

If you have a tractor with a bucket you can also go along the edge of a swampy area and scoop up large amounts of reeds, plants and muck and dump them somewhere high-and-dry to make a big compost heap for your annual gardens.

Gardening in the swamp isn't impossible; it just takes a little balance.

Swamps may not be ideal for standard vegetable gardening, but growing food in a swamp isn't impossible by any stretch. Work with nature, rather than against it and you'll find innovative ways to grow what you need.

And the Beach? Can You Grow BY THE BEACH?

Sure you can. For goodness' sake, there are plenty of edible plants that thrive near the ocean. Prickly pears, tropical almonds, coconuts, cocoplums, hog plum, noni... there are lots of options! I've even seen a thriving tamarind growing in the sand of a Caribbean beach, just feet from the high tide mark. If you wish to grow less salt-tolerant species, shield them with a hedge of cocoplums or other salt-tolerant species facing the ocean to catch some of the salt spray, then plant your other fruit trees behind that. And don't skimp on the coconut palms, unless you're too far north to grow them.

Farther north in the state, you can still grow most tropical species if you live right on the ocean due to the thermal mass of the water keeping frosts from striking overnight. Experiment with that microclimate and see what you can pull off.

No matter where you are in Florida, you can grow a food forest. Pay attention to what farmers and other gardeners are growing and start there, then pay attention to the native vegetation and grow similar species or improved varieties of existing species. With a little detective work, you will find out exactly what works.

And if in doubt, experiment! Nature will let you know what works.

STARTING WITH EXISTING FOREST

I've recently been engaged in discussions with a couple of folks planning food forest systems and there's one question that keeps coming up.

"Should I clear out everything before I plant?"

I wouldn't. Planting into an existing forest can be easier than starting with a bare field.

"But how can that be, Mixmaster D2-tha-T2-tha-G? All that chopping! All those horrible invasive weed trees! All the shade! Heavens... give me a lawn any day!"

Starting with a bunch of huge oaks or towering pines is daunting, but there are benefits to starting with an established and mature ecosystem.

"Like what? My chainsaw budget is already outrageous... and all I've done is carve a manatee mailbox with it!"

Yes, yes... I'm getting to it. Stop interrupting!

A forest is more than trees. It's a huge web of interactions. Birds, mammals, reptiles and insects fill a healthy piece of woodland and things are even more complicated beneath the surface. In the trees' "rhizosphere," i.e., where the roots live, there's an amazing diversity of microscopic activity going on. The complexity of a forest microecology is far beyond that of a simple lawn and you're going to want to keep those interactions going for optimum success in your project.

Remember, a forest floor is what makes trees happy. If you already have a forest, you can work inside of it through selective removal and planting, opening clearings and adding new trees without starting from scratch on a harsh and barren patch of sand.

If you have fast-growing foliage, dense thickets or invasive species on your plot, you can often use many of them to your advantage. Remember what I wrote in chapter three. Take those invasive plants and use them for chop and drop. Use the natives as well. Use everything to feed the trees you're adding.

Let's say you have some scrub oaks, some sumac, some Brazilian pepper and some paper mulberries in a big mess. There's already a canopy in place, along with a microclimate and shaded soil that has better fungal networks and higher humus than a cleared area.

If you have a forest, you have a lot of resources. One mistake I see people making all the time: they cut down trees and shrubs, then burn them to clear the ground. Don't do that! You're literally sending your soil fertility up in smoke. I understand the desire. I've done it myself. But there are benefits to keeping some of that biomass around.

When a tree falls in the forest and a gap is opened in the canopy, seedlings beneath it burst into new growth, reaching for the sky. Annuals and perennials also show up to take advantage of the new light. Meanwhile, they are fed and sheltered by the surrounding trees.

Growing the first trees in my hot and sandy yard was hard, but as the islands grew and the canopy broadened, a whole range of benefits was conferred to the new trees and shrubs I added after the first round was established. I would love to start with an existing forest rather than a lawn! If you have woods, use them.

Make clearings and plant your desired trees, then chop and drop the unwanted species to feed them. By doing so you save on mulch and soil amendments while feeding the all-important soil microecology.

When I first bought my North Florida property, I needed to clear some oaks to make way for my annual gardens. Once they were felled, I was overwhelmed with the amount of debris so I burned them. Instead, I should have just dragged the logs to the front yard and put them around my trees to rot down into soil over time. I kicked myself over that one later, as I struggled to get enough mulch for the front yard food forest.

Some plants grow madly and overwhelm your cultivated varieties. This is where a machete comes in handy. If they grow fast, they are a good source of fast compost! Chop 'em up and their rampant nature isn't a negative—it's a positive. The one plant I find to be the biggest problem in this regard isn't a tree—it's a vine. Smilax roots can be hard to dig and eliminate and the vines will keep coming up from them and grabbing your trees. Some smilax shoots are good eating, though, especially the fat green ones. Others are bitter and have no value that I can discern. If you can't dig them up, you may have luck killing them out with multiple layers of cardboard and mulch, but it takes a long time to kill smilax.

As a note of warning: some unwanted plants will seed themselves over and over again if you let them. The time of your chopping and dropping is key: you want to nail them around bloom time, not after they've populated your forest garden with falling seeds.

And in Central to North Florida, I can't stress enough how much having a bit of tree canopy protects plants and trees that would normally be slaughtered by a hard freeze.

I've seen orange trees bearing fruit in the shade of oaks after nights in the teens without even a touch of frost damage. If you cut down the woods completely, you take away the protection.

Mature trees can handle temperature extremes which young trees cannot. Their canopy acts like a blanket. There is a balance here, of course, since if the canopy is too dense most fruit trees will fail to get the sunlight they need to grow. Half-canopy is better.

Wind is also slowed by existing trees. Water from rains is also kept in the system longer because the shaded ground and leaf drop hold onto it and the breeze and sun can't cause as much evaporation to take place. A forest retains and recycles more moisture than a field, meaning you'll need to water less. It also harbors plenty of beneficial organisms, meaning you're likely to struggle less with pests. As a bonus, it also drops lots of leaves you can use as mulch and likely contains a good web of fungi that can help your young trees reach nutrients they could not get on their own.

Also, as you spend more time on the land, you might find lots of wild edibles that are worth keeping. I've done that on my land and have the muscadine jam to prove it.

It's hard, I know—but things don't have to happen all at once. With patience, observation and problem-solving, you can steer nature to your advantage and gain long-term benefits that go beyond the short-term "problems" of dealing with uncleared land.

My first suggestion is to open up part of the forest canopy and start planting, then work your way through bit by bit, using the existing unwanted trees to feed the new ones rather than burning it all down and starting from scratch.

However, if you can't stand picking your way through a forest and rebuilding it into a food forest bit by bit, I won't judge you if you slash and burn and plant. Just try not to kill anything wonderful when you do. It would be a shame to lose a good persimmon tree or a citrus hiding in the woods. Make sure you have your eyes wide open. If you do burn, consider burning the brush and trees half-way until they are embers, then extinguishing the fire with a hose and spreading the charcoal around. That way you'll at least keep some of the good stuff for your upcoming food forest.

Also, though I talk about using species like Brazilian pepper and paper mulberry for chop and drop, sometimes they can just become too much and need to be eliminated, especially if you don't want to put a ton of effort into your system. Just pile branches on them and burn them to crisps or hire a stump grinder and really get rid of them. Sometimes you can't think in the midst of a bunch of clutter and I understand that. Remember, your first priority is getting food for your family. Don't sweat it if you can't manage every detail perfectly. If you do have to take out a piece of forest, you can rest easy knowing that you're replacing it with an even better forest.

THE PROGRESSION OF A FOOD FOREST

In this chapter we'll run through some things you can expect as your food forest grows and matures, starting in year one.

Year One: The Big Planting

Cardboard weed block and mulch are dropped on site, if possible. Lots of nitrogen-fixing and mulch producing species are planted. Fruit and nut trees are planted in fertile well-mulched islands. Sweet potatoes, Seminole pumpkins, corn, greens, melons, pigeon peas, cassava and other short crops fill in the gaps in the system.

At first, the fruit and nut trees grow slowly. Keeping enough water in the system is tough. Weeds are abundant and should be used as sources for mulch.

Overall, the system looks like a bit of a mess after the first summer and you start to wonder if you should have just left your lawn alone.

Over the winter you catch up on the weeds and knock down some of the more exuberant growth and drop more cardboard and mulch if you can get it.

Yields: roots, pumpkins, leafy greens, etc. Mostly annual.

Year Two: The Long Wait

Spring is exciting as some of your fruit trees wake up and put on some growth. In South Florida, they have just been waiting through the winter and doing almost nothing. In North Florida, some of them are just leafless sticks until warm weather arrives. Some of the fruit trees may bloom in year two, but most will not.

To your delight, the mulberry is now bearing some fruit. The raspberries and blackberries are as well, along with other occasional small fruit here and there. It's also time to dig some ginger and turmeric if you feel like it.

If you mulched a lot in year one, you can dig beneath the mulch in spring and find great humus along with worms, insects, fungi and the best soil you've seen in Florida. You plant more pumpkins and melons and sweet potatoes, and maybe some good veggies in the mulch. If you're growing bananas and papayas and have kept them watered in year one, now they're really jumping! You're going to get some fruit! You can also harvest yams and cassava for the first time.

The support species really start jumping as the weather warms up and the rains begin. In summer, they are totally out of control and need cutting multiple times.

This is great, because it makes more mulch, but man... those fruit trees we planted really are slow, aren't they?

With the last chop-and-drop of fall, you look around and realize everything has gotten bigger and is not quite as thin-looking as it was in year one. Next year... maybe that'll be it!

Yields: roots, pumpkins, leafy greens, bananas, ginger, a few fruits, mulberries. Mostly annuals, but now you're getting bananas and papayas too (frosts permitting!)

Year Three: IT IS HAPPENING

This is the best spring yet, as multiple fruit trees are now blooming happily. You're finally going to get some yield from your fruit trees! The trees have found their footing and are growing in leaps and bounds. The support species are also growing like crazy and need lots of chopping and dropping so they don't choke everything out. At this point, you can remove some of them or just stay vigilant with your machete. It's also time to do some tree pruning. Just drop the branches on the ground to rot down into the forest floor.

The shape of the food forest is really coming together, with your layers meshing. This is a good year to start adding more vines as well as deciding if there's anything you want to graft, remove, encourage or plant more of.

By summer, you are harvesting plums, cherries (of various sorts), apples, mangoes, starfruit, and many other wonderful fruit. Some poky trees, like chestnuts or pecans, aren't making anything yet, but there are lots of others that are moving along.

Your cassavas, sweet potatoes and other short-term crops are running out of space to grow and are less important now. The edges of the system are where you can still plant sun-loving annuals, but there's no longer as much sunshine in the middle of the system.

Be sure to chop and drop and prune through the summer to keep trees under control. Taller species will get away from you fast unless you head them back.

This is a good year to plant lots of yams that can climb into the canopy, as well as passionfruit and grapes.

Yields: roots, pumpkins, perennial greens, bananas, plantains, ginger, some larger fruits, tons of mulberries.

Year 4–7: Everything has CLICKED!

Every year, the system grows in complexity and beauty. You are down to paths between trees and very little grass and weeds. Lots of life has moved in, including birds, bees, beetles, frogs, toads and butterflies. Your fruit yields just get better and better every year. Bringing in mulch from outside is no longer necessary and the soil is marvelous and rich. Your chestnut trees are finally setting a few nuts and some of the seedling trees may start to bloom. The trees you planted at the beginning are really coming into their own and some of the nitrogen-fixers and support species are getting overshadowed. The annual ground covers and vegetables are gone and controlling the influx of weeds is not much of an issue anymore as the system has meshed into a working forest. At this point, you are very glad you planted a food forest. It's beautiful and shady and cool, food is everywhere, and there's so much life! Every day is an adventure as new blooms open and new harvests take place. Lots of gingers and turmeric and other shade-tolerant species can be planted beneath the canopy. It's also important to chop out branches and even entire trees here and there to let in light and keep the canopy from closing completely. Make sure to also divide banana and plantain clumps and spread the pups around in sunny locations—including into your friends' yards.

Yields: yams, perennial greens, bananas, plantains, ginger, lots of fruits!

Year 8+: Florida Food Forest Mastery

The food forest has hit a high level of advancement and would continue to produce just fine even if you walked away for a year or more. Some trees have been defeated in the quest for light, and others tower above, loaded with fruit. Many of the nitrogen-fixers and support species are done, having been replaced with edible species. The forest is a working ecosystem that now creates and maintains its own soil. Occasional pruning helps it out but it will produce no matter what you do now. The nut trees are producing and there is so much fruit in your yard you can't possibly eat it all and have plenty to share.

Congratulations—you have created your own Eden!

I watched the years unfold in two different ends of the state in two very different food forests and was so pleased by the end results that I will never, ever stop planting food forest systems. It's a joyful, exciting, wonderful process that cannot be beaten. At the end, you have a wonderful, cool forest of food and the hot, dry, sticker-filled sand is just a bad memory.

When I started my food forests there was not a book like this one and I made lots of mistakes. The biggest was not building the soil first, which held back my food forest progress by almost two years. You won't make the same mistake. Get that forest floor going, get those trees planted, then watch year after year as the system blossoms like a gangly kid growing into a beautiful adulthood.

Part II

The Species

Now that we've covered the establishment of a Florida food forest system, it's time to consider the many wonderful species we can grow. Some of the plants and descriptions in this portion are taken from my other books but many of them are new to this volume. My great fear in compiling the following lists is that I'll overlook some must-have plants, but I've tried to include more species than I've seen recommended in any other Florida gardening book. There is such a wide breadth of wonderful trees, shrubs, vines, palms and herbs available to Florida gardeners that there is no way I could cover everything. Still, this will give you a deep dive into the possibilities for your food forest project. The species in the following chapters are marked with an (S) for South Florida, a (C) for Central and an (N) for North, based on where they are most comfortable growing. These zones are somewhat fluid so don't be afraid to experiment with pushing zones on tropical species or trying to grow northern species farther south. If I know of working examples of trees growing outside their "proper" range, I'll let you know in the notes on each species. Also included are personal cultivation notes from experience as well as the best means to propagate each species.

As you move north in the state, the species shift from tropical to temperate, making "chill hours" an important consideration. Chill hours are how many hours below 45 degrees a tree receives during the winter months.

As UF puts it:

In order to bloom in spring, deciduous fruit trees like peaches, plums, and nectarines all must go through the plant equivalent of a long winter's nap.

*They need a dormancy period with a certain number of **chilling hours**, when the temperature drops below 45 degrees Fahrenheit. The exact number of chilling hours depends on the fruit tree variety, but it can be anywhere from a hundred to more than a thousand.*

Here in Florida, gardeners should look for special "low chill" fruit tree varieties. Low-chill peaches, plums, and nectarines need just 100 to 525 chilling hours per year, making them better suited for our mild winters.

If a deciduous fruit tree fails to receive enough chill hours, it often fails to bloom or to break dormancy at the right time. If a tree receives too many chill hours, it will often break into bloom before the last frost date, then have all its blooms frozen off along with its new growth. Because Florida often swings back and forth between warm and cold periods during the winter and from year to year, it is a treacherous place for trees depending on a certain amount of cold. My recommendation is to plant trees recommended for inside your growing zone, as well as above and below it. This adds resiliency to your food forest and means that you'll have fruit of some sort every year. This is a Good Gardening Best Practice!

Whether you believe in Global Warming or Ice Age Now, you'll have trees that will live and produce through changes of climate.

Species are organized by their places in the food forest, starting with the canopy, then continuing with the sub-canopy, palms, shrubs, vines, herbaceous plants and ground covers, nitrogen fixers and support species.

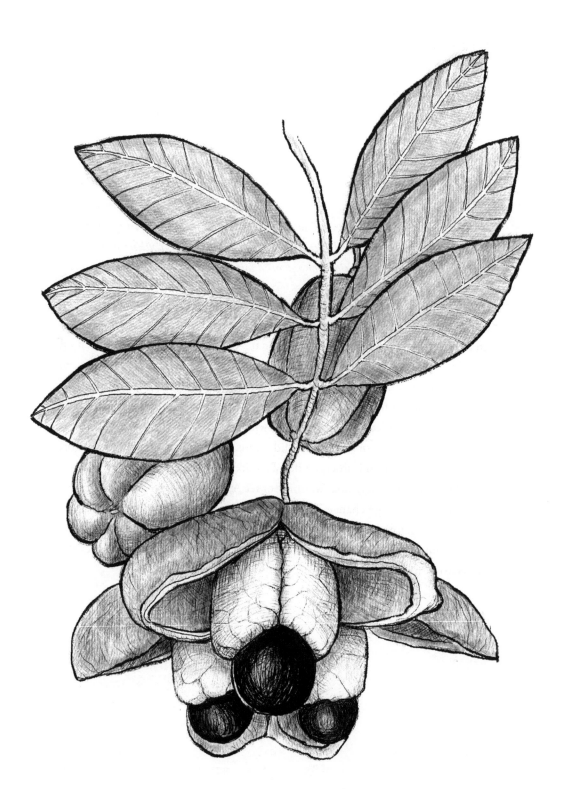

Ackee

CANOPY TREES

The high canopy of your food forest creates the tent poles on which the rest of the system hangs. In this chapter, we'll run through a list of species and cover some tips for growing, as well as their potential sizes and cold tolerance.

Ackee (S)

Latin name: *Blighia sapida*
Cold-hardiness: Can withstand brief cold
      down to the upper 20s
Mature height if unpruned: 30–60'+
Propagation: Seed, air-layering

Ackee is one half of Jamaica's national dish "akee and saltfish" and is somewhat common in South Florida thanks to the Jamaican diaspora. The fruit is poisonous and must be processed carefully in order to avoid unpleasant side effects like death. The arils inside the fruit are the only edible portion and must be harvested after the tri-lobed fruit has popped open, then the reddish-pink feathery portions and the seeds must be removed from the edible portion. Watch out for tiny non-fertilized black seeds that may hide inside the aril. Once the arils are cleaned, they can be boiled or fried, then consumed. The flavor is nutty and delicious, rather like mild peanuts. They are excellent with scrambled eggs. I've seen islanders eat them raw without ill effects but do not recommend the experiment. The tree grows quickly when mulched and watered and can bear fruit from seed in just a few years. It is an attractive specimen, with pale bark and large coarse leaves, growing to a height of perhaps 50 feet if un-pruned. The natural growth of the tree is strongly vertical at first, then it spreads into a nice open canopy. It is quite beautiful when bearing, with its yellow-green leaves and bright orange-red fruits.

WARNING: Ackee is not a good tree for areas where children or pets may attempt to eat the unripe fruit that occasionally falls from the tree. When we rented a house with an ackee tree, my children were warned repeatedly about its toxicity and would throw any fallen unripe fruit into the woods so the younger children wouldn't play with them. If you have a tree in fruit, it is a good idea

to patrol daily for fallen fruit and throw them in the compost so they aren't inadvertently sampled by an unknowing passerby. Children or animals may be poisoned and you do not want that on your conscience!

Fresh ackee seeds germinate readily. Do not store the seed for any period of time as it quickly loses viability. Take it right from the fruit and plant it. Seedlings emerge in a few weeks and can produce fruit in 3–6 years, according to UF.

Avocado (S, C, N)

Latin name: *Persea americana*
Cold-hardiness: Varies by cultivar
Mature height if unpruned: Usually 30–40'
Propagation: Seeds, grafting

Avocado trees can be grown through all of Florida, but not all avocado trees are suited to the northern half of the state. There are tropical varieties and cold-tolerant types. The latter can be identified easily, as crushing one of their leaves releases the scent of anise or licorice. Before you go crushing all the leaves in the local nursery, however, it's better to ask for help from the proprietor, as he should know which varieties are best for your area.

Avocados are easy to grow from pits and can also be grafted. From seed, they usually fruit in about six to ten years. Grafted trees take half that time. Some avocado trees are self-fertile but most prefer a pollinator. This gets a bit complicated, so look up your variety and see which other varieties will pollinate it. Alternately, just plant multiple pits from the same type and they'll be distinct enough to pollinate each other.

Unfortunately, avocados in Florida are sometimes killed or severely damaged by boring beetles that bring in a disease called "laurel wilt." One day your avocado will look fine, the next all the leaves will be wilting. And a week later, the whole thing is brown. This has become quite common. I recommend planting multiple avocado trees and mixing them up with other species to hide them from pests.

Pits germinate easily when planted in moist soil. Use fresh pits, as they die when they dry out. They should germinate within two months.

Avocados may attract hipsters. Plan accordingly.

Black Cherry (C, N)

Latin name: *Prunus serotina*
Cold-hardiness: Far beyond Florida
Mature height if unpruned: 60'+
Propagation: Seed, cuttings, air-layering

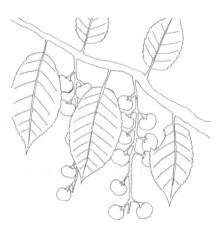

Black cherry is a tall tree with tasty little fruit. Do not confuse it with its poisonous relative the laurel cherry. The tree grows very quickly and is useful for both its fruit and its lumber. Though not the most productive species you can add to a food forest, it is a good-looking tree that is beloved by wildlife. I highly recommend it for larger yards, but it's not the best species for a small food forest.

Stratify seeds in the fridge for 2–3 months to induce germination.

Black Sapote a.k.a.
Chocolate Pudding Fruit (S)

Latin name: *Diospyros nigra*
Cold-hardiness: 32 degrees
Mature height if unpruned: 40'+
Propagation: Seed, grafting

The chocolate pudding fruit in The Great South Florida Food Forest Project is a hit with visitors. The green fruit can be picked when they start to turn a dull yellowy green, then left on the counter for a few days to soften. When the exterior feels soft, open the fruit and enjoy the black, pudding-like interior. It really is like eating chocolate pudding! Do not try the fruit early, however, as they are awful and astringent. They must be soft to be palatable. We've pruned for height on this tree with good success in South Florida. Though Julia Morton reports it can reach 80', I find that highly unlikely in Florida and have mine fruiting well at a controllable 8'. She also reports that mature trees can take brief temperatures below freezing, though I doubt this tree could grow in a location much colder than zone 10.

Seeds must be planted soon after removal from the fruit as they do not keep. Germination takes around a month.

Caimito a.k.a. Star Apple (S)

Latin name: *Chrysophyllum cainito*
Cold-hardiness: 32 degrees
Mature height if unpruned: 25–100'
Propagation: Seed, cuttings, grafting

The star apple has an excellent flavor, but the rind is full of gummy latex and is not pleasant. There are green and purple varieties. Both are delicious. This tree is so beautiful that I would plant it even if it did not bear good fruit. The leaves are deep green and glossy on top and rusty brown beneath, with a graceful angle to their growth on the brown, spreading branches.

Regular irrigation makes star apples grow much faster than if you do not water them. Seedlings can take a long time to produce. There was a tree down the road from me in Grenada that was planted over ten years ago and still has not bloomed. In Florida it would probably take even longer since growth slows to almost nothing in cooler weather. Grafted trees can bear within a year. I would assume the same for trees started via cuttings or air-layers.

Seeds germinate easily and keep for a few months—but better to plant them fast to ensure viability. Eat the fruit, then plant the seeds.

Chestnut (C, N)

Latin name: *Castanea spp.*
Cold-hardiness: Far beyond Florida
Mature height if unpruned: Up to 60'
Propagation: Seed, grafting

The American chestnut tree was almost wiped out by the chestnut blight last century; however, there are now varieties available that are resistant to the blight. Chinese types grow well, as does the "Dunstan," an improved cross of American and Chinese genes with large, sweet nuts.

Dunstan chestnuts are strongly blight-resistant and sold by Chestnut Hill Tree Farm near Gainesville, as well as through various distributors. I called my friend Heather at Chestnut Hill and was told that the trees start bearing in 3–5 years, though not heavily, and will yield around 15–20lb per tree by the time they are 10 years old. These numbers keep going up year after year. A decade later, at their full maturity of 20 years old, they yield 50–100lbs of nuts per tree.

Plant a fresh chestnut seed and it will sprout in a couple of months or so. I grew a few chestnut seedlings on accident by burying a box of moldy nuts out into the food forest, but usually chestnuts need to be pretty fresh to grow. Chestnuts are high in carbs and fit into the diet more like a grain than a traditional nut. They can be dried and made into flour or cooked and eaten fresh. Chestnuts are not good to eat raw. Sometimes they come out bitter when we roast them, but they're always good boiled.

Hickory (Pignut) (N, C)

Latin name: *Carya glabra*
Cold-hardiness: Far beyond Florida
Mature height if unpruned: Up to 135'
Propagation: Seed

Though I did not plant hickory in my food forest on purpose, it still showed up thanks to my children gathering the nuts down the road. They would crack and eat them, as well as use them to play stickball. Some ended up germinating in the yard.

If you have space, they are quite nice trees with plenty of uses. As UF writes:

The wood is a valued lumber, as is the wood of other hickories. It is a hard and heavy wood, and is used to manufacture handles for different tools, basketry, agricultural implements, floorings, cabinets, and veneer for furniture. The wood also makes excellent fuel and the nuts are edible. Historically, the wood was made into wooden wheels because it is dense, has bending qualities, and can withstand compression and shock better than most other woods. Early settlers were able to boil the bark in vinegar to extract a black dye.

The nuts are much harder to crack and eat when compared to its cultivated cousin the pecan. Interestingly, pecans can be grafted onto hickory rootstocks, though the variation in growth speed makes the trees bulge weirdly above the graft.

Seeds sprout after stratification—or plant them in the ground in fall and they'll often show up in winter. Or play stickball in the food forest and see what happens.

Pignut Hickory

Ice Cream Bean (S)

Latin name: *Inga spp.*
Cold-hardiness: 32 degrees
Mature height if unpruned: 60'+
Propagation: Seed

There are various Inga species that are called by the common name "ice cream bean." I had a few in my yard that didn't produce the huge pods you'll find with an image search—and the leaves looked a little different—but they were still "ice cream beans" and were most definitely Inga. The main species grown for its fruit is *Inga edulis*, but it doesn't really matter as they're all nitrogen-fixers. I've also planted *Inga laurina* that I found in the wild. Its fruit is about the size of your index finger but is still good to eat. Nitrogen fixing and fast biomass production are the main benefits of Inga. Its fruit is just a nice addition to the package.

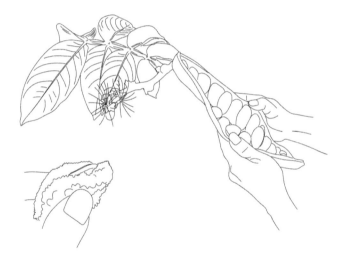

Inga often grows along rivers and creeks in Central American and some of the Caribbean, towering so high you can't reach its fruit. If you want it as a canopy tree, just let it go. It's big and beautiful and will give you plenty of nitrogen in your food forest while providing filtered shade. They make nice stand-alone front yard trees. Unfortunately, they're quite tropical and aren't likely to grow past zone 10, though there may be some potential to grow them in zone 9 as a self-coppicing tree that freezes down and regrows, releasing nitrogen when it does.

Seed must be planted fresh as the beans are soft and do not keep. Plant right away and they'll be up in a month or so.

Jackfruit (S)

Latin name: *Artocarpus heterophyllus*
Cold-hardiness: 32 degrees
Mature height if unpruned: 40'
Propagation: Seed

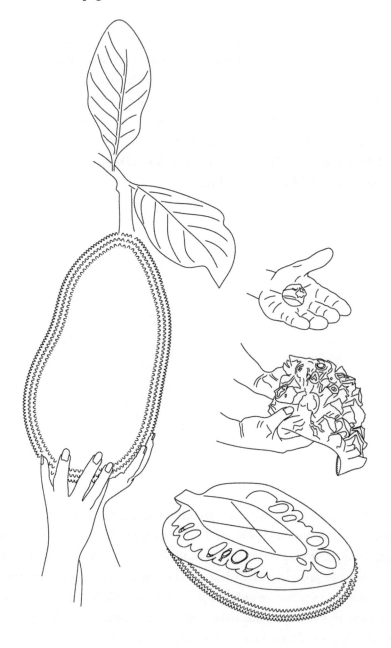

Jackfruit are famous for having the largest fruit in the world. The young, full-size, unripe fruits can be cut and eaten like breadfruit, but the real taste treat arrives when the fruit softens a little and is harvested fully ripe. Inside, you'll find a mess of thready white fibrous flesh with delicious, fat, sweet yellow arils hiding in the webs. You can't eat the thready part, but the yellow fruit is an explosion of tropical fruit flavor, with hints of pineapple, passionfruit and vanilla. Better yet, the large bean-like seeds inside can be boiled and eaten like a nut. I find they taste a lot like boiled peanuts, especially when salted.

Jackfruit is a very attractive tree and grows quickly, bearing in just a few years if it is happy. They like deep mulching and compost and regular water as they grow. The fruits are quite valuable and are relished by Indians and Jamaicans who miss their tropical goodness. Trees like to grow straight up, so don't be afraid to prune to control the height. In Florida they're not likely to grow much taller than 40' and aren't likely to be happy much North of Palm Beach. Mature trees can handle short frosts without dying, but they sure don't like the cold! I've seen a very nice jackfruit tree growing in Winton Manors and bearing literally tons of fruit right in the middle of a typical South Florida lawn.

I've found that jackfruit does not like to be transplanted, so I plant a few seeds directly in the ground where I want a tree, then select the best of the resulting seedlings to be my tree. Seeds come up in about a month and should be sown when fresh. Do not leave them around to dry out.

June Plum (S)

Latin name: *Spondias dulcis*
Cold-hardiness: 32 degrees
Mature height if unpruned: 40'
Propagation: Seed, large branch cuttings

Also known as ambarella, the June plum is a cousin of mango. As Julia Morton writes in *Fruits of Warm Climates*:

The ambarella has suffered by comparison with the mango and by repetition in literature of its inferior quality. However, taken at the proper stage, while still firm, it is relished by many out-of-hand, and it yields a delicious juice for cold beverages. If the crisp sliced flesh is stewed with a little water and sugar and then strained through a wire sieve, it makes a most acceptable product, much like traditional applesauce but with a richer flavor. With the addition of cinnamon or any other spices desired, this sauce can be slowly cooked down to a thick consistency to make a preserve very similar to apple butter. Unripe fruits can be made into jelly, pickles or relishes, or used for flavoring sauces, soups and stews.

Young ambarella leaves are appealingly acid and consumed raw in southeast Asia. In Indonesia, they are steamed and eaten as a vegetable with salted fish and rice, and also used as seasoning for various dishes. They are sometimes cooked with meat to tenderize it.

The June plum has a wonderful, spicy sweet-tart flesh that almost tastes gingery. It's quite a nice, complex flavor, and the juice is delicious. It's very popular as a juice in the Caribbean when in season. We first tried the juice in Grenada where the fruit is called "golden apple." The trees are tall, with weak wood, and they drop the fruit in season. Gather them from the ground and juice away. Just watch out for the hard and spiky pit in the middle.

There is a dwarf variety but I find the fruit to be greatly inferior to the fruit found on full-size cultivars. My friend Josh Jamison at H.E.A.R.T. has used this tree as a coppiced plant for its tart greens, keeping the growth within reach through regular harvests.

June plum germinates from fresh seed and grows quite rapidly. Morton reports that seedlings can bear in as little as 4 years. The tree can also be propagated with large branch cuttings.

Live Oak (S, C, N)

Latin name: *Quercus virginiana*
Cold-hardiness: Beyond Florida
Mature height if unpruned: 60'+
Propagation: Seed

Seeing a beautiful Southern live oak warms me with thoughts of picnics and lemonade, the Antebellum South and my childhood in South Florida. My wife's parents have multiple beautiful live oaks in their Ft. Lauderdale yard, spreading widely and hosting resurrection ferns, birds, climbing cacti, wild orchids, Spanish moss, iguanas and even a colony of bees. Though not a great food tree, they are a common sight in Florida and may be a tree you'll be working around in your food forest system. Though they cast a lot of shade, they also drop a lot of leaves for the forest floor and host so many beneficial species that they are worth keeping. They also make great living trellises for climbing edibles.

Longan (S)

Latin name: *Dimocarpus longan*
Cold-hardiness: 32 degrees
Mature height if unpruned: 40'
Propagation: Seed

Though not as delicious as its cousin the Lychee (see below), longans are still quite good and are popular with Chinese immigrants. It is a good fruit and a beautiful tree. My parents worked closely with friends at a Chinese church who shared the fruit with them from their backyard trees in Weston, Florida. I received seeds but only had one germinate, as they do not keep well. They need to be planted quite soon after being taken from the fruit.

Lychee (S)

Latin name: *Litchi chinensis*
Cold-hardiness: 32 degrees
Mature height if unpruned: Up to 100'
      (unlikely in Florida!)
Propagation: Seed

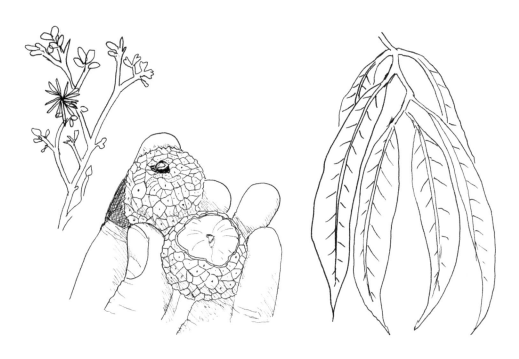

I grew a lychee in a big pot in my North Florida greenhouse and had it fruit in small amounts for me. The fruit is delicious and has a wonderful hint of perfume to it, almost like rose petals.

Though this is a tropical tree, its climatic requirements are strange. As Julia Morton writes:

Groff provided a clear view of the climatic requirements of the lychee. He said that it thrives best in regions "not subject to heavy frost but cool and dry enough in the winter months to provide a period of rest." In China and India, it is grown between 15° and 30° N. "The Canton delta ... is crossed by the Tropic of Cancer and is a subtropical area of considerable range in climate. Great fluctuations of temperature are common throughout the fall and winter months. In the winter sudden rises of temperature will at times cause the lychee ... to flush forth ... new growth. This new growth is seldom subject to a freeze about Canton. On the higher elevations of the mountain regions which are subject to frost the lychee is seldom grown . . . The more hardy mountainous types of the lychee are very sour and those grown near salt water are said to be likewise. The lychee thrives best on the lower plains where the summer months are hot and wet and the winter months are dry and cool.

Heavy frosts will kill young trees but mature trees can withstand light frosts. Cold tolerance of the lychee is intermediate between that of the sweet orange on one hand and mango and avocado on the other. Location, land slope, and proximity to bodies of water can make a great difference in degree of damage by freezing weather. In the severe low temperature crisis during the winter of 1957–58, the effects ranged from minimal to total throughout central and southern Florida. A grove of 12-to 14-year-old trees south of Sanford was killed back nearly to the ground; on Merritt Island trees of the same age were virtually undamaged, while a commercial mango planting was totally destroyed. L.B. Singh resists the common belief that the lychee needs winter cold spells that provide periods of temperature between 30° and 40° F (-1.11° and 4.44° C) because it does well in Mauritius where the temperature is never below 40° F (-1.11° C). However, lychee trees in Panama, Jamaica, and other tropical areas set fruit only occasionally or not at all.

I visited a very accomplished gardener in the Groveland area who had grown a lychee in his yard for multiple years, protecting it from frosts with a frame of wood and plastic he had built. When it reached a solid 16' or so tall, he let it go through the winter on its own... and a freeze killed it. My guess is this is just a zone 10 or warmer tree unless you have a good microclimate.

Though seeds are easy to grow (watch out for those that have skinny, unfertilized pits in the middle—those won't germinate), lychee is better propagated by air-layering to ensure you get a good variety.

Macadamia Nut (S)

Latin name: *Macadamia integrifolia,*
M. tetraphylla
Cold-hardiness: 24 degrees
Mature height if unpruned: 60'
Propagation: Seed, grafting

There is apparently some interest in commercial growing of macadamia nuts in Florida, which makes sense considering how successful they are in Hawaii. We did not try them in our North or South Florida food forest projects because we could not find trees to purchase; however, it is a very valuable nut and is reportedly easy to grow and takes more cold than most tropical trees. For best pollination, plant more than one variety.

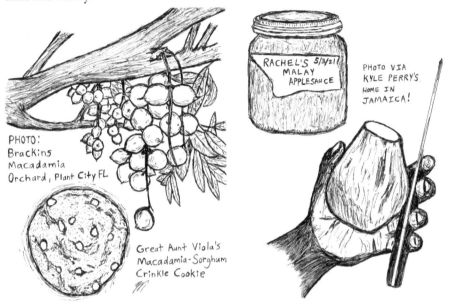

PHOTO: Brackins Macadamia Orchard, Plant City FL

RACHEL'S 5/3/21 MALAY APPLESAUCE

PHOTO VIA KYLE PERRY'S HOME IN JAMAICA!

Great Aunt Viola's Macadamia-Sorghum Crinkle Cookie

Malay Apple (S)

Latin name: *Syzygium malaccense*
Cold-hardiness: 32 degrees (possibly higher)
Mature height if unpruned: 60'
Propagation: Seed, cuttings, air-layering

Morton relates that "The Malay apple is strictly tropical, too tender for Florida and California except under very unusual conditions. It is naturalized and cultivated from sea-level to 9,000 ft (2,740 m) in valleys and on mountain slopes of the lowest forest zone of the Hawaiian Islands, and is grown up to 2,000 ft (610 m) in Ceylon and Puerto Rico. The tree needs a humid climate, with an annual rainfall of 60 in (152 cm) or more."

I'm not sure if that data still holds true, as I know multiple plant nurseries in Florida are selling this tree, but it may just be that we haven't had a bad cold event for a while so they are hanging on. The safest place to grow this tree away from frost is the Keys, as it thrives on other Caribbean islands where temperatures never get close to freezing. The Malay apple is a tall, beautiful tree that loves the wet rain forest and produces a remarkable amount of brilliant pink, feathery flower petals that carpet the ground around blooming trees.

Pits germinated for me within a month of planting. Seed does not keep and should be planted very soon after eating the fruit.

Mamey Sapote (S)

Latin name: *Pouteria sapota*
Cold-hardiness: 32 degrees
Mature height if unpruned: 40'
Propagation: Seed, grafting

The first time I tasted a mamey sapote, I was struck by how much it tasted like a great pumpkin pie. There were undertones of spices and it was an excellent fruit. The tree is a bit big to add to the Great South Florida Food Forest Project, but I planted one on my tropical homestead. They can get very large in the tropics but aren't likely to pass 40' in Florida. The tree itself is quite beautiful and I saw one in the Caribbean that was easily 80' tall with an abundance of fruit. On some of the islands, the fruit are rarely eaten but the large shiny seeds inside are grated as a spice in cooking. For home plantings, grafted trees are best as it can take a decade or more to fruit from seed in Florida and the fruit quality is variable.

Mango (S, C)

Latin name: *Mangifera indica*
Cold-hardiness: 32 degrees
Mature height if unpruned: 80'+
Propagation: Seed, grafting, air-layering

Mangoes may be the best fruit in the world. Almost everyone who has tried fresh mangoes wants to grow a tree. Unless you're like our would-be mango illustrator Laura and are allergic. In that case, please stick to safe and boring fruits like apples.

Mangoes grow excellently in South Florida and get harder and harder to grow as you move north. They are a tropical tree and do not appreciate frost one bit. I planted multiple seedlings in North Florida and they all froze to the ground, but the tree growing in the Great South Florida Food Forest has been bearing heavily for years. Incidentally, the frosts didn't completely kill all my North Florida mangoes—they've been trying to grow back every year for almost a decade—but they sure aren't in any shape to make fruit, unless Global Warming really pans out and the climate switches to Zone 10 before they finally give up. Mangoes are marginal in Central Florida but can be grown in sheltered locations.

If you let mango trees grow to their full height they can be monstrous. I've seen them as tall as big forest oaks in the Ft. Lauderdale area, at least 60 feet above the ground. This makes harvesting difficult but they are really striking trees. Fortunately, mangos can be pruned a lot smaller for little spaces, so long as you keep cutting them back. Mango wood is very beautiful and has been made into furniture and musical instruments. Malaysian luthier Jeffrey Yong is famous for his beautiful mango wood guitars. Tired of importing wood from Europe and South America, he decided to experiment with local tropical woods and discovered that mango is not only lovely but has a remarkable tone.

This space was supposed to contain an illustration of a mango by artist and musician Laura Price. Unfortunately, when Laura brought home a mango to illustrate, she discovered she was horribly allergic. Her hands became so swollen she could not finish her illustration or play the violin for many days. In lieu of her picture, which would have been amazing, we have this limerick by Tom Sensible:

Poor Laura's whole art-gig was stolen
'Cause her hands are all monstrous and swollen
She chose as the art
The dread mango (so tart)!
Now she can't even fiddle with her v'olin.

Fresh seeds are easy to germinate if the husk is cut away and the embryo inside planted. Seeds with more than one embryo produce true to type, but mono-embryonic seeds are wildcards and may produce fruit that is better or worse than the parent tree, depending on the genetic lottery. If you want an exact cultivar, graft scion wood from that type onto a seedling tree. You can also air-layer mangoes, though it doesn't always work. I attempted to air-layer my grandpa's excellent mango tree years ago without success. Last year I tried again with another tree and it worked just fine—and bloomed the first year. Try, try again.

Pecan (S, C, N)

Latin name: *Carya illinoinensis*
Cold-hardiness: Far beyond Florida
Mature height if unpruned: 90'+
Propagation: Seed, grafting

Though pecans are known as a tree of North Florida and beyond, they are not limited to that region. My friend Bob Rose had a beautiful tree growing at his place in Hollywood which produced good harvests of pecans, despite being outside its normal range. As I was working on this book I recalled having seen it years ago so I gave him a call to learn more. He told me it had grown there for years and years and was probably pollinated by another tree growing on Van Buren street near the Hollywood Bible Chapel. Unfortunately, he continued, the tree came down in '05 during Hurricane Wilma, and as Bob said "the Lord brought that tree down... it fell right in between my place and the neighbor's without doing any damage."

Sad to see it go but glad no one was hurt, Bob cut up the tree and removed the stump. About six months later, a new shoot came up from one of the roots and Bob let it grow. Now he has a 30' pecan in his yard which may start fruiting again soon. That's quite a tree!

Pecans are a variety of deciduous hickory tree with excellent nuts that are a taste of the Old South. The trees can get huge and need lots of space. At least two matched varieties should be planted for pollination. If you don't plant types that bloom around the same time, you won't get nuts. As Dr. Charlie Graham, Senior Pecan Specialist at the Noble Research Institute writes:

For most horticultural plants to successfully produce a crop, viable pollen must be present when the female flowers are receptive for pollination. This is true both for bee-pollinated plants and for wind-pollinated plants, such as pecan. Adequate pollination of a pecan tree is critical for the yield and kernel quality of the nut.

Most fruit trees have flowers that are considered complete, with each flower having a pistil (female) and stamen (male) reproductive structures. However, pecans are different because they have separate male and female flowers on the same tree. They are physically located on different parts of the tree, with the female nutlets emerging from current season growth, and the male catkins developing on last year's growth. But in addition to being physically separated, the male and female flowers do not mature at the same time, which is called dichogamous flowering.

If that isn't confusing enough, pecans take it one step further. You can find some trees that mature the male flowers first followed by the maturing female flower, with this sequence being a Type I or protandrous flowering. While another tree matures the female flower first followed by the male flowers maturing, which is known as a Type II or protogynous flowering. If male pollen release does not overlap nutlet receptivity then the tree has complete dichogamy, but if the timing of pollen release does overlap nutlet receptivity then the tree has incomplete dichogamy. Protogynous cultivars typically have long, thin catkins, while protandrous cultivars typically have catkins which are shorter and of greater diameter.

Why do pecans have this type of flowering? The simple answer is to maximize outcrossing which increases genetic diversity in native stands. More genetic variation leads to better pecan tree survival, continued evolution, and better climate adaptation.Trees with complete dichogamy must be cross-pollinated by another tree to set fruit. Cross-pollinated pecans are usually larger and higher quality than self-pollinated pecans. Self-pollination leads to poor nut growth and development, resulting in low quality kernels and increased nut abortion.

What this means, in a nutshell, is that you should make sure you consult a pollination chart when planting pecan trees. OR NUT ABORTION!

I also don't recommend putting all your nuts in one basket by just planting two trees. Plant four, if you have the space, or more. It would be a shame to grow a pair of trees to pollinate each other and then lose one of them eight years later and have to wait for a new tree to grow large enough to pollinate the remaining large one. Pecans are also prone to getting knocked down in hurricanes, so keep that in mind. Plant more, just in case, and don't put them right next to your house. If a tree does fall over, remember that pecan wood is very good for smoking and has a rich flavor like its cousin hickory.

If you want to go the seedling route, let nuts dry in fall, then put them in the fridge for a few months in a bag of potting soil, then pull them out and soak in water for a few hours and plant them sometime in the late winter or spring. Or plant them in the ground in fall and see if they come up after winter.

Grafting is a sure bet and decreases the amount of time required until fruiting, though it's not as fun as growing seeds.

Pecans are an excellent canopy tree for Florida food forest projects—I highly recommend them. If you are in South Florida and decide to grow pecans, please let me know how it turns out.

Persimmon (American) (C, N)

Latin name: *Diospyros virginiana*
Cold-hardiness: Far beyond Florida
Mature height if unpruned: 30'+
Propagation: Seed, grafting

The American persimmon tree is a great fruit so long as you eat it at the right time. The fruits are very astringent until fully ripe and soft, then they are wonderfully delicious. American persimmons are a dioecious species which means you need a male and a female tree for pollination. I've seen them growing in abysmal scrubland soils in Central and North Florida, though they get taller and should bear more on decent soil and some care. Only one male is needed to pollinate multiple female trees. There's no way to tell if a seedling tree is male or female until it blooms so just plant persimmon seeds and see what happens. It's easy to topwork later and graft female scion wood onto male trees. You can even make a self-pollinating tree out of a single persimmon by grafting a male branch onto a female tree or female branches onto a male tree, ensuring that you leave some of the male tree untouched so it will bloom and pollinate the female portions.

Persimmons take some shade and will still fruit. They are often seen mixed into woods and in semi-open areas.

You can plant persimmon seeds in the ground in fall and watch for them to come up in spring or put them in the fridge through the winter and plant them out in spring in pots or right in the ground. Persimmons do not grow from cuttings or air-layers, so seed and grafting are your only options for propagation.

Persimmon (Japanese) (S, C, N)

Latin name: *Diospyros kaki*
Cold-hardiness: Far beyond Florida
Mature height if unpruned: 18'+
Propagation: Seed, grafting

The Japanese persimmon has much larger fruit than the American persimmon, though it is generally a much smaller tree. It could easily be put in the "sub-canopy" portion of a Florida food forest except for its intolerance of shady conditions. I

PERSIMMON

JAPANESE

DIOSPYROS

KAKI

HandDrawnBear

planted four Japanese persimmons in the North Florida Food Forest Project in varying amounts of shade. Two were in full sun, one got a little shade and a fourth was in more than half shade. The most shaded tree simply refused to grow and fruit, but all the others did fine. Japanese persimmons are not dioecious like their American cousins and will fruit without a pollinator, though they may make more if they have a mate. They come in astringent and non-astringent forms. The former have wonderful, complex flavors but must be mushy-ripe to be eaten. The non-astringent types can be eaten right from the tree like a crunchy apple. They taste like honey and sunshine. I would rate their delicious fruit as the closest thing you can grow to a mango outside the tropics.

In a small yard, Japanese persimmons are a great canopy for little food forest projects. We planted a Hachiya persimmon in a 4' wide garden bed and surrounded it with berries, herbs, roses, marigolds and other cool plants to make a mini food-forest bed right in the annual gardens. It did great. I also add them to my Grocery Row Gardens without worrying about them becoming too aggressive, like their American cousins are wont to do.

Seeds grow easily when planted fresh from the fruit. They do not propagate at all from cuttings. Japanese persimmons are commonly grafted onto American persimmon seedlings and if you already have American persimmon trees in your yard, you can "hack" them into producing better fruit by grafting on scion wood from Japanese types.

Spanish Lime (S)

Latin name: *Melicoccus bijugatus*
Cold-hardiness: 32 degrees
Mature height if unpruned: 60'+
Propagation: Seed, air-layering

Though a very common tree in the New World tropics—it's almost a weed in parts of the Caribbean—the Spanish lime, better known as the mamoncillo, is not common in South Florida. It's a tasty fruit, though unimproved types have a lot of pit and only a small amount of sweet-tart flesh. There are two problems that hold this tree back in Florida, yeah three! which keep it less common.

One is the cold. It can really only be grown well in the most Southerly portions of the state.

Second is its need for male and female trees to ensure pollination. That's a frustration, especially if you are growing them from seed. As a tree it takes up a lot of space and time to grow one to fruiting size only to find out it isn't going to produce fruit.

Third, the tree isn't that easy to graft, so you have to grow it with air-layering or risk the seedling lottery.

As UF states:

Mamoncillo may be propagated by seed, however, varieties do not come true to seed and seedling trees may not begin fruit production for 8 to 10 years. Trees may be vegetatively propagated by marcottage (air-layering branches of 2 inches of diameter during the warm part of the year, rooting in 5 to 6 weeks). Grafting or budding onto seedling rootstock may not always be successful.

And Morton writes:

The mamoncillo is usually grown from seed but superior types should be vegetatively reproduced. Air-layering of fairly large branches, at least 2 in (5 cm) in diameter, is successful in the summer and there will be adequate root development in 5 to 6 weeks. Approach-grafting is feasible provided the rootstocks are raised in a lightweight medium, in plastic bags to facilitate attachment to the selected tree. Attempts to veneer-graft or chip-bud have generally failed.

If you have space, it is a lovely tree with smooth gray bark and attractive green leaves with an interesting shape. I would be tempted to plant three seedlings in a single hole to let them grow into a three-trunked mess that would pollinate itself.

Finally, my wife does not like these trees due to the size of the pits inside. As you suck the flesh off, it's almost the perfect size for choking to death. When we lived on the island of Grenada, where this tree is called the "skinup tree," the son of our fellow church member accidentally inhaled one into his lungs and had to be air-lifted out for an operation.

Other than that caution, it is a good fruit.

Tamarind (S)

Latin name: *Tamarindus indica*
Cold-hardiness: 32 degrees
Mature height if unpruned: 40–60'
Propagation: Seed, cuttings, side-veneer
grafting, air-layering

Tamarinds are very hurricane resistant as well as bearing edible fruits and leaves. The canopy casts a heavy shade and the roots seem to compete heavily for resources, however, so not much wants to grow beneath a mature tamarind.

I planted one with my Dad in the front yard of his place and it is now a beautiful tree that is slowly growing to a terrifying height. They can be pruned back—and I recommend doing so when they are young—but that ship has sailed now. Tamarind has sweet and sour versions. The former is good for fresh eating and the latter is better for seasoning. If you've ever enjoyed Worcestershire sauce, you have consumed tamarind, as it's one of the ingredients in the classic condiment. Worcestershire sauce also contains anchovies, which are the bacon of the sea. And it has garlic and onions, which is more pedestrian. Reports that it also contains orangutan toenails and fermented snail organs are almost certainly false so I won't discuss that in this book, only noting that I don't care at all and will still enjoy Worcestershire sauce on beef and in stir-fries where a hint of alpha-keratin and mollusk guts may enhance the dish.

The wood of the tamarind is very white, with striking black streaks through the heart. I saw a beautiful table made from it by my friend Pak David Rus in Indonesia.

Large trees can take some frost and will grow back. There are reports of trees freezing to the ground and re-growing. If you are in a marginal area, I recommend protecting young trees until they are large enough to suffer less damage. Tamarind trees are also remarkably salt-tolerant and can grow by the shore.

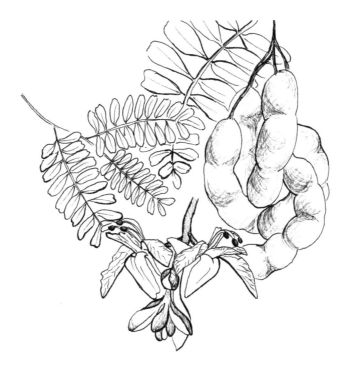

Seeds germinate best if you nick them first and soak them overnight before planting. They'll come up in a couple of weeks. We have not tried cuttings yet, but it's worth trying as the time to fruiting should be less than with seedlings.

Tropical Almond (S)

Latin name: *Terminalia catappa*
Cold-hardiness: 32 degrees
Mature height if unpruned: 40'
Propagation: Seed

Though these trees "officially" can get really big, they don't usually grow super tall in Florida. That said, they do grow wide and fast, so plant accordingly. I've had to prune the one I planted in my parents' Ft. Lauderdale yard because it was rapidly reaching over the neighbor's lawn and dropping lots of leaves and nuts. Unlike many nut trees, the tropical almond fruits very, very quickly. My seed-grown tree fruited 18 months after planting. They also grow very fast. Did I mention that? Really fast! And as they grow, they develop an attractive multi-tiered growth pattern.

Tropical almond lumber is hard and works very well. It's often an inexpensive wood in the tropics and makes quite nice furniture, despite being relatively unknown compared to popular tropical hardwoods like teak and mahogany. If I had the land I

would plant extra trees just to use for future building projects. My friend Moses cut a fallen tree into slabs with his sawmill and gave me some of it. I built a very nice little bookshelf from the wood. It sands well and looks attractive when varnished.

The fast growth of this tree and its ability to grow in terrible soil also makes me think it has value as a pioneer tree that could be chopped and dropped to feed other species. As a mature tree it drops lots of leaves that are valuable for mulch, along with an abundance of fruit. The kernels inside do indeed taste like almonds. By nature a beach-hugging species, tropical almond can take all the salt thrown at it, making it a valuable canopy tree for seaside plantings.

Some varieties have larger nuts, though they can be hard to find. Go on nature walks near the beach and hunt for large tropical almond seeds and break some of them open to see how large the kernel is. If you find a large type, plant seeds from that tree. Just dig a little hole in the ground and plant a few fallen nuts, skin and all. Some of them are bound to sprout. Mine came up in about a month.

Acerola Cherry

SUB-CANOPY TREES

Acerola Cherry (S)

Latin name: *Malpighia emarginata*
Cold-hardiness: 30 degrees
Mature height if unpruned: 20'+
Propagation: Cuttings

The acerola cherry, also known as the Barbados cherry, is a delicious sweet-tart tropical fruit with an exceptionally high vitamin C content. The trees can get big and bushy if unpruned and bear off and on through the year unless there is a drought. Ever seen vitamin C tablets that claim to contain "acerola?" That's this guy. It is very tolerant of pruning and some cultivars bear almost year-round if mulched and watered. Acerola also makes an impenetrable privacy hedge.

Though Morton and others note this tree as a shrub not exceeding 20' in size, I have seen a tree nearing 30'. Generally, it's small and is very easy to keep that way with occasional pruning. The natural shape of the plant is a big round dome shape with lots of branching inside.

Germination of the seeds is sketchy but cuttings root easily if kept from drying out. I once stuck some cuttings in pots of soil and put them in white plastic bags to keep them from drying out. Then I forgot the bags under my potting bench for a few months. When I found them again, I opened the bags expecting to have dead, dried-out cuttings. Instead, I found pots full of happy little well-rooted trees.

This is a very good small fruit and quite worth growing in a food forest. You could likely push it all the way up into the middle of the state if you find suitable microclimates in your yard, as they can take a couple degrees below freezing without kicking off.

Allspice (S, C, N)

Latin name: *Pimenta dioica*
Cold-hardiness: 28 degrees
Mature height if unpruned: 30'
     (unlikely in Florida)
Propagation: Seed, cuttings

Allspice is a beautiful tropical spice tree whose dried fruit is well-known to bakers and chefs. It grew abundantly near our home in the Caribbean and self-seeded through the jungle; however, it's much less common in Florida.

Though it's a tropical tree, enterprising gardeners have grown it successfully up into Zone 9. I got in contact with expert gardener and nurseryman Randy Myers in Tampa to ask about his experiences in growing allspice in his area. He writes:

I have not gotten mine to produce fruit. It has bloomed a number of times, but no fruit sets. The species is known for being dioecious, so that is not surprising, since I only have the one specimen. So I feel pretty confident in saying that you could get fruit here if you had both male and female plants. I never actually looked at the flowers closely enough to determine which sex mine is.

I do use the leaves in flavoring Cincinnati chili,. And I use the leaves on a barbecue to create smoke in order to make jerk chicken, which is how it is traditionally done (not with a spice rub). The leaves must be used fresh, as they lose their aromatic qualities if they are dried, unlike the dried fruits which do retain their flavor.

Randy is a good resource for Florida food foresters as he grows and sells a lot of rare species in his nursery Randy's Tropical Plants, which you'll find at buyraretropicalplants.com.

Allspice grows easily in South Florida and is very attractive in the landscape, with deep green leaves and peeling bark. Propagate by planting fresh seed.

Apple (S, C, N)

Latin name: *Malus domestica*
Cold-hardiness: Far beyond Florida
Mature height if unpruned: 8–16'+
Propagation: Seed, grafting

Though not usually considered a Florida fruit tree, apples may be grown throughout the state with some success. UF recommends low chill hour varieties such as Anna and its pollinator Golden Dorsett, as well as the Israeli selection Ein Shemer; however, I have heard from others in the state that they have also had luck with King David, Granny Smith, Gala and other cultivars. My recommendation is to plant whatever apple varieties you want to grow and see how they do. There's a very useful book by Kevin Hauser titled *Growing Apples in the Tropics,* which I own. It can be purchased from the Kuffel Creek Nursery website at www.kuffelcreek.com. One of Kevin's recommendations for apples in warm climates is that if they don't bloom for you, strip all the leaves off by hand, which makes them think they've gone through dormancy and induces a bloom cycle. This should work particularly well in South Florida.

Dad and I planted an apple in his backyard before it was the Great South Florida Food Forest Project but it only fruited once. It sat back there and did nothing for a long, long time. Eventually it was overgrown by something else and died. If I had known about hand-stripping the leaves, we probably would have had fruits many times—and we wouldn't have neglected the tree!

Apple trees are really easy to graft. Starting seeds is easy as well. Just put seeds from a fresh fruit into some slightly moist potting soil and stick them in a baggie in the fridge for a few months. Once they sprout, pot them up. Do not give the seedlings too much water or they'll rot. Seedlings can then be grafted with whatever variety of apple you wish to grow, or grown out to see what happens. I saw mature fruiting apple trees in the equatorial tropics which were grown from seed by my friend Camillo. It can be done!

Apple Cactus/Peruvian Apple Cactus (S, C, N)

Latin name: *Cereus repandus*
Cold-hardiness: 20 degrees +/-
Mature height if unpruned: 30'+
Propagation: Cuttings, seed

A beautiful columnar cactus. I planted several in the North Florida Food Forest but have not seen them fruit yet. They grow slowly at first and are very easy to start from cuttings. The fruit is reportedly delicious and it's often grown as an ornamental for its lovely shape and flowers.

As my friend Kevin Espiritu at Epic Gardening writes:

> *Also known as "night-blooming cereus cactus", it produces large, cream-colored flowers that only open for one night—so don't miss your chance to see your apple cactus flowers! It produces thornless fruits called Peruvian apples or pitaya. The color of fruits can vary from violet-red to yellow. The edible interior of the fruit is small and white, having crunchy seeds. Quite delicious, if you ask me.*

Scrubland Farmz owner Sam Singleton's son Zeke grew one of these cactus from a potted plant I gave him years ago. It's now as tall as his house and bearing good fruit. They have germinated its seeds by surface-planting in light potting soil and have continued to propagate the variety from large stem cuttings.

Atemoya

Atemoya (S)

Latin name: Annona squamosa x A. cherimola
Cold-hardiness: 29 degrees
Mature height if unpruned: 30'
Propagation: Seed, grafting

As its Latin name reveals, the atemoya is a stable hybrid of the sugar apple (*A. squamosa*) and the cherimoya (*A. cherimola*). In English, they are often called the "custard apple." They grow easily from fresh seeds but do not root from air-layers or cuttings. The trees are more cold-hardy than some of their cousins—soursop, I'm looking at you, you wimp!—and fruit in just a few years from seed. The University of Florida does not recommend planting them in shade or they may fail to fruit. The atemoya is a good species for the edge of your food forest where it gets plenty of light.

Bamboo (S, C, N)

Latin name: *Subfamily Bambusoideae*
Cold-hardiness: Varies
Mature height if unpruned: Varies
Propagation: Division

In my own demented opinion, bamboo is a must-have in a food forest project. If you have a wish to cause rampant mayhem and destruction, plant running types. If

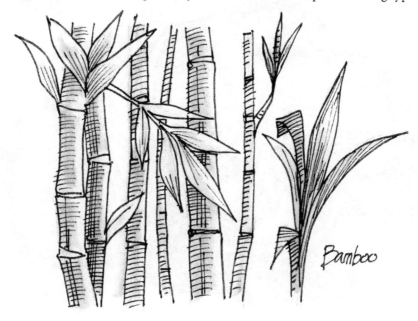

Bamboo

you instead wish for a beautiful source of edible shoots and building material, plant a clumping type.

I made the mistake of planting a running bamboo (it was legitimately a mistake—it was supposed to be a clumper!) near the back of the North Florida Food Forest Project and it ended up becoming a big problem. I eventually got rid of it by selling the property and moving 1500 miles away so the runners couldn't reach me.

Don't be like me. Plant a clumping type. And don't buy bamboo from guys in trench coats in dark alleys.

Many varieties of bamboo have edible shoots. If you can get a variety with edible shoots that also makes good fishing poles/tomato stakes, you're in good shape. Larger types can be used for building material and fuel for fires. Just don't throw entire unsplit sections in a fire as they explode like bombs and shoot splinters everywhere.

In my tropical food forest system I planted four varieties of bamboo for fishing poles, shoots, privacy, building material and more. It's so useful to have, you won't know what you did without it.

To propagate bamboo, divide off pieces of the root mass with some shoots or young (small) canes on them. Some types also grow from cuttings of stem segments but I have not had luck that way.

Banana/Plantain (S, C, N)

Latin name: *Musa spp.*
Cold-hardiness: Varies, damaged during frosts
Mature height if unpruned: 6–18', depending
      on variety
Propagation: Division

Bananas and plantains are easy to grow in South Florida, moderately easy to grow in central Florida, and slower and harder to grow in North Florida due to freezing temperatures in winter. In the tropics, you can basically live on bananas and plantains. Ripe, they are sweet and delicious. Bananas are good off the stalk and ripe plantains are good fried, baked or roasted in a fire. If you pick bananas or plantains green, they can be peeled and boiled, added to stews, boiled and mashed into a porridge with sugar and spices or sliced and fried in oil. It's like the best of a root crop and the best of a fruit crop. Some banana trees mature quite rapidly and produce fruit within a year of planting if well-fed and watered. Others take longer. The key to bananas is regular feeding and watering. They love to sit next to seeping water. I had excellent luck running my sink drain into a stand of bananas. As denizens of the rainy tropics, bananas thrive on more water than Florida gets from the sky. It's estimated that they like around 100 inches of water per year, which is roughly twice the rainfall Florida

gets. If they are not watered, they grow slowly and may spend years without fruiting. This is what happened with the unirrigated bananas in my North Florida yard and in my parents' South Florida food forest. Their thirstiness makes sense when you cut down a banana stalk. It's like a huge column of water held together with tough fibers. Bananas really like to drink.

To start bananas, it is necessary to take donor plant material from an existing stand of trees. Get a sharp shovel or your trusty machete and dig out a "pup" tree from alongside the main clump, making sure you get the bulb at the bottom. Shoot for a pup that is roughly 2–4' tall. Smaller pups take longer to grow and produce. If you chop off the stem and don't get the roots, it will die. Alternately, you can chop down a larger non-fruiting stalk to a foot or so from the ground and dig out the stump, separating it from the main clump of banana trees, then plant that. Big trunk sections with a large piece of root mass are called "bull heads" and will make a few small trees that shoot up quickly and grow faster than transplanted pups.

When you plant bananas, give them a space in full sun if possible, though they can still fruit in half sun. In North Florida, plant them along the south side of buildings or close to warm walls and water tanks so they have an easier time on freezing nights. Dig a nice hole and throw in a handful or two of wood ashes if you have them, then plant banana pups at about the same depth they were before. Some people plant a couple of bananas next to each other in each station to help create a sheltered microclimate. Plant larger banana and plantain varieties at about 8–10' apart. Dwarf types, like the diminutive Dwarf Cavendish, can be planted at about 5–6' apart. Mulch around the newly planted trees and don't let the weeds crowd them or vines cover them. Feed with lots of nitrogen. Peeing at the base of the trees a few times a week is a Good Gardening Best Practice (TM). They also like plenty of compost, some chicken manure, or high-nitrogen fertilizers. A generous sprinkling of wood ashes now and again helps provide potassium, which as we all know is one of the nutrients provided by what may be "the world's most perfect fruit," as the old ad put it. Alternately, you can feed them with a high-potassium commercial fertilizer.

Once bananas start to make a clump and spread, the fruit arrives with regularity and you'll get plenty of calories for only a little work. They like some shelter from wind. Bananas in full sun and wind in the middle of a field alone will suffer greatly. It's better for them to have eastern exposure rather than western if they aren't in full sun. They also love humidity, which is why it's good to plant bananas near each other to hold in some moisture and shade the ground.

The largest stalk in a clump will go into bloom when it's ready. A large, heart-shaped inflorescence emerges from the crown of the stalk and starts moving downward, unfurling and making bananas as it goes. The bananas are the female blooms. After the tree finishes making those, the inflorescence keeps moving down, making male blooms, which are smaller and do not have banana-shaped ovaries at their bases. These attract insects and hummingbirds but will not make bananas. When the bananas on the stalk grow nice and fat and start to turn a light dull green color, you can cut them down. Or you can wait until the first few bananas turn yellow and cut the stalk down. Once cut, bananas ripen rapidly—sometimes faster than you can eat them. If need be, freeze extras to store for the future. Or cook some of the green bananas as if they were potatoes and eat the ripe ones out of hand. Plantains usually need cooking to be palatable, even when ripe and yellow.

Once a banana "tree" has produced a stalk of bananas, it's done. Cut it down to the ground and chop it up to use as mulch or compost. Once it's out of the way, other stalks in the clump will fruit and new pups will replace it. Over time, one banana tree will grow into a clump of bananas and eventually into a big stand of bananas. They will not be as productive this way, however. It's better to cut down the big stalks after they fruit and remove all but 1–2 of the other stalks around it to encourage the plant to make more fruit rather than more stalks. You can always chop out a few pups to plant elsewhere or give away if you feel bad about paring down the clump.

Bananas love organic matter and rich soil. Florida often lacks both, so be sure to keep your bananas happy by mulching them and throwing in whatever humus-building material you have. Old coffee grounds, grass clippings, kitchen scraps—just throw them in and around the clumps to rot down. When you're chopping down weeds or stripping vines off the fence, just feed them to the banana monster.

When temperatures drop in the fall and winter, bananas quit growing. They love days in the 80s and wet weather, but cold and dry weather makes them slow down or stop altogether. Frosts kill the fruit and foliage and sometimes kill the trunks right to the ground. However, this isn't always the case. North Florida gardeners often remove all the brown leaves or chop the trunks off after a freeze, making the plants regrow from lower down. I do not recommend this! If it's winter and you get a freeze that toasts your banana trees, just leave them alone. I don't care how ugly they look—leave them alone until spring. The dead leaves help keep the remaining trunks warm in case of a further freeze. In spring once the danger of frost has passed, you can go ahead and take off the dead leaves but don't attack the trunks right away. Wait and see what happens. Often, a new leaf will emerge from the top of what looked to be a dead trunk and the tree will keep on growing. If you chop it all down to make it look nice, you won't get fruit as quickly. If the trunks get rotten and start to collapse, go ahead. Otherwise, wait and see. An exception is if a stalk was already blooming when Jack Frost arrived. If the bloom and/or young bananas are toasted, cut the whole stalk down—it's done. You'll have to wait for the next "tree" to produce.

Bananas will take some shade but do best with more sun. Put them in the wettest portion of your food forest system where they get at light for at least half the day. Bananas and plantains are serious staples—don't overlook them in your food forest plan!

Bay (S, C, N)

Latin name: Laurus spp., Persea spp. Pimenta
  racemosa
Cold-hardiness: Varies by species
Mature height if unpruned: 20–40' for *Laurus*,
  Persea. 20–30' for *P. racemosa*
Propagation: Seed

Florida has multiple native bay tree species in the *Persea* genus that often show up in North Florida food forests without invitation. In the south of the state, you may have to introduce your own bay trees. The West Indian Bay (*Pimenta racemosa*) is a beautiful slow-growing tree for South Florida that takes sun and shade. The "real" bays are in the *Laurus* genus. *Laurus nobilis*, the true bay, is subject to laurel wilt disease like its cousin the avocado. I have seen it growing in Ocala, so it is cold-hardy enough to survive. Bays can take lots of shade and do well.

On Florida's native bays, Green Deane writes:

> *The unsung natives have leaves that can be used for seasoning, just like a bay leaf, and their leaves can be used to make a tea. Better, no matter what your environment you're in, one of those Three Leafleteers is near you.*

P. humilis ... *likes it very dry and is found in scrubby areas.* P. palustris ... *likes it feet very wet so it is a denizen of swamps.* P. borbonia ... *likes it between. Fresh or dried leaves from all three can be used for tea and seasoning.*

Once you spot what you think is a native bay, just crush its leaves and you'll soon know for sure by the aroma. Bays propagate easily from seed.

Bignay (S, C)

Latin name: *Antidesma bunius*
Cold-hardiness: Probably mid-20s
Mature height if unpruned: 10–26'
Propagation: Seed, cuttings, grafting, air-Layering

Bignay is a lovely tree when covered in sprays of fruit. The fruits are eaten fresh or made into juice, jam, wines and jelly. It is dioecious and must have a male present to pollinate females and induce fruiting. Shade tolerance is unknown. I have been unable to find and grow this tree myself, though it has been planted at Fairchild Tropical Gardens.

Bilimbi (S)

Latin name: *Averrhoa bilimbi*
Cold-hardiness: 32 degrees
Mature height if unpruned: 12'
Propagation: Seed

Bilimbi is a beautiful but barely edible relative of starfruit. If you have kidney stones, stay away from these things as they are loaded with oxalic acid. The fruit is very acid and can be used for relishes and sauces. The best thing about bilimbi is how the fruit grow like weird semi-translucent cucumbers hanging right off the trunk of the tree. It looks like a pickle tree—and is sour enough to fit the look. I grew a bilimbi tree from seed and it bloomed four years later. It is reportedly less cold-tolerant than starfruit and will not grow well outside of USDA zone 10.

Get seeds from a fresh fruit and plant them. They'll come up in a month or so and are tolerant of neglect.

Breadfruit (S)

Latin name: *Artocarpus altilis*
Cold-hardiness: Probably 40 or so
Mature height if unpruned: 60' (highly unlikely
in Florida)
Propagation: Grafting onto breadnut seedlings,
root cuttings

Though a fantastic staple crop elsewhere, breadfruit is not happy in Florida and rarely does well. It is an ultra-tropical tree which likes high humidity and lots of rain. There are occasional sad-looking specimens in South Florida. If you can manage to get it to grow and fruit well, you will have a ready market for the fruits which can fetch high prices inside the US. I recommend growing it with lots of mulch and water and near a canal or lake if possible. Breadfruit do not make seeds and must be propagated via grafting onto breadnut (Artocarpus camansi) or from root cuttings. Sometimes if you chop here and there into the ground around a breadfruit with a shovel, you'll cut through a root and a new sucker plant will appear at the wound site a few months later. These can be dug and transplanted.

Bilimbi

Breadfruit Tree

Cacao (S)

Latin name: *Theobroma cacao*
Cold-hardiness: 32 degrees
Mature height if unpruned: 25'
Propagation: Seed, grafting

Like breadfruit, cacao is poorly suited to most of Florida, though gardener David Harold has about 400 cacao seedlings, a few dozen air-layers, and two trees in the ground in the Coconut Creek area. His mature trees are fruiting and produce pods regularly. Part of the success of David's trees may be because he is both an excellent gardener and he is also located in a sheltered area on a canal which helps with humidity. Cocoa trees like warm weather, some shade and plenty of humidity

or they will not thrive. They cannot take dry conditions without losing their leaves. My cousin attempted to grow one in a pot indoors and lost it due to the dry air.

This is a true tropical tree of humid climates but David's experiences in South Florida make it obvious that it may be a good understory candidate in South Florida food forests.

Fresh seeds are hard to find. Plant them immediately and they germinate within a couple of months.

Canistel (S)

Latin name: *Pouteria campechiana*
Cold-hardiness: 32 degrees
Mature height if unpruned: 25'
Propagation: Seed, grafting, air-layering

When we visited the Fruit and Spice Park in Redland almost six years ago, we had the chance to try fresh canistel fruit for the first time. It is yellow and crumbly inside, almost cake-like rather than pulpy or juicy. The seeds are shiny and beautiful. Our baby ate the fruit like it was going out of style, making a complete mess of her stroller, her hands and her face. The fruit is pleasant and filling and the trees are beautiful, looking rather like the unrelated mango.

Canistel sprouts readily from seed, provided the seed is super fresh. Do not let them dry out or sit around! Seriously, they will die. You have to plant canistel seeds within a week or two of harvesting them from the fruit or they lose viability.

According to UF, "Seedling canistel begin to produce fruit in 3 to 6 years."

Let's hope so, as I have two seedlings I am waiting on! One is planted in The Great South Florida Food Forest Project and has been in the ground for about eight years without fruiting. That said, the sandy soil is very bad and it has not had much care. Still, it's taller than me now. The second one I planted is a year old and is growing on my old tropical homestead. It was planted in excellent soil over the mortal remains of my childrens' pet rabbit, may he rest in peace. It's thriving and is about knee-height now. I grew it from a single seed Farah Chaffin saved for me from a good variety growing at the home of one of the members of the Rare Fruit & Vegetable Council of Broward County. Don't worry if it takes a couple of months for a canistel seed to sprout. Just plant them fresh and wait—they usually germinate.

If you graft canistel seedlings from a mature tree, you will get fruit faster than if you wait for them to fruit on their own.

Canistel

Carob (S, C)

Latin name: *Ceratonia siliqua*
Cold-hardiness: Probably mid 20s
Mature height if unpruned: Up to 50', though
     unlikely in Florida
Propagation: Seed

I successfully germinated carob seeds by nicking their hard seed coats, then soaking them overnight and planting them in pots. Some of the trees were given to a friend with a food forest but I have been unable to find out if they are still living. The tree is reported by Morton to be slightly more cold-tolerant than orange and should do just fine in south through central Florida.

The pods are a chocolate substitute and reportedly taste good. This tree is a likely candidate for the pods mentioned in the parable of The Prodigal Son, told by Jesus in Luke 15:11–32.

A certain man had two sons. And the younger of them said to his father, "Father, give me the portion of goods that falls to me." So he divided to them his livelihood. And not many days after, the younger son gathered all together, journeyed to a far country, and there wasted his possessions with prodigal living. But when he had spent all, there arose a severe famine in that land, and he began to be in want. Then he went and joined himself to a citizen of that country, and he sent him into his fields to feed swine. And he would gladly have filled his stomach with the pods that the swine ate, and no one gave him anything.

But when he came to himself, he said, "How many of my father's hired servants have bread enough and to spare, and I perish with hunger! I will arise and go to my father, and will say to him, "Father, I have sinned against heaven and before you, and I am no longer worthy to be called your son. Make me like one of your hired servants."

And he arose and came to his father. But when he was still a great way off, his father saw him and had compassion, and ran and fell on his neck and kissed him. And the son said to him, "Father, I have sinned against heaven and in your sight, and am no longer worthy to be called your son."

But the father said to his servants, "Bring out the best robe and put it on him, and put a ring on his hand and sandals on his feet. And bring the fatted calf here and kill it, and let us eat and be merry; for this my son was dead and is alive again; he was lost and is found." (NKJV)

The carob tree is a native of the Mediterranean and should probably be planted in a dry, well-drained area of your food forest. Morton reports "The carob is slightly hardier than the sweet orange. Young trees suffer frost damage. Mature tees can endure a temperature drop to 20° F (-6.67° C). Frost during the blooming period will reduce or prevent fruit-set. The tree does best in a Mediterranean-type climate with cool, not cold, winters, mild to warm springs, and warm to hot summers with little or no rain."

Not ideally adapted to Florida, obviously, but still an interesting tree to add.

Cashew (S)

Latin name: *Anacardium occidentale*
Cold-hardiness: 32 degrees
Mature height if unpruned: 35', probably less
    in Florida
Propagation: Seed

Dad and I planted a cashew tree in The Great South Florida Food Forest Project some years ago. Unfortunately, its location was forgotten amidst the many chop-and-drop plants we planted at the same time, so the tree was cut to the ground repeatedly.

Multiple years in a row! Despite that, it has grown back and is doing well again. This is a tough tree.

Cashew tree sap is toxic, and the branches should not be burned. If you are allergic to poison ivy, you may not want to plant this tree as it's loaded with the same toxic oil. The fruit itself is supposed to be edible and is often juiced, but the juice scratches my throat up due to its high oxalic acid content. If you want to grow it for its nuts—which is why most people grow it—know this: the nuts are surrounded by a nasty, caustic, burning, oily sap that will totally mess you up. To process them, they must be picked off the bottom of the fruit and dried, then the toxic stuff burned off. It's a heckuva process. Sure, it's cool to have a tree, but I do not bother planting them anymore, even where they grow well. Cashew trees grow quickly from fresh seed and will bear in just a few years. Seeds should be planted quickly as they lose viability if stored. Store-bought cashews, even if raw, will not germinate.

Cattley Guava (S, C, N)

Latin name: *Psidium cattleyanum*
Cold-hardiness: Around 20 degrees
Mature height if unpruned: 12'+
Propagation: Seeds, cuttings

Also known as the "strawberry guava," the cattley guava is a severe invasive in Hawaii, though it doesn't seem to spread in Florida. Unlike the truly tropical guava, it can take some cold and will grow back after most frosts even up in North Florida. There are two varieties, red and yellow, though I believe the yellow version to be less cold tolerant. The trees can take some shade and still fruit without issue. I've seen a very productive tree growing in Citra despite winters that have gone below 20 degrees.

The fruit is delicious and abundant and tastes much like tropical guavas. Cuttings take some time to root and do best under mist.

Cherry of the Rio Grande (S, C, N)

Latin name: *Eugenia involucrata*
Cold-hardiness: Low 20s
Mature height if unpruned: 15–20'
Propagation: Seed

Cherry of the Rio Grande is an attractive relative of the more common Surinam cherry. Its fruit is quite delicious, tasting much like a good Bing cherry. The cold-hardiness of this species allows for it to be grown throughout the state. Plant seeds from fresh fruit and do not store them long as they'll lose viability. Seedling growth is slow and it can take half a decade for the plant to fruit. Cherry of the

Rio Grande can be grown as a small tree or a shrub and will still fruit in some shade.

Chinese Chestnut (C, N)

Latin name: *Castanea mollissima*
Cold-hardiness: Far beyond Florida
Mature height if unpruned: 40'
Propagation: Seed, grafting

The Chinese chestnut is a smaller chestnut tree with nuts that aren't as sweet as the American or Dunstan chestnut but are still quite good to eat. Two are needed for pollination. This is a good nut tree for smaller yards and responds well to pruning. They grow easily from fresh seed and can also be grafted with improved varieties.

Cinnamon (S)

Latin name: *Cinnamomun verum*
Cold-hardiness: 32 degrees (allegedly)
Mature height if unpruned: 20'
Propagation: Seed, cuttings, suckers

Cinnamon is easy to grow in the southern part of Florida and can be purchased from a variety of plant nurseries. It's usually coppiced and the re-growth of branches is harvested for the bark when they reach an appropriate size after two years. If done in the rainy season, the bark peels easily. It's possible that cinnamon can be grown farther north into the state than is commonly recognized, as its invasive cousin the camphor tree—which is also consider tropical—easily grows up beyond the Ocala area. Cinnamon grows easily from seed.

Citrus (various) (S, C, N)

Latin name: *Citrus spp.*
Cold-hardiness: Varies by species
Mature height if unpruned: 12–35'
Propagation: Seed, grafting, air-layering

Though the orange was once Florida's most popular fruit tree, the arrival of citrus greening has destroyed a chunk of the industry. Citrus used to be one of the easiest fruit trees to grow in Florida. When I was growing up we had a huge grapefruit tree in the backyard. It was so big my dad built my brother Brian and me a tree fort in its branches. It's gone now, having succumbed to disease. If you want to grow citrus, I recommend not getting too attached to the trees you plant because they're probably going to die. My North Florida food forest has multiple successful citrus trees in it, in part because there are no sick trees or groves nearby from which they could catch greening. Additionally, I mixed the trees in with a bunch of other species, including lemongrass, *Eleagnus spp.*, guavas, and *Tithonia diversifolia.* I believe the polyculture has helped keep disease-bearing insect pests away.

Citrus can fruit in some shade and do better in sheltered microclimates in the top half of the state. Young trees are quite subject to frost damage. Key limes and Eureka lemons do best south of Orlando, but some citrus, such as kumquats, grapefruit and mandarins grow well in the northern half due to their increased cold-hardiness.

Lemon

Oranges fare well in the middle of the state but occasionally get destroyed by frost in the north. I don't recommend planting citrus anymore, but I understand the desire to do so. If greening can be beaten, citrus will reclaim its pride of place in Florida. It is easy to grow from seed and generally makes good fruit, though commercial growers use grafting to maintain cultivars. A seedling calamondin or key lime can fruit in as little as three years. Lemons take a little longer, oranges longer still, and grapefruit may take 8–10 years to fruit from seed.

Curry Leaf Tree (S, C)

Latin name: *Murraya koenigii*
Cold-hardiness: Unknown
Mature height if unpruned: 12'
Propagation: Seeds, suckers, cuttings

This is a wonderful, peppery spice tree with small edible fruits, though I have not seen it fruit in Florida. When I was a child our Indian neighbors had one in their backyard. The leaves, when crushed, smell like a combination of bay, citrus, cumin and rich curry powder. The trees are small and quite pretty and will grow just fine in some shade. Leaves are very good added to soups and stews. The trees can sucker abundantly from the roots and invade surrounding spaces, so you'll have to keep on top of it. It is classified as invasive but has not been so for me. It's always a popular plant to share with guests, as the aroma of the leaves is surprisingly delicious. Propagation via suckers is easy—just dig a good one out of the ground and keep it watered until it is happy.

Elderberry (C, N)

Latin name: *Sambucus nigra (subsp.) canadensis*
Cold-hardiness: Far beyond Florida
Mature height if unpruned: 20'
Propagation: Division, cuttings

ELDER

BERRY & FLOWER

Florida has many wild elderberries growing along roadside ditches as you head north on the interstate through the middle of the state. Do not get them confused with their relative, water hemlock, as the growth is similar. Though they like wet spots, they will tolerate some drought.

Improved varieties from farther north may or may not thrive in the state. We planted a few improved cultivars from up north but they were not happy compared to the vigorous and smaller-fruited local variety. They like half to full sun and thrive along edges and wetter areas.

All parts are poisonous except for the fully ripe berries, though stems can be dried and used for whistles. We put elderberry fruit in the dehydrator to make tinctures for treating colds, as the fruit is anti-viral. Put some dried fruit in vodka and it will soak up the essences. If you drink enough, you will no longer care that you're sick.

The best propagation method I have found is to divide off shoots from the bottom of a clump and plant them in pots or right in the ground. Water well to get them established. They tend to grow in big clumps but I have also seen elderberry pruned into a tree form.

Fig (S, C, N)

Latin name: *Ficus carica*
Cold-hardiness: Far beyond Florida
Mature height if unpruned: up to 25', but usu-
    ally no more than 12'
Propagation: Cuttings

There are many varieties of figs that grow in Florida though some are less productive than others. The classic "Mission" fig fruits poorly, but the common Brown Turkey and Celeste types are well-suited to the state. A variety known as Texas Everbearing also does quite well and bears abundantly.

Figs may suffer from frost damage but grow back in spring. We grew them successfully in Tennessee where they would freeze to the ground, then regrow and bear the next year as a shrub. There is an absolutely monster fig in a Gainesville apartment complex growing in a mess of boulders to a height of more than 20'. For some reason, figs seem to like growing next to rocks and buildings. If they grow large in a pot and are then transplanted they do worse than if you plant a small one in the ground and let it get established in place. Figs like dry and rocky places though they do appreciate mulch. They will fruit sporadically in half-shade but do best in full sun.

Fig

Figs respond well to pruning and root easily from short branches stuck into pots and left in the shade someplace obvious where you'll remember to water them regularly.

Governor's Plum (S, C)

Latin name: *Flacourtia indica*
Cold-hardiness: 26 degrees
Mature height if unpruned: 16'
Propagation: Air-layering, suckers, seed

Governor's plum is a tasty fruit very similar to a regular plum, though smaller. The trees are scrappy and easy to grow with brutal thorns on the trunks. They make great edible death hedges and grow quickly. According to CABI:

The fruits can also be fermented and used to make alcoholic beverages. The flavour is variable from sweet to sour and the fruit can be found in the local markets in Africa. The leaves are eaten as a vegetable in Madagascar and leaves and bark are thought to be used as flavouring in the making of rum. (...) The timber is very hard and heavy and is used as rough lumber and to make charcoal. The tree is planted as an ornamental and living hedge. In India the branches are lopped for fodder and in a number of places it is planted to form impenetrable hedges or windbreaks. Although slow growing, it responds well to coppicing and is used as a source of firewood.

Governor's plum grows from seed and also grows from air-layers, as reported on Ken Fern's site Useful Tropical Plants.

Grumichama (S, C)

Latin name: *Eugenia brasiliensis*
Cold-hardiness: Upper 20s
Mature height if unpruned: 25'+
Propagation: Seed

We planted a grumichama around eight years ago in The Great South Florida Food Forest Project. Right now it's still only a couple of feet tall.

As Morton writes, "The grumichama is of slow growth when young unless raised in a mixture of peat moss and sand and then given a thick layer of peat moss around

the roots when setting out, and kept heavily fertilized. In Hawaii, it has taken 7 years to reach 7 ft. Fruiting begins when the plants are 4 to 5 years old."

Maybe that's it, but holy moly, that thing is a dog. Having read about its delicious fruit and beautiful appearance, I eagerly planted one, then it sat. For years. I'm sure it doesn't like the lousy sand, but it has been mulched and fed now and again, though not regularly. It has been way outpaced by the other trees and still refuses to grow much, though this year it bloomed, then failed to set fruit. What a tree! How amazing!

If you decide to grow a grumichama, maybe you'll have better luck. They should grow from fresh seeds, if you can find them, and should definitely fruit within three hundred years of germination.

Guava (S, C)

Latin name: *Psidium guajava*
Cold-hardiness: 32 degrees
Mature height if unpruned: 20'+
Propagation: Seeds, root-cuttings

Though guavas are a tropical tree, they regrow well after frosts. The trunks are quite attractive and the fruit ranges from bland and musky to very good, though they are quite subject to worms. The color inside the guava may be pink or white.

In North Florida they cannot take freezing nights so they are best grown next to a south-facing wall. Or better, plant the more cold-hardy Cattley Guava, also known as strawberry guava. That species is a terrible invasive in

Hawaii but does not seem to be invasive in Florida. I've seen a very productive guava tree in Polk County but the trees I planted north of Ocala froze to the ground and died. Guavas can take lots of pruning and still fruit the next year, so if your tree gets out of control, cut away.

Seeds are an easy way to start guavas. They can also be grafted. Morton notes:

Pruned branches may serve as propagating material. Cuttings of half-ripened wood, 1/4 to 1/2 in (6–12.5 mm) thick will root with bottom heat or rooting-hormone treatment. Using both, 87% success has been achieved. Treated softwood cuttings will also root well in intermittent mist. In Trinidad, softwood, treated cuttings have been rooted in 18 days in coconut fiber dust or sand in shaded bins sprayed 2 or 3 times daily to keep humidity above 90%. Over 100,000 plants were produced by this method over a 2-year period. Under tropical conditions (high heat and high humidity), mature wood 3/4 to 1 in (2–2.5 cm) thick and 1 1/2 to 2 ft (45–60 cm) long, stuck into 1-ft (30-cm) high black plastic bags filled with soil, readily roots without chemical treatment.

In India, air-layering and inarching have been practiced for many years. However, trees grown from cuttings or air-layers have no taproot and are apt to be blown down in the first 2 or 3 years. For this reason, budding and grafting are preferred.

Some guavas have better flavor than others. My favorite are the ones with white flesh, fully ripe from the tree. The guava is a must-grow in the tropical food forest, just based on its use in Cuban guava-and-cheese pastries. That alone makes it worth growing.

Jabuticaba (S, C)

Latin name: Plinia cauliflora *(and friends)*
Cold-hardiness: Allegedly to the mid-20s.
Mature height if unpruned: 12–16'
Propagation: Cuttings, seed

This small Brazilian tree bears delicious fruit about the size of golf balls. The common jabuticaba has black fruit, but there are related species with differing fruit. Interestingly, the fruit grow right out of the trunk—and the trunks themselves are quite ornamental. Imagine a non-blooming crepe myrtle tree with perfect spherical gumballs glued all over its trunk and you have a good idea what the jabuticaba looks like. Since my North Florida food forest was too far north in the state for these babies,

I grew one in a pot on my porch. If you have a climate that's warm year-round with plenty of rainfall, your jabuticaba can bear 5–6 times throughout the year. That beats the living daylights out of any temperate fruit!

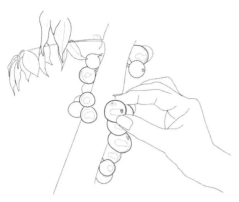

There are some excellent specimens in South Florida. If you try it in the middle of the state, I highly recommend protecting it through winter freezes until it is a large tree and its cold-tolerance is higher. They take some shade and bear well. Seeds are easy to germinate when planted fresh, though tree growth is slow. They can be sped up with lots of water and compost. Jabuticaba is a rainforest tree. If it's dry, they don't grow much at all. Rich soil and abundant water make it grow much faster. Fresh seeds are easy to germinate, and air-layering should work well for starting trees that will fruit faster than seedlings.

Jamaican Cherry (S)

Latin name: *Muntingia calabura*
Cold-hardiness: 32
Mature height if unpruned: 25'
Propagation: Division

I don't know what it is with people naming tropical fruit trees after cherries, but there you go. The Jamaican cherry is also sometimes called the "strawberry tree" because of its blooms but it's not the same strawberry tree that grows up north (*Arbutus unedo*) which is named that because its fruits resemble strawberries. These guys taste really, really good. Like cotton candy mixed with popcorn. The trees grow quickly and bear continuously in warm weather. If you live in zone 10 or

warmer, grab one. It's awesome. They have zero frost tolerance, and my tree was completely killed during one freezing night in North Florida—despite being covered with a blanket! They often make shoots from the roots which can be carefully divided off and planted to grow new trees. Seed germination is very iffy and I have not been able to sprout them.

Japanese Raisin Tree (C, N)

Latin name: *Hovenia dulcis*
Cold-hardiness: Far beyond Florida
Mature height if unpruned: 30'+
Propagation: Seed, cuttings

According to UF, this tree grows from USDA zone 6A—10A, meaning it should grow in South Florida. However, Plants for a Future only places it down to zone 9. It may grow just fine in South Florida, so if you find the species interesting, give it a try.

We planted a tree in the North Florida Food Forest where it grew well for a few years before we moved. Before we sold the property, a friend dug the tree up and took it to his farm. It is an attractive tree, though I have not yet tried the fruit. Ours was in partial shade and did well, though it supposedly prefers full sun. I have no data on propagation.

Jujube (S, C, N)

Latin name: *Ziziphus jujuba,*
          Ziziphus mauritiana
Cold-hardiness: 32 degrees, more or less
Mature height if unpruned: 20'+/-
Propagation: Seed, suckers

Both Chinese and Indian jujube will grow in Florida. The former is more cold-tolerant than the latter. The plants handle a wide range of conditions, both dry and wet, and seem to be tolerant of bad soil. Though frost may knock the trees back, they regrow rapidly. Both are shrubs to small trees and produce fruit rapidly from seed. We've also had good luck dividing off suckers and planting them.

Loquat (S, C, N)

Latin name: *Eriobotrya japonica*
Cold-hardiness: Foliage—low teens. Flowers and
fruit: mid-20s
Mature height if unpruned: Up to 40', but half
that is more common
Propagation: Seeds, grafting

This is one of the easiest fruit trees to grow in Florida. There are many loquat trees in the state which have been planted as ornamentals rather than as serious fruit trees, though most of the fruit I've tasted are still decent. Improved varieties have better flavor and are sweeter with smaller pits inside. Loquats bear well in full sun and so-so in half shade. In full shade, they fail to bear anything.

This is a very easy and care-free tree which can bear twice a year in South Florida. Unfortunately for North Floridians, they flower during winter and the blooms are much less cold-hardy than the foliage, meaning that ill-timed frosts will sometimes take away all your fruit for the year, even though they don't damage the tree itself. Still, loquats often fruit in the north of the state and are well-worth growing.

The tree is evergreen and casts deep shade. Leaves can also be made into an herbal tea. Seeds germinate in a couple of months when planted in pots or in the ground and kept watered, but the sprouts are subject to damping off so do not overwater them. From seed, they generally bear in about six years. Grafting loquats is very easy and greatly shortens the time to bearing. Grow seedlings then graft on scion wood from improved varieties for best results.

Loquat

Malabar Chestnut (S)

Latin name: *Pachira aquatica/P. glabra*
Cold-hardiness: 32 degrees
Mature height if unpruned: Less than 20'
Propagation: Seed, cuttings

The Malabar chestnut is a beautiful tree. It can often be found sold in a group of braided seedlings as the "money tree." The seeds are edible raw or cooked, though some have reported becoming ill from eating the raw nuts.

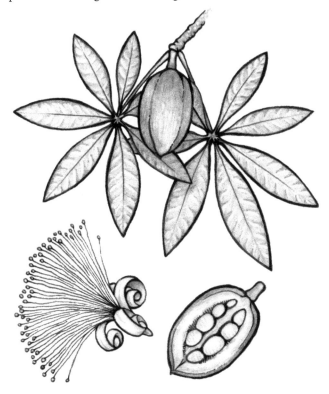

According to the California Rare Fruit Growers:

The nuts of the Malabar chestnut are harvested when the seed pods burst. The raw nuts taste like peanuts and will keep for months in a cool, dry place. Roasted or fried in oil they have the flavor of chestnuts, and can be ground into a flour for bread baking."

In South Florida it usually isn't a huge tree, though in the full tropics it can hit 60'. That said, there is an absolutely massive *Pachira* of some sort growing at the Riverland Preserve park in Ft. Lauderdale, so be ready to prune. Large chunks of branches and trunks can be planted in the ground and root successfully. Seeds should be planted soon after harvest as the viability drops rapidly. A few years ago, I planted some seeds in the Great South Florida Food Forest Project and forgot I had done so. Now there is a good-sized little tree growing there which I initially thought was a *Schefflera* seedling due to its leaf shape and location near where we cut down a large tree some years ago.

Moringa (S, C, N)

Latin name: *Moringa oleifera*
Cold-hardiness: 32 degrees
Mature height if unpruned: 30'
Propagation: Seed, cuttings

Moringa, "the Miracle Tree", is touted as a cure-all and has now been planted in yards all over Florida. Moringa is a fast-growing tropical tree species with multiple uses. In its native range, the tree's large pods are picked young and served as a delicious vegetable comparable to asparagus. Unfortunately, gaining consistent pod yields in Florida isn't easy, so here the moringa is often grown for its tiny edible and medicinal leaves.

Because of the tree's remarkable ability to mine the ground for nutrients, the leaves are loaded with nutrition—and even contain complete protein, a relative rarity in the Vegetable Kingdom. There are claims that the tree also kills fungal infections, fights cancer, gives you the ability to fly, etc. I'm not sure about all those bits and pieces,

but its nutrition has been proven in the lab and on the ground in Africa, where dried leaves are used as a powerful antidote to malnutrition in infants and nursing mothers.

Beyond those benefits, moringa also grows at a ridiculous rate. The first time I planted seeds, the trees shot towards the sky at an astounding speed, reaching 20' before winter frosts knocked them back to the ground. This rate of growth means you'll have plenty of leaves to harvest. Bonus: moringa leaves are excellent livestock feed. The tree is also good for chopping up and adding to compost piles, since its soft wood deteriorates rapidly. It's a staple chop-and-drop tree in my tropical food forest projects. I've also dried the thin leaves in my greenhouse and then crushed them into powder. I then sprinkle that dust over newly prepared garden beds for a little extra dose of fertilization. Moringa seems to give young plants a kick.

In South Florida moringa grows year-round without protection but in Central and North Florida, it stalls in winter. The trees cannot stand frost, and the entire tree— including the thinner trunks—with turn into soppy mush if it gets much below 32 degrees, though the tree usually resprouts from the ground once the weather warms up in spring. I had a friend who planted some moringa trees, lost them all in a brutal freeze, then figured they were dead and started pulling them up in the spring—until she noticed tiny shoots rising from the ground where one of the young trees had been. These trees are tough! They don't always come back, but they usually do. North Floridians suffer through occasional freezes down into the teens which is way too cold for the above-ground growth of a moringa tree.

To give my trees a head start on next year, and to increase leaf yield, I coppice my moringas at about 3' tall in the late fall before the first frost. I then put a 2' diameter ring of 4' tall chicken wire around the trunk, stake it in, then stuff the ring full of leaves or pine needles. Sometimes I'll also throw a blanket or tarp on top of that for additional frost protection and to keep the rains from rotting the remaining trunk. This method keeps the main above-ground trunk from getting whacked by frost. When the tree comes back in spring, it beats the living daylights out of the ones that weren't protected. I have seen claims that moringa not subject to frost can reach 60' in height, but have never seen anything near that height happen in Florida.

Moringa is propagated from seeds and cuttings, though the first method gives you much stronger plants. Cuttings sometimes take and sometimes don't. If you want to give cuttings a try, lop off a branch ranging in diameter from 1–2" and at least 2' long and bury the bottom third in the ground. It usually starts sprouting new growth in a few weeks—or it decides to rot. I might use cuttings for an instant barrier fence, but seedling moringa trees can reach 20' tall in their first year so I usually just grow those. I don't like the weak root system on cuttings.

Beyond being good fertilizer and livestock fodder, moringa leaves are nice added to soups, salads, stir-fries and eggs. Snapping the large, compound leaves off the tree is easy, and once you do that, you can strip the little leaflets off into whatever you're cooking. If you expect freezing weather, strip all the leaves from the trees and spread them out to dry indoors on a tarp, then you'll still have them to add to soups or to make tea from. This plant is a nutritional powerhouse. A little moringa each day keeps the doctor away.

Seeds don't want to germinate in cool weather, so if you are starting them in a cool, North Florida spring, I recommend putting your seedling trays on top of a heat mat.

Mulberry (S, C, N)

Latin name: *Morus spp.*
Cold-hardiness: Far beyond Florida
Mature height if unpruned: Varies
Propagation: Cuttings, grafting

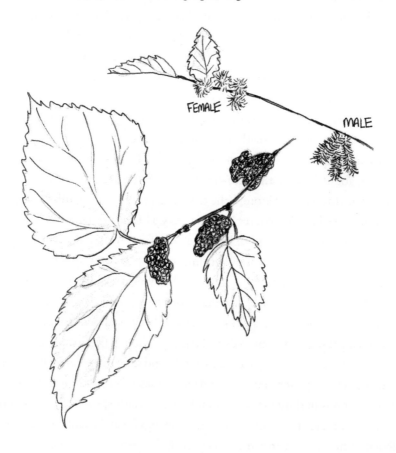

Mulberries aren't just a northern tree. Some species grow well and bear even in the tropics. This low-maintenance and easy-to-grow tree will produce more sweet fruit than you can handle. If you have a small yard, no worries—just prune them back after they fruit. You can cut the living daylights out of mulberries and they'll regrow. Mulberry leaves are a good animal forage.

Try to avoid planting purple-fruited types near driveways or areas where you're likely to step on them and track purple juice into your house and onto the carpets. They drop a lot of fruit all at once. There are also white-fruited varieties which do not stain and can be planted wherever you like. White fruits taste like honey and are quite pleasant. The long-fruited Pakistan varieties are less vigorous than other types and did not do as well for me as Illinois Everbearing or the 5th Street mulberry propagated by the Edible Plant Project in Gainesville. New, large-fruited selections are becoming available thanks to the work of Florida fruit enthusiasts such as Josh Jamison and Craig Hepworth, so look for those.

The common Dwarf Everbearing type is a little slow to get going and does not make the best fruit, though it bears abundantly and is easy to control in a small space. We have one growing well in the Great South Florida Food Forest Project along with a 5th Street mulberry. Unfortunately, the latter does not fruit much at all in South Florida.

The best variety we've encountered for the entirety of the state is one I named "Rachel Goodman," after my wife. This variety is currently propagated exclusively by Scrubland Farmz nursery north of Ocala. The flavor is excellent and the tree is attractive. The mother tree is from Ft. Lauderdale and grew on my wife's street when she was a little girl. Later it was destroyed in a hurricane, but cuttings were saved by gardener Guy Seligman, who started multiple new trees in a lot across the street from the location of the original mulberry. When Rachel and I went looking for the tree we had visited as children, we saw it was gone—and then met Guy, who showed us the children of that original tree and shared cuttings. Great save! It's a nice tree, not too large, with an umbrella-like canopy.

As for species varieties, the native "red" mulberry can become a very large tree and grows in the central and northern part of the state, though the fruit is generally not as good as the "white" (*Morus alba*) or "black" (*Morus nigra*) mulberries. To make things more confusing, the black mulberry and the red mulberry both bear black/purple fruit and the white mulberry bears black/purple or white fruit.

Seedling mulberries can take 10 or more years to bloom and come in both male and female forms. Males produce only pollen; females produce only fruit. However, pollination is not required for fruiting—and without a male, you get seedless fruit—so there is no need to keep male mulberries around. Unless you're trying to breed a new variety, it makes much more sense to start mulberries from cuttings or grafting than from seed. If vegetatively propagated, mulberries will often bear in their first year after planting.

Noni (S)

Latin name: *Morinda citrifolia*
Cold-hardiness: 32 degrees
Mature height if unpruned: 20'
Propagation: Cuttings, seeds

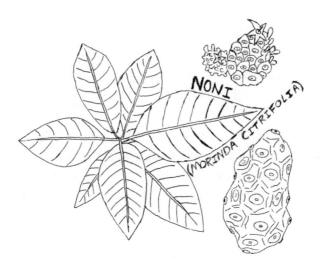

I love the look of noni trees and their very alien fruit. The trees are very attractive with broad green leaves. The ripe fruit smells like vomit and cheese and tastes rather like that combination as well, though with an aftertaste of black pepper. I eat them anyhow, because they're supposed to be good for me. If the fruit tasted great, I would have to doubt the health benefits, as we all know only nasty-tasting things are really, really good for you. The tree is quite tropical and handles high salinity without any trouble. They'll grow right on the beach.

Noni makes a very nice plant for property boundaries because it's a nice, dense privacy hedge, though the fruit is messy. Seeds germinate readily and happy seedlings can fruit in less than two years. I have spit seeds into a garden bed and covered them with my foot, then dug up the resulting seedlings months later. Stem cuttings also take decently.

Olive (S, C, N)

Latin name: *Olea europaea*
Cold-hardiness: Beyond Florida
Mature height if unpruned: 25'
Propagation: Cuttings, grafting

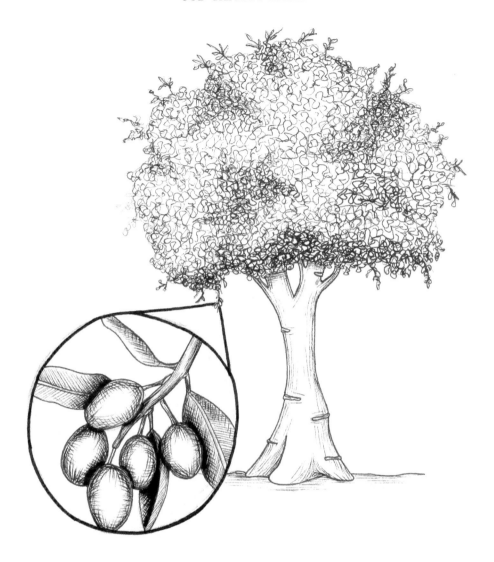

Though olive trees are very common in the Mediterranean, olive production in Florida is still in its infancy. Our humid climate is not ideal; however, many people are still finding good luck with certain varieties, Arbequina being one of the most popular. I planted two of them, along with a Mission for pollination, and got some olives in the fifth year of growing. The young trees are subject to frost damage and may even freeze to the ground on a very cold night. Older trees sail through just fine. There are some very nice fruiting olives at the Marion County Extension Office in Ocala which are worth visiting if you are interested in growing this tree. The trees are beautiful, with silvery green leaves and attractive trunks. They need full sun to fruit well. Olives are mostly self-infertile so it is important to plant a few varieties to ensure pollination. Avoid planting olives in shady or wet areas. Highly fertile soils can also reduce fruit yields. We planted ours alongside our driveway slab and they did well there in the heat. Cuttings from young wood generally root well with the mini-greenhouse method. I have not tried growing them from pits.

Otaheite Gooseberry (S, C)

Latin name: *Phyllanthus acidus*
Cold-hardiness: Probably mid 20s
Mature height if unpruned: 25'
Propagation: Seed, air-layering

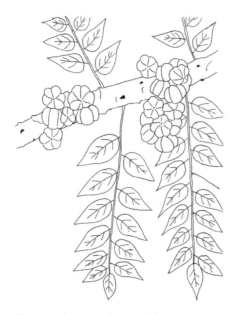

An easy-to-grow shrub to small tree, the Otaheite gooseberry bears a ridiculous amount of small acidic fruit. My children like to eat them right off the tree. As one of them said, "they taste really sour, but once you eat one, then you want to eat more!" My wife and I do not relish them raw as the children do, but I would plant the tree just because it's weird and interesting. With lots of sugar, the fruit can be cooked and the pits strained out for a good, if somewhat grainy, jam. According to Morton, "The Otaheite gooseberry is subtropical to tropical, being sufficiently hardy to survive and fruit in Tampa, Florida, where cold spells are more severe than in the southeastern part of the state. It thrives up to an elevation of 3,000 ft (914 m) in El Salvador."

The plants are quite salt-tolerant. We have seen them growing by the ocean at a boat marina and bearing abundantly.

Otaheite gooseberries are easy to grow from seed. Let your children eat the flesh, then plant the pits. They germinate in about a month and can fruit in just a few years.

Papaya (S, C)

Latin name: *Carica papaya*
Cold-hardiness: 32 degrees
Mature height if unpruned: 6–18'+,
   depending on variety
Propagation: Seed

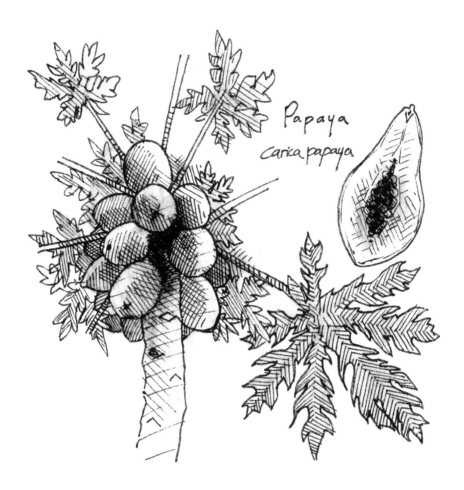

Papaya
Carica papaya

Papaya are a truly tropical tree, though they can be pushed out of their zone somewhat. I don't recommend growing them in North Florida unless you're a bit of a nut, but I'll give you help on how to do it anyhow, as you're already a bit of a nut if you're reading this book.

In South Florida you can grow papayas year round and keep planting more, but the papaya fruit fly, also known as the papaya wasp, often ruins the fruit. The female fly stings green fruit and lays her eggs inside. When the fruits ripen and you cut them open, they are rotten inside and filled with grubs. Bagging them early keeps her out but is a lot of work. I prefer to just plant trees here and there and burn any infected fruit I find.

Papaya are very easy to grow from seed. Just take some of the guts out of a store-bought papaya and plant some of the slop in a spot you want a papaya tree. Plant them in stations 6' apart. When the seedlings come up in 2–4 weeks, let them grow to a few inches tall then thin all but the strongest on the hill. Alternately, you can leave three papaya on each station. Here's why: papaya are a little complicated, as they come in

male, female and hermaphroditic plants. The latter two will produce fruit but the males only produce blooms. Having a male or two around for pollination is a good idea, but you want more of your trees to be females or hermaphrodites - hence leaving three trees to grow in each station. Once they bloom, it is easy to tell if papayas are male or female and you can cut down the two trees you don't want.

If well-fed and watered, papaya can produce within a year. They are greedy plants and want lots of water and food to grow well. You almost cannot overfeed them, but if their roots stay soaked for more than a day or so they often rot and die so keep them well-watered but also well-drained. Green papaya are edible cooked or raw in Thai salad. Some are allergic to the sap of green papayas so be careful not to eat too much unless you know you can take it. Pregnant women should avoid papaya altogether as some enzymes in them can cause her to abort her unborn child. Green papaya are a good cooked vegetable when peeled and the insides removed. Chop and saute or cook in stews. A good ripe papaya is like a tree melon, delicious served with breakfast.

In the northern half away from the shore, they tend to get knocked to the ground by frosts and do not recover well, but if you can keep them protected or have a lucky winter, you'll get good fruit, especially because the loathsome papaya fruit fly does not live up there.

I've been told it's "impossible" to do in North Florida's climate, but nevertheless, in the fall, we ate homegrown papaya for breakfast on a regular basis. A master gardener once visited and saw my trees, then remarked "Oh. Papaya. Too bad you can't grow those here!" They were serious.

Here's how to grow papaya in North Florida. Papayas are a tender plant, and if it gets cold, the tree will rapidly wilt and burn from the frost. A hard freeze that lasts any period of time will kill a papaya tree right to the ground. Fortunately, papaya trees grow very quickly and bear fruit rapidly, even from seed. If you want to eat papaya, you need to start your trees one year in pots, then plant them out in the spring of the next year.

If you start papayas from seed in the spring, by fall they'll be 6' or more tall and will start fruiting. Then the weather cools and their growth stops. Then it freezes, killing them to the ground and ruining all the green fruit. Therefore, put them in pots the first year so you can get lots of fruit in the second year.

In spring when all danger of frost has passed, plant your papaya trees in rich soil in a somewhat sheltered location. Against a south wall is great. RIGHT AGAINST the wall is good. This should help you get fruit for longer into the fall, and they may even live through the winter. Growing dwarf varieties of papaya makes them easier to protect. It's possible to grow them in-ground and erect a greenhouse over them if you really like papayas. You can't do that with the tall types.

If a frost threatens and you have a tree out in the open, pick the fruit and bring it indoors to ripen. Some of them will ripen on the counter, and you can eat the green ones in salads and pickles or however else you like to eat them.

Growing papaya in North Florida may not be the most efficient way to spend your gardening time, but the flavor of ripe papaya along with their health benefits makes them a great addition to your homestead. In South and Central Florida, it's much easier to grow them and they are easy to pop into a food forest, as their vertical growth takes up very little space. They are also very productive very quickly, capable of bearing 200lbs of fruit per tree in their second year! I recommend planting papayas every year for a continuous supply, as the trees tend to decline and die at a few years of age.

PawPaw (C, N)

Latin name: *Asimina triloba, Asimina spp.*
Cold-hardiness: Beyond Florida
Mature height if unpruned: 25' on *A. triloba,*
          others vary
Propagation: Seed, grafting

Pawpaws are not to be confused with papayas, even though both are commonly called "pawpaws." True pawpaws are a temperate climate tree. Florida has eight native varieties of pawpaws that are not the better-known pawpaw of northern fame. These include *A. parviflora, A pygmaea, A. obovota,* and *A. reticulata.* They are all edible, though some are bland, and I've never had a good *A. pygmaea.* According to my friend Terri Pietroburgo, "The Florida pawpaws don't taste as good as the northern *triloba* because it has been cultivated to taste certain ways. The Florida pawpaws have a tropical taste that isn't the same as anything I have eaten. I have tasted six of our eight species and liked them all. Like anything else you pick in the wild sometimes you get one that's not that good but overall I have liked the taste. My grandson eats them as fast as I can get the seeds out!" Terri also told me that the best fruiting native Florida pawpaw variety is *A. parviflora.*

These native trees can be hard to find, but they are worth adding to a Florida food forest. The common pawpaw, *A. triloba,* is uncommon in Florida but has been seen fruiting well in the Gainesville area.

PawPaws are basically an understory tree—they don't like a lot of sun when they're small, so plant them in at least half-shade. This makes them ideal as a food forest tree, as they fit right in under the canopy and still fruit, unlike some other fruit trees.

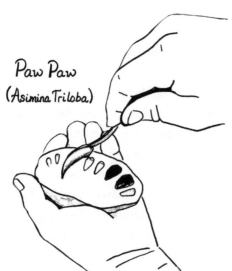

Paw Paw
(Asimina Triloba)

PawPaw trees are a bit funny about pollination. Their flowers are fly-pollinated and smell faintly of carrion. Unfortunately, flies are not very good pollinators so if you want fruit, it's a good idea to hand-pollinate the trees when they bloom. There are reports of farmers hanging chicken necks in their pawpaw orchards to attract more flies, but as a homeowner or small grower of trees, you'll probably have more luck with a paintbrush. Go get a little artists' brush and touch the inside of the flowers on one tree to get the pollen, then go touch the brush to the blooms on another tree. Then go back to the first tree, do it again, then do the second tree again.

Pawpaw seed germination requires a few steps. It's about a half-year process but it's not hard. It just takes time.

If a pawpaw seed dries out, it is dead. If you have old seeds, they'll fail. Unless they've been taken from a ripe fruit and popped right into the refrigerator and kept slightly moist, the embryos dry out and die. Pawpaws are not like beans—you need fresh seed.

Asimina triloba seeds need to be stratified to germinate. Pop them in the fridge for four months in a baggie of slightly moist peat moss or potting soil. Native Florida varieties may or may not need stratification—I have not experimented with them.

Once you've had the seeds in the fridge for four months, plant them in spring. They will germinate a couple of months later in early summer. I have a flat of fifty of them sitting beneath the magnolia tree behind my house.

You can plant your seeds right in the ground after stratification or you can plant them in pots. Deep pots better accommodate pawpaw taproots. You can transplant pawpaw trees if they're first started in pots, but if you plant them in the ground first, good luck transplanting them! They do not transplant well at all as the taproot is ridiculous. As they get older, pawpaw trees can handle more sun.

Pawpaw can fruit from seed in 3–4 years. They do not propagate from cuttings.

Peaches and Nectarines (C, N)

Latin name: *Prunus persica*
Cold-hardiness: Far beyond Florida
Mature height if unpruned: 18'+
Propagation: Seed, grafting

As the citrus industry has gone into free fall thanks to greening, peach production has replaced some former orange groves. If you haven't eaten homegrown peaches, you haven't eaten peaches. I never liked peaches as they were rubbery and awful—until I tried a fully ripe one from the tree. It was like a completely different fruit.

You can get away with growing peaches pretty far south into Florida, especially with super low-chill types like UFSun and UFBest, though Tropic Beauty goes pretty far south as well. However, the varieties you can grow and your chances of regular fruit increase as you head farther north in the state. I recommend growing a few varieties of peaches, with a variety of chill hours that are both above and below the recommended amount for your area. That way if the climate gets hotter, you still get peaches. If it gets colder, ditto.

Nectarines are non-fuzzy peaches. There are a variety of low-chill types for Florida, including Sunraycer, Sunmist and Suncoast, and the patented UFRoyal and UFQueen varieties from the University of Florida. We grew a Sunraycer in the North Florida Food Forest Project and it was a beautiful tree with lovely fruit and red leaves.

Pruning peaches and nectarines is a very good idea. Chop them down to 2' tall after planting so they make multiple leaders that branch low, then you'll have a shorter tree with more fruit. Don't worry. You won't kill them. They like a good bit of sun, so don't plant them in the shade. Some peaches make way too much fruit for the tree. If you have a ton of fruit on a tree, pick off at least half to 2/3 of them when they are the size of marbles and let the rest grow. If you don't, you get a bunch of small peaches that are mostly pit, instead of a good selection of big fruit.

Peaches and nectarines are easy to grow from seed and have always made good fruit for me. Locally grown fruit are more likely to meet your chill hour requirements, so I recommend using seed from those.

To germinate them, clean the flesh off the pits. If you crack them open, this may improve the germination rate, but it isn't necessary. Soak the pits in water for a few hours, then stick them in slightly moist potting soil in a baggie, then put that baggie in the fridge. In a few months, they will develop roots. At this point you can take them out and plant them in pots. When the weather is warm, they will grow like crazy. I have had a peach tree bloom only 18 months after planting the little seedling. Peaches and nectarines are subject to nematode damage, so I recommend planting the trees in holes with compost, then keeping them well-mulched to keep organic matter around the roots, suppressing nematode activity.

Pear (C, N)

Latin name: *Pyrus communis*
Cold-hardiness: Far beyond Florida
Mature height if unpruned: 25–40'
Propagation: Seed, grafting, air-layers

Like my experience with peaches, I didn't care for pears until I tried them fresh and fully ripe. Years ago, we bought a house in Tennessee with mature pear trees growing in the yard. They were some variety of dessert pear, pale green and yellow when ripe, and endowed with a wonderful melt-in-your-mouth flavor. My opinion of pears as hard, watered-down apples with unpleasant texture was transformed.

Now I love pears.

When I moved to Florida, I was afraid I wouldn't be able to grow any varieties worth eating. Fortunately, I was wrong. You can grow good pears from about the middle of the state north. Further south than that and you'll have chill hour issues and may have to mess around with forcing dormancy by leaf stripping, etc... and that's a topic for another day. Growing pears in Florida is easier than you might think.

Unlike apples, peaches, plums and nectarines, pears are relatively care-free trees. The biggest disease issue they face is fire blight, a nasty bacterial infection that usually starts at the ends of branches and works its way down towards the trunk. Fortunately, if you're observant, you can often head off the infection with a good pair of pruning shears and a spray-bottle of alcohol.

Sterilize your pruners with alcohol, then cut at least 12" further down each infected branch than the closest patch of infection. The infection is easy to identify since it looks like the name implies: charred brown leaves and wood. Make sure to sterilize your shears between each cut so you don't inadvertently spread the disease.

Once you've removed all the infected wood, burn it. Don't throw it in your compost or let it fall around the base of the tree. You want it gone.

Beyond the occasional brush with fire blight, Florida has some good pear varieties to get excited about. We can grow the classic Kieffer pear, the old-fashioned Pineapple pear (which apparently has a touch of pineapple flavor to the fruit), gourmet Oriental pears and other good varieties like Hood, Spalding and the low-chill UF cultivar Flordahome.

In the North Florida Food Forest I planted a Hood, a Kieffer, a Flordahome, an Asian and a Pineapple. All did well and didn't complain a bit about the bad soil.

When you plant pear (or any other) trees, make sure you keep the grass back from around the trunks to a distance of 4–5'. Grass will consume your tree's resources and choke it. A ring of mulch is always a good idea.

Pears take a few years to get big enough to bear well, so plant them as soon as you can. The wait is worth it. We used to harvest hundreds of pounds off our two trees in Tennessee. That made for a lot of delicious pear butter, salsa, slices in syrup, pear sauce, dried pears and pear hooch.

Pear trees are also beautiful beyond their functionality. I've come to love their interesting shape, the rough bark, the wild branches and the lovely blooms in spring. Though they're an easy survival tree for Florida, they don't make my top three (which are mulberries, loquats and persimmons) but they're a very close four at the moment. Plant a few for extra-good pollination and redundancy.

Pears are easy to propagate via grafting onto pear seedlings, ornamental pear varieties or even onto some varieties of hawthorn. Graft just before they break dormancy in the spring for best results.

Plum (C, N)

Latin name: *Prunus (var.)*
Cold-hardiness: Far beyond Florida
Mature height if unpruned: 20'
Propagation: Seed, grafting

Plums are generally easy to grow and take pruning well. They can also be used as rootstocks for peach and nectarine grafts, though the grafts may outgrow the plum itself and must be supported with poles. The native Florida Chickasaw plum works very well as a rootstock for better plum varieties, peaches and nectarines as it can survive in miserable nematode-infested soil and keep growing. The Nemaguard peach rootstock is also used for plums as they are plagued by nematodes, especially in very sandy soil.

The common Santa Rosa plum never did well for me in Florida. I had at least three of them die in the North Florida Food Forest. The "Gulf" varieties of plums from the University of Florida did great. Plums like full sun but can take a little shade and still fruit. Plant more than one variety of plum for pollination. Chickasaw plums are easy to propagate via digging up suckers during their late winter dormancy and potting them. The fruit is not usually very good, so they are better as rootstocks, animal food or for jams, with occasional sweet exceptions. The same is true of the fruit of the more attractive native Flatwoods plum. Both of these native plums make good preserves as the tarter fruits are good with added sugar. They are also a glorious announcement of a North Florida spring as they explode in a snowfall of white blooms. Plums can be propagated from seed, cuttings, air-layering or grafting.

Pomegranate (S, C, N)

Latin name: *Punica granatum*
Cold-hardiness: 10–20 degrees
Mature height if unpruned: Around 16'
Propagation: Seed, cuttings

Pomegranates are a beautiful and ancient fruit of sub-tropical arid climates. It's not ideally suited to Florida but some varieties do well. In my North Florida Food Forest I planted a half-dozen of them, of which two wilted and died to the ground after thriving for a few years, due to some strange disease issue. The dwarf types are much tougher and can fruit in a year from seed, though the fruit is barely worth eating. Wonderful is the most common full-sized variety and does okay in Florida. The fruit is often blotched and mottled, unlike the beautiful pomegranates we are used to seeing from California. Less of a tree than a big old ball of shrub, the pomegranate doesn't need training. Just plant it and let it grow. They usually fruit in the third or fourth year after planting. Seedling trees fruit in just a few years. Pomegranates do not fruit in the shade. Hot and dry locations are best. Don't overwater pomegranates. Though usually cold-hardy into the low teens, I have had pomegranates badly frozen back after an unexpected frost. Pomegranates are not hard to start from woody cuttings in early spring. Seeds germinate within a month and grow quickly.

Purple Mombin (S)

Latin name: *Spondias purpurea*
Cold-hardiness: 32 degrees
Mature height if unpruned: 16'
Propagation: Seeds, cuttings

The purple mombin is a popular fruit of the Caribbean and across the American tropics. The tree is small, with thin bark and very weak wood. The fruit is not amazing but it is sweet-tart and refreshing, though the pit is large and the flesh not particularly thick. My children greatly enjoy them.

Cuttings root very easily when rammed into the ground during the rainy months. If you start them in pots, be careful during transplanting as the roots are very weak and break easily.

Pomegranate

Sapodilla (S)

Latin name: *Manilkara zapota*
Cold-hardiness: 30 degrees
Mature height if unpruned: 40'
Propagation: Seed, grafting

The sapodilla is a delectable fruit that tastes like rich brown sugar and melts in your mouth.

Weirdly enough, this excellent fruit tree has been "assessed by the IFAS Invasive Plants Working Group as invasive in south and central Florida and is not recommended by UF/IFAS for planting."

Far be it from me to argue with UF, but... WE DON'T CARE! Seriously, if there was a tree I *wish* would seed itself in my yard, it would be sapodilla.

I found photos of a beautiful old sapodilla tree growing in Key West on the grounds of the Kimpton Winslow's Bungalows. I called the office for information, however, and was told by a very snippy man that "all he knew was that it was a tree." I asked if it fruited and he said yes but had no more information or a contact for the previous owners of the property. He wouldn't help me out at all, so I gave up chasing that lead. Come on, man. When someone is writing a book and calls and says he wants to write about a tree on your property, you gotta do better than that. Are you working in tandem with the invasive police at UF or something?

The sapodilla grows easily from seed and takes a half-decade or so to fruit. Grafted trees should be much faster. Though it can get quite tall, it is controlled easily with pruning.

Sea Grape (S)

Latin name: *Coccoloba uvifera*
Cold-hardiness: 30 degrees
Mature height if unpruned: 30'+, but more commonly 20'
Propagation: Seed, cuttings

Most people don't think of sea grapes as edible. Some of them are even delicious. When I was in college, there was a huge tree in the middle of the campus which bore abundant clusters of fruit. I helped myself, much to the bemusement of my classmates. Sometimes that was my only lunch.

Though the fruit tend to get soft and overripe quickly, they can be made into a good sea grape jam—and the trees themselves are highly ornamental. They are common along the coastline and can handle plenty of saltwater around their roots. It's a great beachside tree to hold back salt spray from more tender trees inland.

The wood is beautiful and pink-orange, though it twists quite a bit while drying. I carved a spoon from seagrape wood while sitting next to a fire and it turned out beautiful that night but started curving later. In a later project, my friend Moses used his sawmill to cut me some thicker planks from a large seagrape trunk which I used as steps inside a cabin I was building. They were beautifully orange-pink when varnished and almost glowed.

Seagrapes grow from fresh seed and cuttings. Seedlings transplant easily.

Soap Nut (S, C, N)

Latin name: *Sapindus saponaria*
Cold-hardiness: Probably low 20's.
Mature height if unpruned: Roughly 30'
Propagation: Seed

If you're a back-to-the-land sort or an alternative health, organic-market-shopping type, or a plant lover, you may have heard of the "soap nut" before. Or, more likely, their Indian cousin *Sapindus mukorossi*.

The Florida soapberry, *Sapindus saponaria* is a native tree, though it's only seen in the middle of the state when planted on purpose. I've been told by Dave Chiappini of Chiappini Native Farm and Nursery that its only common range in the state is scattered across a few islands on the coast.

According to UF, it's hardy to USDA Growing Zone 10. This is demonstrably false since there are large specimens growing in Gainesville and bearing fruit quite happily right at the edge of USDA zone 8.

The fruit, erroneously called a "soap nut", is loaded with saponins. Dry them (and pit them if you like) and they can be used to wash your hands or do a load of laundry when placed in a mesh bag. They last quite a few washings.

I first heard that the trees take 8 years or longer to produce fruit when grown from seed, however my friend Alex Ojeda told me that his soapberry trees bore fruit only three years after germination. The same was true of my friend Sam's trees at Scrubland Farmz. Three years, then fruit.

The soapberry needs a mate for pollination, so it is important to plant a few trees if you want fruit. Trees come in male, female and hermaphroditic varieties. Only females and hermaphrodites will bear soap nuts. If you plant three, chances are good that at least one or two of them will fruit for you. I planted five in the North Florida Food Forest Project.

Soapberry trees grow tall with an airy, open habit, looking a lot like the despised Chinaberry tree that's invaded railroad tracks and roadsides across the state, though unlike Chinaberry they have almost white bark.

If you have a small yard, I recommend planting three in a tight triangle so they grow like a triple-trunked tree and will pollinate each other without taking up too much space. That's what I did, spacing them about 6' apart, though if I were to do it again, I would plant three in the same hole at about 18" apart.

Soap nut trees are tolerant of poor soil and grow rather quickly into airy, lovely trees that don't cast particularly dense shade. If you want your own soap without bothering with lye and fat, tuck some in on the edge of your food forest.

Germination is easy with soapberry trees. I scarified a bunch of fresh seeds and planted them in little pots and got almost a 100% germination rate. When I planted older seeds, however, I got a much lower germination rate of only around 25%. I do not know if the tree can be air-layered or started from cuttings, but I assume not.

Soursop (S)

Latin name: *Annona muricata*
Cold-hardiness: 32
Mature height if unpruned: 30'
Propagation: Seed

Soursop, known as guanábana in Latin America, is a delicious fruit that makes excellent ice cream. It is white, creamy, tart-sweet and delicious, with quite a few black seeds inside that are almost as fun to spit as watermelon seeds. Don't eat the seeds as they are reportedly toxic.

Soursop is a tropical relative of pawpaw and cannot take cold weather. The leaves are often used as a tea to kill cancer cells, though the tea doesn't taste particularly good. The trees can take some shade and have attractive glossy green leaves. In the Caribbean, the fruit is often stolen and resold, as it fetches a high value at market.

There was a beautiful and productive soursop tree in Ft. Lauderdale my friend Eddy planted across the street from my parents' place, however, the house was sold, and the new owner cut it down and replaced it with a crappy little plastic shed.

An nescis, mi fili, quantilla prudentia mundus regatur?

What a waste. Every tropical yard should have a soursop. And zero stupid plastic sheds.

Soursop grows easily from fresh seed which germinates in a month or so.

Starfruit (S, C)

Latin name: *Averrhoa carambola*
Cold-hardiness: A little below freezing
Mature height if unpruned: 25'.   18' is more
　　　　　common
Propagation: Seed, grafting

Starfruit, also known as carambola, is one of my favorite fruits.

There is a beautiful tree growing in The Great South Florida Food Forest Project which has provided baskets and baskets of fruit over the years.

Starfruit usually bears two crops a year in non-freezing climates. I used to grow one in a pot in North Florida, but I gave it to my friend Curtiss who planted it in the ground at his place a little north of The Villages. Knowing that it was a tropical tree, he planted it against a wall in a protected microclimate. Despite the climate, he is getting abundant fruit.

If you've only had starfruit from the grocery store, you haven't tasted starfruit. Those bland and watery things are terrible. Fresh starfruit has a juicy sweet-tart tropical goodness that's very refreshing. Don't eat too many if you are subject to kidney stones, as they are high in oxalic acid.

The trees do not get very big. They spread sideways and have attractive bark and feathery leaves. Many years ago, I stood transfixed beneath a 15' tree in my friend Gary Paul's yard, looking up towards the sky. It was the first time I saw a starfruit tree up close. The sight of the semi-translucent fruit hanging like Chinese lanterns in the tropical sun was transcendently beautiful. I could have just sat down and stayed there for hours, staring up through the branches.

You can propagate starfruit via seeds or grafting. Some seedling types taste sour or have bitter skin, though some are very good.

Sugar Apple (S)

Latin name: *Annona squamosa*
Cold-hardiness: 32 degrees
Mature height if unpruned: 14'
Propagation: Seed

The first time I saw a sugar apple was in the back yard of the Indian neighbors who lived across from my parents when I was a kid. I had no idea what the tree was, and it wasn't particularly pretty, but the fruit was fascinating. I don't recall trying one back then but I have had them as an adult and they are quite pleasant, if rather too sweet. It's really like eating grainy sugar.

The sugar apple is very easy to grow and produces decent crops even when young. The fruit are ready when the "joints" in them really expand and the fruit starts to soften. Don't pick and eat them early as they are awful before they ripen.

Trees grow and fruit in just a few years from seed.

Sumac (Winged) (C, N)

Latin name: *Rhus copallinum*
Cold-hardiness: Far beyond Florida
Mature height if unpruned: Roughly 16'
Propagation: Division

I added the first winged sumac to my North Florida food forest right at the beginning of the project. I dug one up from the edge of a housing development in Citra and took it home to the food forest, where it quickly grew into an ugly, spindly tree. They won't win any beauty contests, but they are a useful species to have. Over time, more sumac planted themselves into the food forest, likely with the help of birds. Though some know of sumacs only through an encounter with the winged sumac's evil cousin, poison sumac, it is easy to tell the species apart, especially when in fruit,

Winged Sumac

as poison sumac has white berries. The winged sumac is all over the place in North Florida and is the only species I've seen in the state.

When I planted my winged sumac, I counted sumacs as more of a minor native edible than as a particularly useful tree.

Over the years, however, I've also found them to be a decent chop-n-drop plant that functions as a fast-growing mulch provider. The suckering habit of sumacs means there are always a few growing here and there, often some feet from the parent tree.

They are also great for attracting wildlife.

One day I was out in the front yard, wandering through the food forest, when I heard a powerful buzzing sound overhead. At first, I thought I was hearing a swarm of flies or the buzz of electricity, then I saw that the masses of sumac blooms over my head were absolutely covered with bees and other pollinators.

The variety and activity were incredible! For being such tiny flowers, they sure attracted an abundance of buzzing things.

You'll read online that you can make sumac "lemonade" from the fruit. I haven't found that to work well. And we can grow lemons, so why bother? Sumac looks its best in fall when the leaves turn a violent red.

Winged sumacs are easy to propagate by digging up suckers.

Wax Apple (S)

Latin name: *Syzygium samarangense*
Cold-hardiness: 32 degrees
Mature height if unpruned: 25'
Propagation: Seed, cuttings

The wax apple is a lovely small tree with beautiful fruit borne in large clusters on the branches.

The slightly underripe fruit have a flavor like a green apple, but the fully ripe fruit are sweet with a hint of a rose-like bouquet on the palate. They retain their crisp, apple-like crunch even at peak ripeness.

The tree's fluffy white flowers betray their relation to guavas, though you'd never know it by the flavor.

Wax apples are very tropical and cannot take the cold, though you could likely grow them in large pots in the northern half of the state. My friend Eric Moulton has a beautiful and productive wax apple tree growing in Ft. Lauderdale near my parents' food forest.

Some wax apples have a single pit in the center, though some fruits are empty. If you get a pit, plant it before it dries out and it will sprout in about a month. The trees can also be propagated via air layering and occasionally cuttings.

Yaupon holly (C, N)

Latin name: *Ilex vomitoria*
Cold-hardiness: Far beyond Florida
Mature height if unpruned: Roughly 20'
Propagation: Seed, cuttings

The yaupon holly is an unassuming shrub or small tree which wouldn't catch your eye if you saw one during a woodland stroll. On closer inspection, it does have its own beauty. The bark is pale and smooth, the leaves small, dentate and glossy green. Female yaupon hollies set the familiar red berries of holly jolly Christmas fame. These berries are eaten by birds but not by man.

In Florida the yaupon holly is often planted as a native landscape plant for its evergreen foliage and attractive trunk. In the panhandle, yaupon is a very common understory tree in pine woods. So common, in fact, that people hate them and consider them a weed.

For those of you who really enjoy aesthetics with your tea, varieties of yaupon have been found and bred by the landscaping industry in a wide range of shapes. I have seen rigidly columnar forms, weeping forms, the tiny 2' dwarf forms I mentioned above, and, as I planted in my yard, the full-size wilder form. Some of these are better for leaf production than others. You could plant a little tea hedge of dwarf yaupon trees or go big with a full-size tree. It's possible to prune for more leaf production and to keep the leaves in reach for harvest, but you may not end up with a pretty tree that way, especially if you are butchering back a graceful full-sized specimen.

I harvest yaupon when the weather is dry. I go outside with one of my wife's stainless mixing bowls and a pair of nippers. Then I prune the last six inches of younger yaupon shoots into the bowl; leaves, twigs and all.

To make quick yaupon tea, I simply chop up some of the leaves and small twigs and pour boiling water over them and let them steep for a while. This makes a light, pleasant green tea.

For stronger tea, chop up and dry the leaves first, then make tea. The flavor is pleasant, earthy, and much like a middle-of-the-road English tea. Excellent.

One way I really like to do them now is to take the green leaves and twigs from the tree, then chop and toast them on a hot cast-iron pan until they dry and singe to a pale brown. This creates a smoky, rich flavor that is very nice and reminiscent of yaupon's South American cousin yerba maté.

Some readers have told me that toasting or roasting is necessary to free up the caffeine in yaupon holly but I have been unable to find any details on that. Plus, I lack a lab and can't test it. My internal caffeine sensors aren't delicate enough thanks to years of black coffee consumption. I should probably give some green yaupon tea to our two-year-old as a test.

Yaupon holly tea is delicious. It cannot really replace coffee, sadly, since nothing can do that, but it is a good way to get your morning (afternoon, evening, midnight) buzz.

Quick note: don't chew the raw leaves—they'll irritate your mouth.

If I were to pick one source of caffeine for Florida, this would be it. Sure, I would miss espresso—but I wouldn't miss the work involved with growing coffee.

Yaupon grows from seed and probably cuttings, though I have not tried either.

Yaupon Holly

Cabbage Palmetto

PALMS

Cabbage Palm (S, C, N)

Latin name: *Sabal palmetto*
Cold-hardiness: Beyond Florida
Mature height if unpruned: 65'
Propagation: Seed

Cabbage palms are everywhere in Florida. The fruits are edible and sweet, though they have almost no flesh. Roasted, you might be able to grind the seeds, but otherwise, they're like buckshot. The "heart of palm" in the center of the growth bud at the top of the tree is the very best part of the cabbage palm but that requires killing the tree. If I had plenty of land, I might harvest them selectively and let the birds replant. They take a long time to get to any size. Heart of palm is mild and nutty and the texture is wonderfully fine. It's truly an excellent vegetable, but I would consider it much more of a luxury than a staple. When a neighbor cut down a cabbage palm, we readily harvested the heart and enjoyed it, but I've never cut down a tree on purpose to get one.

From seed, cabbage palm grows slowly. As UF relates:

Sabal palm seeds are not difficult to germinate, but should be planted when fresh for best germination. With uniform moisture and high temperatures (86°F–95°F), germination can occur in as few as 18 days, with 50% of final germination occurring within 33 days (Carpenter 1987; Sento 1970). Newly emerged seedlings look much like grass, but each succeeding leaf has an additional leaf segment that adds to their width. The slow-growing seedlings can take 15–30 years to develop a visible trunk under natural conditions, but in nurseries this can occur much faster (McPherson and Williams 1996).

They don't take up much space in a food forest and are rugged and attractive, hosting birds and other species as well as bringing an Old Florida feel to the homestead.

Coconut Palm (S)

Latin name: *Cocus nucifera*
Cold-hardiness: 32 degrees
Mature height if unpruned: 40'
Propagation: Seed

Coconut palms can be considered a survival gardening staple in South Florida. The nuts are highly nutritious and filling when fully ripe and can be processed to make coconut oil and coconut milk. The coconut water in immature nuts is excellent for your health and can stand in for lunch when you're working in the garden. I find that it fills me up and reinvigorates me as I farm. When wet, coconut husks stay soaked. I bury them at the bottom of container gardens or let them rot in wet piles for a year or more to use in potting mixes. Sea salt is a good amendment for coconut palms, increasing their vigor and yields. You can just carry home buckets of seawater and dump it at the base of coconut palms—just be careful not to soak less salt-tolerant plants around them. If you can grow coconut palms in your food forest, I highly recommend doing so.

An easy way to germinate the nuts is to grab a bunch of coconuts and bury them half-way in the ground on their sides in a group under a hedge or someplace out of the way, then transplant whatever nuts sprout. Sprouts usually appear in a few months.

Pindo Palm (S, C, N)

Latin name: *Butia capitata*
Cold-hardiness: Beyond Florida
Mature height if unpruned: 25'
Propagation: Seed

The pindo palm is a Brazilian native that is quite cold-hardy. I planted two pindos in my North Florida food forest because I was so impressed with the flavor of pindo palm jelly. Pindo palm fruit are not great off the tree, but the jelly tastes incredible.

Coconut, pineapple, passionfruit – you taste notes of different tropical delights in it. Very, very good.

I once harvested about 50lbs from the Ocala agricultural extension offices and made jelly with them. They often just fall on the ground unused and are available for the asking. And the aroma of the fruit is intoxicating. Pindo palms are often sold in ornamental nurseries. Their silvery foliage and cold-hardiness make them very popular. I got my first two trees from Home Depot and have encouraged many food forest enthusiasts to add a few to their plans. You won't regret it.

Seeds take some months to germinate and initial growth is slow.

Autumn Olive

SHRUBS

Autumn Olive (N)

Latin name: *Eleagnus umbellata*
Cold-hardiness: Far beyond Florida
Mature height if unpruned: 12'
Propagation: Seed, cuttings

This is an EVIL INVASIVE PLANT™ with edible berries and nitrogen-fixing capability. It was once planted extensively to reclaim old mine sites but is no longer recommended. I had a handful of them growing in my North Florida food forest and they grew well, but not invasively. The fruits can be made into ketchup. If the shrubs get too tall or bushy, chop them way back. They'll live and drop nitrogen at the same time. As a dual-use edible and nitrogen fixer, autumn olive is a very useful species.

I found it hard to root cuttings, but not impossible.

Blackberry (C, N)

Latin name: *Rubus spp.*
Cold-hardiness: Far beyond Florida
Mature height if unpruned: 5'
Propagation: Tip layering, cuttings

There is an excellent series of blackberries that was developed by the University of Arkansas blackberry breeding program in recent decades. I've grown quite a few of them. They are named after various Indian tribes. I grew Apache up in Tennessee and it did great. Down in Florida I've grown Natchez, Ouachita, Kiowa and Arapaho. All did well.

More and more blackberry U-pick farms have been popping up across North Florida and it seems that our conditions support most of the University of Arkansas releases.

If you're going to grow blackberries in Florida, it's important to give them extra water and feeding in the spring when it's dry, otherwise they don't set much fruit.

I've also found some decent blackberries growing in the wild. Taste every plant you find and if you find a great one, take some cuttings and plant it. They'll be perfectly suited to your area already, though they're a lot smaller than the commercial varieties. I've noticed bitterness is a problem with a lot of blackberries, even cultivated ones. I believe it may be a combination of harsh conditions, low water and so-so soil. Another problem is picking before they're completely ripe.

Blackberries like lots of sun. The ones growing in the shade fail to fruit for me. The ones along my driveway in full sun did a lot better.

A slightly acid soil (pH 5.5–6.5) is good for blackberries. Mine thrive on compost and coffee grounds. They also appreciate a good mulching plus a quarter cup of Epsom salts in the spring. Err on the side of LOTS of organic matter, rather than just a little. If your pH is a little high, work in some sulphur and mulch with pine debris, whether needles, mulch chips or just forest duff.

Once you get too far south, growing blackberries gets difficult. It might be worth trying as an experiment, but I wouldn't count on them.

To start lots more blackberries, bury the tips of some of the branches in the ground and they'll root there, putting up new shoots. Transplant these wherever you like.

Blueberry (C, N)

Latin name: *Vaccinium genus*
Cold-hardiness: Far beyond Florida
Mature height if unpruned: 12'
Propagation: Cuttings, Grafting

In the panhandle there are vast areas of blueberries growing wild under pine trees and in mixed woods. They love acidic soil, and you'll find them once you know what to look for. Some species have small fruit, others larger, but if you want the biggest and best fruit, buying or propagating commercial cultivars is the way to go.

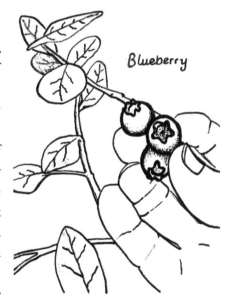

The Southern Highbush blueberry is the most common commercial variety with a wide range of different cultivars. Its range runs on down to the south of Polk County, though I don't think they'll produce well all the way down into truly tropical South Florida. A little chill is good for them. For the Central part of the state and northwards, I much prefer rabbiteye blueberry varieties. They are tough and scrappy, take much less work than Southern highbush blueberries and stand a wider pH range. Sometimes you can find them growing in the wild.

There are also various interesting native varieties of blueberries, such as the tiny "Shiny Blueberry," (*Vaccinium myrsinites).* The fruit are itty-bitty but have an out-sized blueberry flavor. Some native plant nurseries carry this delightful variety, which grows excellently in acid scrubland sand. There are also blueberry relatives of various degrees of flavor and palatability, including deerberry (*Vaccinium stamineum*) and sparkleberry (*Vaccinium arboreum*). We eat both in season.

Sparkleberry can be used as a root stock for better varieties of blueberry, including rabbiteye and Southern highbush. This is a great idea for two reasons: first, sparkleberry does not need to be grown in a bunch of pine bark mulch to be happy and second, sparkleberry can handle a wider range of pH, rainfall levels and soil types than commercial blueberries can. Sparkleberries are grainy and not very flavorful.

Take their ability to thrive in tough conditions and use it as a base for better types, grafting on top in late winter and early spring.

Commercial blueberries have various chill hour requirements. Check the varieties you plan to buy to make sure they fit your region of Florida. As blueberries love acid soil, most people dig in lots of rotted pine bark or commercial "blueberry mix" soil before planting. I have grown rabbiteyes just in the sand, but I mulched them on top with pine bark and gave them elemental sulphur to acidify the soil.

Blueberries fruit in half-sun but do best in full. Rabbiteyes are much longer-lived and have less disease issues and irrigation needs than do Southern Highbush. The latter produces earlier in the season and has berries with thinner skins which are the common ones you'll see in stores. Blueberries make beautiful hedges and landscape plants, so think of them next time you want to do some front-yard landscaping. Some of the rabbiteye types have almost blue foliage with pink new growth, and in the spring all blueberries have lovely bell-like flowers which hang like little white dresses from the canes.

Pruning blueberries is a good practice if you want lots of fruit. When I interviewed Bill Hall of B&G Blueberries in Ft. McCoy back in 2019, he told me:

On the Rabbiteye you don't do anything but take the oldest wood out. Like on this one (pointing to a rabbiteye bush), when I get ready, I've looked at this cane and say, "Well, this cane's weak." I get down there and maybe cut it off all the way down here (points to bottom of the cane). Cause I want it to sprout out, and be thicker and bigger. And so if you had 10 canes on a Rabbiteye plant, we'd want to take out 20% of the growth of the canes and take the oldest and tallest out. And if you did that every year, every five years, you wouldn't have any wood that's over five years old. And so my experience is that after five years they start getting more diseases and funguses, but if you keep cutting it out and getting it out of the patch, letting new stuff come in, the Rabbiteyes will really last, and they'll produce. And another reason for don't take it all off to cause in a Rabbiteye the next year you won't have any berries if you take it all down. For the Southern Highbush, they'd go in and they top them, and they depend on the new growth for all their berries. They cut them completely down, maybe about two and a half, three foot tall. The Southern Highbush are pruned, basically I call it a flat top or a rooftop. And I use a gasoline-powered trimmer and get two tall boys to walk along here and hit them. And you can see they do it about the same height every year. And then they'll just come back with a vengeance until they get real old and die.

To start blueberries from cuttings, use semi-hardwood cuttings under mist or use the pot and baggie method to make a mini-greenhouse. I have rooted them on the windowsill in my kitchen. It takes about 3 months for them to root. I have not tried growing blueberries from seed.

Cassava (S, C, N)

Latin name: *Manihot escuelenta*
Cold-hardiness: 32 degrees
Mature height if unpruned: 5–10' (depends on variety)
Propagation: Cuttings

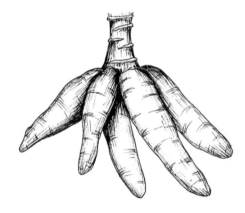

Cassava is a serious staple crop. It is low maintenance and more filling than anything else in this entire book. It's got about twice the calories as regular white potatoes, with nutrition-rich leaves which are edible after boiling for 20 minutes.

Cassava is a tropical crop and is not happy in cold weather. I grew it in North Florida but it would freeze to the ground in winter and took eighteen months to make decent-sized roots. When I grew it in warmer Frostproof, it produced roots within a year and grew through the winter without issue. When you read about cassava, you'll read that it contains cyanide and that there are both "sweet" and "bitter" varieties, the latter being very high in cyanide and only edible with extensive processing. That's not the type you want to grow. Stick to the "sweet" types, which are probably all you'll find in Florida anyhow, as the "bitter" types are usually used for commercial starch production rather than home gardening. Spanish-speakers know cassava as "yuca." Caribbean islanders know it as cassava or manioc. Jamaicans, Puerto-Ricans, various islanders, Indians and Central Americans often have cassava to share or know where you can get planting material. Grower Jim in Orlando usually has it as well, as do permaculture gardeners and other eccentrics around the state. I got my first cassava cuttings from an older missionary who got his from Indian friends, then I grew the

Vertical, diagonal and horizontal cassava planting methods.

plants for years and shared it with many friends. Do not confuse "yuca" with "yucca," despite what the spell-check on your stupid phone tells you. "Yucca" is an unrelated species and not even close to cassava, despite the similar name.

To grow cassava, plant 10–16" mature pieces of cassava stem in mounded banks or loose soil, 3–4' apart. Bury them about half-way into the ground so the top of the stem is sticking out, then water them in. If you have drier conditions, the stem cuttings may be buried diagonally or even on their sides a couple inches beneath the ground. They sprout slower that way but grow well.

If they are happy and warm, you will have roots in a year. I know people will say "six months," but you almost have to be a wizard to pull that off in most of Florida due to the cool season and lack of rain in spring and fall. Unless you find a fast-producing variety. Propagative material isn't all that easy to find, even for the long-season types.

After a year, do some archaeology around the roots, digging carefully, to find the roots. They grow in spokes out from the central stem. If you have good-sized roots (2" diameter or so, or larger), chop the bush down and carefully pull them up from the sand. Be careful not to damage the roots as you dig around the plant. They are easy to chop through with a shovel. Once you have your roots, it is easy to make a slit in the sides about a quarter-inch deep and peel off the outer bark layer, then cut the roots open and remove the woody threads in the very middle of each. Once dug, cassava roots only keep for a few days before starting to darken and spoil inside, so dig them when you need them or leave them in the ground. You can sneak a root or two from the sides of a growing plant if you do not want to dig the whole thing, but generally I just dig a plant all at once, peel the roots, plant the canes I cut down, then give the clean roots to my wife so she can cut them up and remove the woody centers and cook them.

Boil cassava in an open pot until it is soft, then it is safe to eat. Do not eat the raw roots, as they contain some cyanide precursors that are removed by boiling. The leaves can also be boiled for twenty minutes and eaten. Younger leaves are more tender, but all of them are a bit papery, though high in protein and nutrients. Recently we put some through the blender then cooked them into a soup. It was edible.

A good-sized cassava patch is excellent food security, especially if you are regularly replanting. The plants suffer from few issues in Florida and can be planted whenever you like as it is a non-seasonal crop. It grows much faster in warm weather and when the rain is falling but it will tolerate cool days and dry weather. In winter, it makes sense to plant canes on their sides a couple inches deep to protect them from frost. I've found that it will spring up just fine when the soil warms, even if planted months earlier. In colder areas of the state, above-ground growth will freeze down but comes back in spring. This is a top survival crop if you can get planting material. Once you have some plants, you can always make more.

Roots from the store are unlikely to grow—stem cuttings are the best. If you can feed your cassava with a balanced fertilizer or compost it will do better than if it is just left to its own devices. It also seems to appreciate being mulched.

In a food forest setting, put cassava at the sunny edges. It's also a good crop to plant all around a new food forest system when there's still plenty of sunshine. More sun = happier cassava with bigger roots. They will not do much in the shade.

If you live in North Florida and want planting material for spring, cut canes down before the first frost. Then dig a pit and put some straw or leaves in it and carefully fill it up with longer pieces of cane, then cover with more leaves and straw and a layer of dirt or a tarp. You can dig them up in spring to plant out after all danger of frost. They'll keep beneath the ground just fine and may even start rooting and sprouting for you before you dig them.

Chaya (S, C, N)

Latin name: *Cnidoscolus chayamansa,*
C. aconitifolius
Cold-hardiness: Around 32 degrees
Mature height if unpruned: 15'
Propagation: Cuttings

Chaya is a perennial shrub growing 6'+. The leaves are a good edible, though they should be boiled for 20 minutes before eating to off-gas the cyanide precursors. I know, that sounds scary, but it's not a big deal, especially for this prolific, delicious, pest-free and nutritious plant. The young leaves and shoot tips are the best to eat. Chaya freezes to the ground during tough winters and regrows vigorously in spring. To grow it, take cuttings, break off most of the leaves, then let them sit somewhere in the shade for a few days or weeks for the cut portions to heal up. Then, plant them

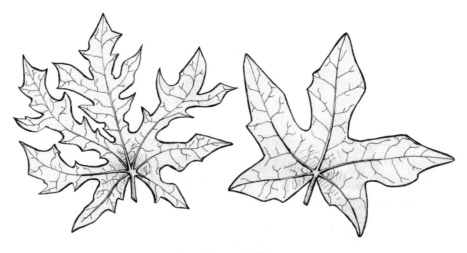

Two Types of Chaya

with at least a few inches of stem in the ground or in a pot or soil and let them root. They take a while to get started but once they're happy, they grow fast and produce a lot of edible leaves. Chaya stems are prone to rotting if you just stick them straight in the ground or try to root them in water. Chaya plants make good edible hedges and grow in full sun or half shade. In full shade they get very leggy and don't produce well.

Cocoplum (S)

Latin name: *Chrysobalanus icaco*
Cold-hardiness: 32 degrees
Mature height if unpruned: 10'
Propagation: Seed

A couple of years ago my sister Steph and I went foraging at a park by the beach and discovered a bunch of delicious cocoplums.

As there was an abundance of plants in fruit, I tasted all the cocoplums I could and saved seeds from the tastiest and largest specimens.

Cocoplums are a remarkably easy-to-grow Florida native. So long as you don't have freezing temperatures, they grow happily in a wide range of conditions and they handle salinity just fine. You'll see them as hedges around gas stations and growing behind apartment complexes in terrible, dry, lousy dirt. It's a survivor.

The pits are large compared to the fruit and the skins can be a little bitter. Green Deane writes: "The large kernel removed from its shell is edible raw or cooked. Some think it has the faint flavor of almond. To me it tastes like granola. Many think the

kernel is far better when the fruit and kernel are both pierced so the juice of the pulp is allowed to seep into the kernel."

To germinate cocoplums, eat the plums, scrub the flesh off the pits, then plant them. My last round took a remarkably long time to emerge – some took as long as 90 days. One final one sprouted about 10 months after planting! The earliest came up around two months from planting, however, and when they come up they grow quickly.

Coffee (S)

Latin name: *Coffea (spp)*
Cold-hardiness: 32 degrees
Mature height if unpruned: 20'
Propagation: Seed

Though coffee is a tropical plant, I grew *C. arabica* along the south-facing wall of my North Florida home and it sailed through nights that hit the teens further out in the yard. That wall radiated warmth overnight and was basically USDA Zone 10, even when the yard dropped into USDA Zone 8 territory.

In South Florida you can pop some coffee plants into your yard and they'll grow without too much care.

I grew a coffee tree in a large pot for about four years and it paid me with a few handfuls of fruit a year. During the freezes I kept it in my greenhouse. During the spring, summer and fall, it resided in a shady spot outdoors, happily blooming every spring and producing coffee cherries in the fall and winter.

For the time I owned that first productive coffee tree, all the beans were used to grow baby coffee plants which I sold through my nursery.

A word on those "beans": they're not really beans. They're the seeds inside a small fruit called a "coffee cherry." Coffee cherries taste a lot like sweet red bell peppers with a bit of spice to them.

Eat the fruit, spit out the seeds, then roast and grind them. Or plant them.

From germination, it takes about 3 years for your new coffee tree to start blooming. Coffee is self-pollinating, so you'll be able to get beans off a tree without it needing a mate. They grow moderately quickly if you keep them in acidic soil and supplied with nitrogen. I fed my North Florida trees with rabbit manure and coffee grounds. Blood meal is another good choice.

Coffee takes well to growing in a pot and can be grown as a houseplant year-round. The leaves are attractive, the blooms are lovely and the fruit is a fascinating conversation piece.

Note: when you keep a plant in a pot, it's easy to over or under-water. Just give it a good soaking when the top inch or so has dried out. About once a week should be good. Coffee is pretty forgiving of less than regular waterings, but it will droop and let you know when it's not happy.

The plant itself is a glossy-leaved and attractive fellow that flowers in early spring and fruits along its stem in clusters. They almost look like plastic and make a nice houseplant. From flowering to fruiting takes nine months, so be patient.

Once your harvest ripens, you can break open the red fruit or simply eat it and spit the "beans" out to be saved for roasting. We just toast ours in a cast-iron pan, turning them regularly.

It's hard to kill coffee when it's growing in good soil and warm conditions. If you move it into full sun, it will burn the leaves and make it unhappy. If it goes without water for too long, it will wilt but usually recovers rapidly when water is reapplied. Just keep it fed and watered and it will reward you with plenty of rich, glossy leaves and abundant blooms and fruit. I met a man at the Kanapaha plant show in 2015 who was growing coffee trees in his yard somewhere around Gainesville. They're brought in during freezes, but he told me he's had great success with fruiting and production.

According to my non-scientific estimates, a serious coffee drinker will require about 25 bushes to stay caffeinated through a year. An occasional coffee drinker will only need a few. They bear more and more every year and can grow into a decent-sized tree under good conditions; however, taking care of that many trees and staying on top of picking, drying and roasting will be a pain. Can you imagine keeping 25 coffee trees inside your house? Crazy, but it would be kind of awesome.

Gardener Alison Golwick posted on my blog that she was having luck growing them outside their "natural" tropical range:

I am growing arabica coffee plants in Brandon, Florida, a community just east of Tampa, Florida. It is zone 9b, I live on a ridge with a slight slope so planted the coffee plants along a south facing slope with an oak canopy. They get a little morning sun and some part shade during the day. I planted them two years ago and they are doing great. This year they produced their first fruit.

The fruit is still green in November, so I am worried that it is getting too cold for it to complete ripening, as this takes 37 weeks from flower to red fruit. The coffee plants range from 3–5 feet and are beautifully lush shiny green leaves – very healthy looking. I will be giving them more TLC over these colder months with compost tea and some extra water.

From the beginning I decided to plant them as a privacy plant along my property line, so in the end if they didn't produce coffee beans, they would still be a beautiful border plant. I originally ordered 18 plants – that is what is recommended for 2 cups of coffee a day for a year, 18 plants can supply enough coffee for that. Later I added another 10 plants just to finish the property line and have extra coffee!

I love my coffee plants and I am glad they seem happy as well.

Oh another tip, when we had a bad frost, I used Tyvek home wrap insulation teepeed'd over them in a long row to protect them from the frost. It worked great! Tyvek does not let moisture in, so it keeps the frost out. Anyway, it protected the plants, and it is easy to roll up and use again. Now that the plants are taller it will take more material, but it is cheaper than other frost protection options.

If I lived in South Florida, I would plant a plantation of coffee in my yard and sell my own Florida-grown small-batch coffee. I really think its potential is overlooked. It wouldn't even have to be *C. arabica*, the commonly grown expensive coffee. *C. liberica* tastes just fine and can handle lowland growing in a variety of conditions and needs way less care. We grew it in Grenada at about 250 feet above sea level and it thrived. I also planted some near the beach right at sea level and they were happy. Though coffee growers often use this species just as a root stock and do not use it for commercial production, I think *Liberica* has massive potential. The beans are huge, and the trees easily grow to 20' plus with massive yields.

As a huge bonus in a food forest situation, coffee grows great in the shade, making it a perfect understory. Just be sure to prune it now and again to maintain production. Maybe you'll be the one to start a Florida coffee plantation! Let me know if you do.

Coffee trees take a little bit of time to propagate. Cuttings can be rooted under mist, allegedly, but my greenhouse rooting experiments were all failures, so I only grow them from seeds now.

You must use fresh seed which is hard to find. Roasted Dunkin' Donuts beans will not work. "Green" coffee beans are probably already too dry to grow.

Once you find fresh seeds, they usually take a month or two to germinate. Germination is uneven and imperfect. Maybe 50–75%. Bottom heat helps. I've had them come up in less than a month with a heating pad beneath my seed trays. You need to keep them moist during this time. I put the seed trays on a large baking tray with a little water in the bottom so they don't dry out. That works well.

Cranberry Hibiscus a.k.a. False Roselle (S, C, N)

Latin name: *Hibiscus acetosella*
Cold-hardiness: 20-something degrees
Mature height if unpruned: 6'
Propagation: Seed, cuttings

Cranberry hibiscus is a perennial, somewhat cold-hardy shrub with leaves that are edible raw or cooked. Its tart, deep red leaves are highly ornamental and are excellent in Caesar salads. The blooms are red-pink to dark red-purple with deep maroon throats. It handles sun and shade and is easily propagated from seed and cuttings. This is a nice addition to salads, but the leaves are a little small to be particularly useful as a perennial green. Do not confuse this plant with Jamaican sorrel, AKA Florida cranberry, which produces large edible calyxes which can be made into punches and preserves. The cranberry hibiscus makes only edible leaves. Cranberry hibiscus starts easily from seeds and cuttings.

Edible-leaf Hibiscus a.k.a. Sunset Muskmallow a.k.a. Hibiscus Manihot (S, C)

Latin name: *Abelmoschus manihot*
Cold-hardiness: 32 degrees
Mature height if unpruned: 8'
Propagation: Cuttings, Seed

This edible hibiscus is a perennial shrub reaching 10' under ideal conditions. The huge leaves are edible raw or cooked and are mucilaginous with a sweet taste rather like a mild lettuce. A few big leaves can make a whole salad. The rare blooms are large and pale yellow. Mine didn't bloom or set seed pods in the South Florida Food Forest but it did bloom for me in Grenada and set seed. This is a truly excellent salad green. It did not live through winters in North Florida, though I tried. There I kept it alive in pots. Cuttings root easily and the plant usually regrows after a frost.

Goumi Berry (C, N)

Latin name: *Eleagnus multiflora*
Cold-hardiness: Far beyond Florida
Mature height if unpruned: 8'
Propagation: Cuttings, Seed

Goumi berries are edible and rich in antioxidants. As a huge bonus, the plant is a nitrogen-fixer that is short and tucks in well next to larger trees. The bushes are drought-tolerant, attractive and basically care-free.

Though goumi berries don't grow as fast as their cousin the silverthorn, goumi berries grow at a decent rate and are easy to shape however you like.

I'm not sure how they'll do in South Florida, but they did well in North Florida, though the yield of berries was small. Its other relative, autumn olive, was more productive but is much more invasive and not as pretty.

I tried propagating these from cuttings under mist but had a terrible success rate, with only about 1 in 50 rooting. We have not tried seeds yet.

Grape Mahonia a.k.a Leatherleaf Mahonia a.k.a Oregon Holly Grape (C, N)

Latin name: *Mahonia bealei,*
Mahonia aquifolium
Cold-hardiness: Beyond Florida
Mature height if unpruned: 4–10'
Propagation: Unknown

These lovely shade plants are a striking addition to any landscape or food forest. My friend Guda Taylor called *Mahonia bealei* the "grape mahonia" when she had them at Taylor Gardens Nursery, whereas the University of Florida calls it the "leatherleaf mahonia." I list both names here in case you have a hard time finding one. *Mahonia aquifolium* is the true Oregon grape holly and is similar in growth and fruit flavor. The fruits are sweet-tart and seedy but good to eat. Birds love them, but if you get

there first, they can be made into jams. As an understory for shade, mahonias are perfect.

We planted multiple leatherleaf mahonias beneath the oaks in our North Florida food forest where they did well despite the dry soil, roots and full shade.

Mahonia propagates via seeds or cuttings.

Katuk (S, C)

Latin name: *Sauropus androgynous*
Cold-hardiness: 32 degrees
Mature height if unpruned: 10'
Propagation: Cuttings, Seed

Katuk is a tropical perennial shrub with edible leaves that can be consumed raw or cooked. Raw, they are unpleasantly zippy but when cooked they lose their weird flavor. Some sites say their shoot tips can be cooked like asparagus, but I have never found them to be tender or large enough to make it worthwhile. Overall, it's a so-so edible. I much prefer the edible-leaf hibiscus or even moringa. If you live where it freezes, plant katuk in a protected location or keep in a pot. It thrives in half to full sun. Katuk often self-seeds and is also easy to start from cuttings.

Katuk

Miracle Fruit (S)

Latin name: *Synsepalum dulcificum*
Cold-hardiness: 32 degrees
Mature height if unpruned: 8'
Propagation: Seed

The first time I tried miracle fruit was when I visited Craig Hepworth in Citra. He had miracle fruit growing in his greenhouse. I had heard of the fruit and its remarkable effect on the palate but hadn't ever seen them in person, let alone eaten one. Craig picked some from an unremarkable looking little bush, then picked a lemon and a starfruit and we headed back to his porch.

First, he had me taste the starfruit, which was quite sour. Then he handed me a miracle fruit.

"Eat this miracle fruit and chew it for a while, making sure it coats your tongue. Then try a slice of starfruit," he said.

I did. The miracle fruit was somewhat sweet but didn't taste like much. After eating it, I took a slice of the sour starfruit. Now it tasted explosively sweet and delicious—like starfruit candy!

After the starfruit, I ate a slice of lemon. All the sourness and acidity were gone and it tasted like super-sweet lemonade.

It's an incredible experience and the effects of eating a miracle fruit last for some minutes before fading.

Miracle fruit isn't a great fruit in its own right, but it is a great experience. I was given seeds and they took 30–90 days to germinate when outside temperatures were in the 80s. Air-layering may work as well but I have not tried it. Miracle fruit likes acid soil and grows quite slowly.

Mysore and Other Raspberries (S, C, N)

Latin name: *Rubus (spp.)*
Cold-hardiness: Varies
Mature height if unpruned: 5'
Propagation: Division, cuttings, tip layering

There are multiple raspberries which grow in Florida; the easiest to grow and most productive being the Mysore. The Mysore raspberry is a tropical relation of the northern raspberry. It can produce multiple times a year but is endowed with vicious spines which make harvesting painful without good gloves and long sleeves. Plant where you don't want intruders—and be sure to cut back the canes now and again so you don't end up with an impenetrable raspberry thicket. They prefer half shade to full sun.

Mysore is a black raspberry, not a red one like you'll find up north. We found the fruit somewhat watery and bland in our gardens, but that's supposedly atypical for the species.

I've enjoyed growing Mysore raspberries ever since my friend Andi blessed me with a little baby one in a pot a years ago. It grew into a monster plant and bore many times. It also rooted into the ground outside of its bed here and there. Wherever the canes get a little buried, they'll start a new plant. I was able to share quite a few thanks to this habit. They seem to like some shade better than full sun.

Besides Mysore, there's another raspberry called "Dorman Red" that's sometimes recommended for Florida but it's very marginal. I only got one fruit from mine in three years, then it died. Raspberries in general don't like the heat here and I also believe the winters aren't cold enough to stimulate them into decent production.

Another variety of raspberry you'll sometimes see in Florida is the Southern selection "Caroline". This one produced more fruit for me than Dorman Red, but I only had them growing in pots in my old plant nursery. It needs more testing to see if it'll be worth growing here long-term.

I believe both Dorman Red and Caroline appreciate some shade. Both are very cold-hardy. Mysore doesn't seem to mind the heat, though it may freeze down during a cold snap that reaches into the low 20s.

A final variety of raspberry we started testing this year is named "Heritage." Its range is from zones 5–8 and it seems well-suited to the panhandle (though not near the warmer coastal areas). This variety produces twice a year and has a better flavor than Mysore, but is unlikely to be happy south of Gainesville or so.

Raspberries can be propagated easily by dividing off suckers or digging up a root ball and breaking it apart into multiple plants.

Naranjilla (S, C, N)

Latin name: *Solanum quitoense*
Cold-hardiness: Probably 32 degrees
Mature height if unpruned: 4'
Propagation: Seed

Naranjillas are a perennial member of the *Solanaceae* family that looks like a mutant, spiky eggplant bush. They allegedly taste a bit citrusy, but I haven't tried a good one yet. The one plant I grew had seedy fruit that weren't worth eating, though the bush itself got a lot of comments. Better varieties are good for juicing or can be eaten fresh. They are supposed to like full sun but mine fruited in a mostly shady area. They will freeze back in winter but often survive. Naranjilla start easily from seeds and adapt well to living in containers. They look like they'd also grow easily from cuttings.

Natal Plum (S, C)

Latin name: *Carissa macrocarpa*
Cold-hardiness: A little below 32 degrees
Mature height if unpruned: 8'
Propagation: Cuttings

The natal plum is a shrub native to Africa that is quite attractive in the landscaping. My dad planted one years ago and called it a "boxwood," though it isn't. I had no idea the pinkish-red fruits on it were edible until decades later when I was working on the backyard food forest project. The fruit on that shrub is delicately sweet and somewhat raspberry-like with a little bit of a bitter undertone.

All parts of the plant are poisonous (though not horribly so) except for the ripe fruit. The blossoms are lovely and smell like jasmine. The shrub is thorny and makes a good boundary. Dad planted his to stop people from cutting through his landscaping when going up the front walk and it's worked well for that. Though it's a tropical shrub, I kept one alive in a sheltered location in my North Florida food forest. You'll see this plant for sale in plant nurseries but there seems to be some variability in fruit size, productivity and flavor. I've eaten much better ones at a botanical garden than the ones growing at my parents' place. Natal plum likes full sun and good drainage, tolerating lots of abuse and drought. Cuttings rooted under mist, though often rotted as well. I have not yet tried growing this species from seed.

Pereskia a.k.a. Barbados Gooseberry (S)

Latin name: *Pereskia aculeata*
Cold-hardiness: Probably 32 degrees
Mature height if unpruned: Unknown
Propagation: Cuttings, seed

Pereskia aculeata is a cactus that looks like a shrub or vine with fleshy leaves. It features vicious thorns as well as delicious fruit and edible leaves, making it a useful multiple-purpose species, though it may have some invasive potential in Florida. As Infogalactic states:

Although Pereskia aculeata *is edible and of high nutrition quality, making it a useful alternative to conventional food crops, this plant is a declared weed in South Africa where it does extensive damage to forest areas by smothering indigenous trees. Infestations occur in some KwaZulu-Natal forests and are embedded in the canopy and difficult to remove. The plant has a tendency to form large, impenetrable clumps and the spines on the stems make control of large infestations difficult. The plants can regrow from leaves or pieces of stem. One specimen that had infested a tree had its stems cut at the base, but after four years the 'dry' stems of the* Pereskia *that fell from the tree still set root and regrew.*

Nevertheless, I grow it and love it. "Invasive" just means "easy-to-grow," right?

I originally grew this plant from seeds harvested at the Rare Fruit & Vegetable Council of Broward County. They were in a baggie with a bunch of other seeds and I completely lost track of which were which. On sorting through the seeds later, I thought at first they were limeberry (*Triphasia trifolia*) and planted them in pots labelled as such. After a month or so they emerged and grew

vigorously—yet they didn't look a bit like limeberry seedlings! Unable to determine the species or even the genus, I posted a picture to my Instagram account where it was quickly identified by one of my readers as a *Pereskia* species. As it grew, bloomed and fruited over the next year, I finally pinned it down as *Pereskia aculeata*. In my Grenada food forest, I planted them at the bottom of pollarded nitrogen-fixing trees for climbing support. It's likely not hardy to much below freezing. The fruits are sweet-tart and quite good. *P. aculeata* is very easy to grow from seed or cuttings.

Pigeon Pea (N, C, S)

Latin name: *Cajanus cajan*
Cold-hardiness: 32 degrees
Mature height if unpruned: 8'
Propagation: Seed

Pigeon peas are a staple in Central America, India and the Caribbean. The plant is a short-lived perennial shrub or small tree that bears an abundance of pods containing small peas in the fall and winter. The variety we grew in North Florida took too long to produce and the pods froze off too early for eating, though they still had utility as a nitrogen-fixer. There are varieties that produce earlier in the year which should work better. I have seen them setting pods in Alabama, zone 8b, so it is possible to get a harvest. If you get a mild winter, they'll produce better. In the Central to Southern portions of the state, they should give you peas right through winter and into spring. Once they're done producing in spring, you can cut them back and use the greenery to feed and mulch fruit trees and perennials. The pea plants will then grow back and fruit again in fall.

The woody stems are quite hard and make good cooking fuel for rocket stoves. The peas can be used for shelling when green and the pods are plump, or you can let the pods dry on the branch and then shell out the dry peas later. Pigeon peas are usually day-length sensitive, which means they will not start blooming until late in the year. Plant the seeds from February through May for fall and winter yields.

Pigeon peas produce their own nitrogen and do not generally appreciate being fertilized, though they like good soil, loose ground and compost. A good way to cover recently cleared ground before you plant a food forest is by covering it with pigeon peas. The resultant growth will suppress weeds and enrich the ground with nitrogen. Plant your pigeon peas in stations 4–6' apart with 2–3 peas in each station (wider-spaced pea plants will produce more peas each) rather like you would plant corn in stations.

In fact, you can intercrop corn and peas by planting them in stations along with the corn in early spring, adding a couple of peas with your four corn seeds. The corn will produce in 3–4 months, then can be cut down, allowing the pigeon peas to take over the stations and produce a few months later.

Plant peas 1–2" deep and water them in. Germination is better if you soak peas overnight before planting. As a bonus to their edibility, pigeon pea shrubs produce a lot of nitrogen on their roots and biomass above. They can be chopped and dropped to feed your fruit trees, compost pile or herbivorous animals and will grow back again. This is not good for yields however, so do not chop down the peas before they produce for you unless you are just growing them for nitrogen and biomass. In Grenada I grew pigeon peas to maturity, harvested them, chopped the pea bushes down to a foot or so high, then had them grow back and produce for me again the next fall and winter.

Boil or steam green peas for a few minutes before eating. Dry peas are harder to digest and are best soaked overnight, then boiled until soft or added to stews. Pre-soaking the seeds increases the germination rate.

Prickly Pear (S, C, N)

Latin name: *Opuntia spp.*
Cold-hardiness: Beyond Florida
Mature height if unpruned: Varies
Propagation: Cuttings

Most of us are familiar with the prickly pear fruit. Upscale grocery stores sometimes carry them as a novelty in their fruit sections, and some ethnic markets carry the edible "nopale" pads. The true prickly pear fruit is about the size of a plum with a rich red/purple juice and a berry-like flavor, though there are all kinds of cactus called "prickly pears" with varying fruit sizes. Just watch out for the seeds – they're hard as rocks. A prickly pear is worth growing just for its fruit; however, it gets better than that. as the "pads" are a good vegetable. They have a flavor somewhere between green beans and okra, with a little bit of saltiness to them.

Preparation is key with cactus. If you pick the pads young, before their spines develop, you're good to go – but if you pick them after spines appear, be careful. Even the tiny glochids are really, really annoying. They'll itch and sting and burn for quite a while and they're really hard to see and pull from your tormented skin. Many "spineless" varieties still have these little fuzz-like spines, so watch out.

Some people will tell you that a blast of water is the best way to remove these little spines. I haven't found that to work well. My favorite method is fire. Skewer a pad and turn it over an open flame. Voila! No glochids.

Big spines are easy to remove with the sharp tip of a carrot peeler. Just core them right outta there. Once the spines are gone, chop up the pads and use them however you like. I enjoy them in stir-fries and with eggs, but they're also really good in Dave's Cactus Chili of Death. Want the recipe? Alright, here you go.

Dave's Cactus Chili Of Death (serves 8)

Ingredients:

1–2 lbs ground beef or sausage
1 or 2 large onions
1 #10 can of kidney beans
A couple cans of tomato sauce or tomato paste and extra water
2–3 cactus pads with spines removed
Hot peppers
Spices and more hot peppers and stuff

Directions:

Fry ground beef/sausage in lard (if you have it, if not use whatever wussy oil you have laying around) along with chopped up onions, some hot peppers (I like cayenne, habanero and jalapeno varieties) and diced cactus pads in the bottom of a big pot. When they look good and cooked, pour in your beans and tomato sauce or paste.

You want it thin enough so it doesn't burn, but not so thin that the chili is watery. At this point, you make magic happen by adding in as many of these things are you have available: Mexican seasoning, chili powder, paprika, ground red pepper, smoke seasoning, garlic powder, cumin, steak seasoning, Texas Pete hot sauce (or equivalent), black pepper and salt. Taste regularly to make sure you're balancing the flavors correctly. You want a meaty, smoky, spicy chili. Keep messing with it until it's perfect.

Serve in a big bowl with shredded cheddar and a large dollop of sour cream. Unless you're very pregnant, be sure to also drink at least 24 oz of beer with it. 36 oz is better. 48 oz is too much.

Prickly pear cactus like full sun but will live in half-shade. There are a wide range of native types, some of which have 2" thorns and tiny fruit. Those are best planted in a death hedge, rather than the food forest. Pads can be cut off the plant and left to heal for a few days or weeks, then buried part-way in well-drained soil to root and grow. I have not bothered growing prickly pear cactus from seeds.

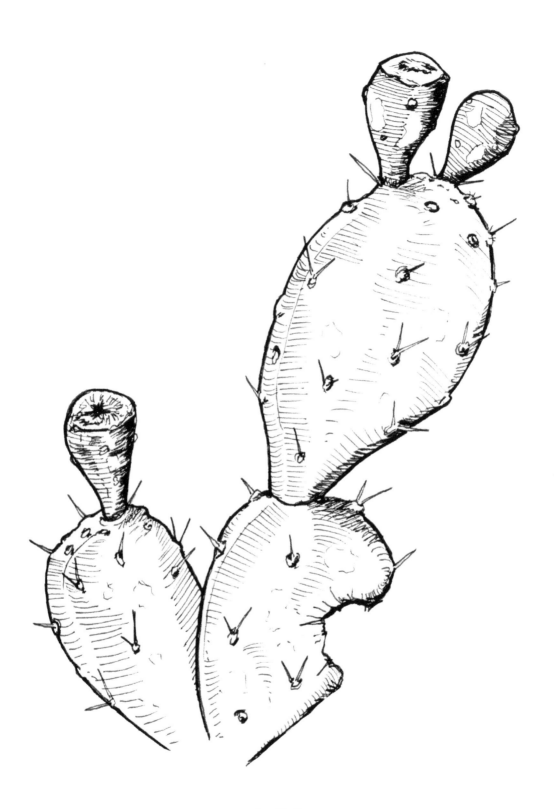

Prickly Pear

Rosemary (S, C, N)

Latin name: *Salvia rosmarinus*
Cold-hardiness: Beyond Florida
Mature height if unpruned: 3–5'
Propagation: Cuttings

Rosemary can live for years in Florida, provided it's happy. The plant does not like full shade or consistently wet soil and thrives in large containers and along sidewalks and driveways. I saw a nice large rosemary bush growing in a parking lot island at the United Bank in Atmore, Alabama, a few miles over the Florida line. It was joined by a few jalapeno plants mixed in with ornamentals. That's my kind of gardening.

Rosemary is a good plant for the borders of your food forest, as well as rocky and gravelly areas. Rosemary roots from stem cuttings, provided you don't let them get so wet they rot.

Roselle a.k.a. Jamaican Sorrel a.k.a. Florida Cranberry (S, C, N)

Latin name: *Hibiscus sabdariffa*
Cold-hardiness: 32 degrees
Mature height if unpruned: 5'
Propagation: Seed

Roselle, or Jamaican sorrel, is one of the coolest-looking edibles you can grow. It's also delicious. Roselle is a member of the hibiscus family (which also includes okra) and like many hibiscus, has multiple edible parts.

The blooms, leaves, and pods on this plant are all edible – but the reason most people grow Jamaican sorrel is for the calyxes.

What is a calyx, you ask? It's the pointy red bit at the base of the flower. The plants are day-length sensitive and start blooming and fruiting in the fall.

After blooming, the flower withers and the pod inside the bud begins to swell. After a few days, the calyx around it is large and juicy – ready for picking.

Chop the stem end off, slit one side and pop out the green fruit in the middle. (They're like freaky little okra babies. I send them right out the door to the chickens.) Then save the calyxes in the freezer until Thanksgiving – they're a dead ringer for cranberry, though not as bitter, hence its third common name Florida Cranberry.

Here is my wife's recipe for Florida Cranberry Relish:

Rachel's Florida Cranberry Relish

1 1/2 c. orange or apple juice
1 1/3 c. sugar
1/2 teaspoon ground cinnamon
1/2 teaspoon ground nutmeg
a couple of dashes of ground cloves
24 oz. Florida cranberries
1 c. raisins (golden or ordinary)
1 c. chopped pecans

In a saucepan, combine juice, sugar, cinnamon, nutmeg and cloves. Cook over medium heat, stirring frequently until sugar is dissolved. Add Florida cranberries and raisins, bring to a boil.

Reduce heat, simmer 3–4 minutes.

Remove from heat, stir in nuts. Chill for several hours.

The light cycle affects when roselle starts blooming, so keep that in mind. You'll have lovely flower-less bushes until sometime in October, then the blooms arrive in profusion. Pick regularly to keep the plant going, which it will until frost.

Another great thing about these plants: the leaves have a lemony-tart and satisfying flavor that's perfect in Caesar salads.

We start our roselle from seed in the spring and then transplant the seedlings out to the garden when they are around 6" tall. They'll grow like crazy with a little care.

Simpson Stopper (S, C, N)

Latin name: *Myrcianthes fragrans*
Cold-hardiness: Lower 20s.
Mature height if unpruned: 15'
Propagation: Seed, cuttings

Much like the coco plum, Surinam cherries, and natal plums, the Simpson stopper is a plant with decent edible fruit that has somehow been relegated to the "generic hedge plant" category.

I was shopping at Taylor Gardens Nursery some years ago and saw a big Simpson stopper in full fruit. I picked a handful as I was talking to Dave Taylor, the owner. He eyed me incredulously as I popped the fruit into my mouth.

"Now you're gonna die," he told me.

"No, I'm not. These are edible. They're delicious!"

"Nope. You're gonna die. I'm not talking about the stupid fruits, you fruit."

Dave then ran me through with an African spear. As the berries fell from my now-limp hand and my eyesight dimmed, I could hear his gravelly laugh as he carefully wiped my blood off the gory instrument of my death.

"Simpson stoppers don't kill people. I kill people!"

Simpson stoppers are at their very best when fully ripe. They have a nice, sweet taste on the front end, followed by a slight bitter grapefruit aftertaste.

One day I hope to harvest enough of them to make Simpson Stopper jam.

Simpson Stoppers can be propagated from fresh seed. They grow slowly but larger specimens are often available at decent prices from Florida nurseries as it is a well-known native species.

Sugar Cane (S, C, N)

Latin name: *Saccharum spp.*
Cold-hardiness: 32 degrees (above-ground)
Mature height if unpruned: 10'
Propagation: Cuttings

Sugarcane is easy to grow in Florida and does not require flooded conditions to produce. I cover it in the appendix of *Totally Crazy Easy Florida Gardening* and in *Florida Survival Gardening* but in short, all you need is a good hunk of sugarcane with a few intact nodes (those are the joints in the cane). Since sugarcane is usually harvested in the fall, that's the time you're likely to see the canes for sale. Most grocery stores don't carry sugarcane, but a lot of farm stands do in the fall—and fall is when you want to plant, at least in North Florida. Buy a couple of stout canes (they're usually 5–6 feet long with about 8–12 nodes, depending on the cultivar), and you're well on your way. When you get home, cut your canes into segments with at least 3–4 nodes each, pick a good spot to plant them, then put those pieces on their sides about 4–6 inches down, and cover them up well.

All winter, those pieces will sit down there in the ground until the soil warms up in the spring. When I planted sugarcane in a North Florida November, new shoots popped up for me sometime in March or April. For each cane you bury, you'll usually get a couple of good shoots emerging from the ground. If you really don't want to trust the earth to take care of your little baby sugarcane plants, you can just stick some chunks of cane in pots with a node or two beneath the dirt and keep them someplace that doesn't freeze, like a sunroom. They'll grow.

When my baby sugarcane plants appeared in the spring and I was sure it wasn't going to freeze again I would fertilize them with chicken manure. You can also use lawn fertilizer. (They're a grass—they like lots of nitrogen.) Throughout the summer they'll get nice and tall and sometime in July or August you'll really see the canes starting to thicken up, but don't chop them yet (unless you really can't stand to wait).

In North Florida, wait until it's just about time for the first frost of fall or winter, then go cut the canes down so you'll get the largest harvest possible. If you don't cut them down and you get a freeze, you're going to lose all the above ground growth and you may even lose the plants. Harvest by cutting the canes down close to the ground, and then put the sugarcane roots to bed for the winter by mulching over them with some rough material. Leaves are good for this, but probably any mulch would work fine. My sugarcane came back even when I barely mulched over the roots.

In its second year, sugarcane bunches out and gives you more canes than it did the first year. In South Florida, just bury some canes whenever you have them and keep them fed and watered. Unless you have a sugarcane press, you'll have to enjoy your cane by peeling pieces of the cane and chewing the sugar out of it. They're delicious. Don't try using your home juicer on it. I had a great one and it couldn't handle the hard fibers inside. A cheap juicer will burst into flames, melt, shoot sparks, implode, then violently explode if you try to run sugarcane through it. We have chopped up cane and boiled it to get the sugar out, then boiled the juice down into cane syrup. It's labor-intensive and inefficient compared to cane juice, though. In Grenada I fermented some cane juice to see if I could make a drinkable beer. Two weeks later, I drank it. It was... drinkable.

Plant sugarcane in at least partial sun around the edges of your food forest for a sweet treat on hot days.

Surinam Cherry (S, C)

Latin name: *Eugenia uniflora*
Cold-hardiness: Upper 20s
Mature height if unpruned: Maybe 20'
Propagation: Seed

The Surinam cherry used to be a common hedge plant in Florida, often just called "cherry hedge."

When I was a kid, our neighbors had a cherry hedge across the front of their porch, and we would occasionally eat the weird, resinous fruits. They had a strange taste, almost like you licked a battery while eating an artificially flavored sweet tart. If they weren't fully ripe, they were awful. When they were fully ripe, they were edible but still had an undertone of varnish.

As Green Deane writes:

I will freely admit these little red pumpkins are an acquired taste. Most folks are expecting some kind of cherry taste and they don't have that. No matter how ripe, there is a resinous quality. To be blunt, you either like them or you definitely do not. More so, they must be picked when absolutely ripe or they are a very unpleasant edible experience. What is absolutely ripe? There is orange red, the color of cars, and there is blue red, the color of old-time fire trucks and blood. Surinam cherries are edible when they are a deep blood-red. Let me repeat that: A deep blood-red. An orange red one won't harm you but you'll wish you hadn't eaten it. And I know you will push the envelope and try one that is not deep, blue-blood red. Don't blame me. I warned you. You won't die or throw up or the like but your mouth will disown you and the next time you will pick a very ripe one.

An improved Surinam cherry variety has as much in common with its plebeian hedge-dwelling relative as a ripe, sun-warmed Honeycrisp apple has with a crab apple.

I used to think the best varieties of Surinam cherries were the black ones. The black varieties are much better than their common red counterparts, as Julia Morton wrote:

There are 2 distinct types: the common bright-red and the rarer dark-crimson to nearly black, which tends to be sweeter and less resinous.

The key word is "tends," as I later discovered a very good red variety. This particular red Surinam cherry has a large fruit with a lot of flesh and a small pit. The resin flavor is a background spice to the fruit, rather than a dominant flavor, and they taste good even when not fully ripe. That means there are both excellent red and black types. Seeds from black varieties will grow into black varieties and red types grow true from seed as well.

Sometimes we give up on fruits too easily. Imagine if the gardeners of antiquity had decided not to bother propagating citrus after tasting wild sour oranges! Seeking out good varieties and propagating them is a great thing. Because the common forms of Surinam cherry are, at best, an "acquired taste," it doesn't mean all of them are. The black varieties I tried at the Broward County Rare Fruit and Vegetable Council were delicious right from the tree, as was the red variety I tasted in Grenada. I saved seeds from both and planted and shared the seedlings.

If you find a great Surinam cherry fruit, I recommend you do the same. There seems to be quite a bit of variation in quality.

Tea (S, C, N)

Latin name: *Camellia sinensis*
Cold-hardiness: Beyond Florida
Mature height if unpruned: Unknown—
    usually kept short
Propagation: Seed

Think tea grows only in China and Japan? Think again. There's actually a working tea farm in South Carolina: the beautiful Charleston Tea Plantation which is owned by the Bigelow Tea Company.

True tea, known in Latin as *Camellia sinensis*, is also an attractive plant. A member of the camellia family, you could easily grow a few bushes in your landscaping and people would just think you liked flowers.

If you're a tea drinker, you might be surprised to know that black tea, green tea, oolong, white, orange pekoe and a plethora of other incarnations of "tea" (unless they're "herbal" teas, which are not from the true tea shrub) are all from the same plant, just processed in different ways.

Like coffee, tea can be successfully grown in a pot. A big benefit to tea over coffee is that you use the leaves rather than the fruits. That means there's not much waiting for harvest time. You simply gather leaves as you need tea, dry them, and brew away.

Tea Plant

Tea Growing

If you can grow camellias, you can grow tea. Tea likes a somewhat acid soil and a little bit of fertilizing, but not a lot at once. I met some folks with a tea nursery, and they told me their tea plants were happiest with regular feedings of fish emulsion, a mild fertilizer with a good range of minerals. My tea plants grow slowly for me though your mileage may vary. They can tolerate full sun but if you live in an area with brutal summers, I recommend you put them in a place where they'll miss some of the hot Western sun of the afternoon. My tea leaves would burn a bit in the heat of a Florida summer, so I gave them some shade. Tea doesn't really need a lot of water, but more water doesn't hurt them either if the soil is well-drained. If you don't have naturally acid soil, you can pot them in "blueberry" or "azalea" mix potting soil. Coffee grounds are also a good amendment to provide some slow-release nitrogen. We found true tea to be harder to grow than most of our food forest plants.

Unfortunately, you're going to need a goodly few backyard tea plants for a decent harvest. The young leaves and center bud are all that one traditionally harvests to make tea. You're looking for the tender new growth. Just visit your plants when they're putting on a flush and snip or pluck off the whole shoot – usually 2–3 leaves.

And remember, how you process tea determines the final flavor.

To make black tea, roll the fresh leaves around in your hands to bruise them, then let them dry for a few days and store away.

For green tea, let your freshly picked leaves wilt in the shade for a few hours, then dry the leaves in your oven for about 20 minutes at 250 degrees. This stops the enzymes in the leaves from breaking down, giving it that crisp, light bitter flavor instead of the rounder, broader flavor of black tea.

Older, tougher tea leaves have been used in some ancient Chinese blends but are no longer commonly brewed. That doesn't mean you can't experiment, of course.

Tea plants make a nice hedge and in some older Japanese home gardens a small tea plantation was an integral part of the landscape.

Though tea plants can be started from cuttings, seeds are the better option. Rooting tea takes some time, and the young plants are rather weak compared to seed-grown specimens. It takes about the same time for them to grow to a good size, so if you can start with seeds, why not do so? Seeds pop up in about a month but take about 2–3 years before you can start harvesting many leaves. If you only have cuttings, root them in loose soil or vermiculite, ensuring the pot is in the shade. Put a stick in the pot and rubber-band a clear plastic bag over the top of the pot as a humidity tent to keep the cutting from drying out. Roots will usually start to form in a few months. Baby those cuttings – they really can't take much abuse and will also suffer great damage and likely die if you move them into the sun all at once.

VINES

Beans (S, C, N)

Latin name: *Various*
Cold-hardiness: 32 degrees
Mature height if unpruned: N/A
Propagation: Seed

Beans are a good survival staple if you grow them to the dry stage. Dry beans are not super productive for the space they take up, though they are worth growing for their protein content and how they improve the soil for subsequent crops. I grew multiple varieties of beans in North Florida over the years and had problems with getting dry beans. Green beans? No problem! But not dry beans. This is due to Florida's weather and how beans grow. Beans are a warm season crop that cannot take frost, so they are commonly planted in Central/North Florida in March/April and will make beans in June/July, leading to dry beans in the middle of the summer rainy season. This means that as the plants are starting to dry, the monsoons come and soak the pods repeatedly leading to moldy and sometimes sprouting "dry" beans. In South Florida you'll probably have better luck letting them dry down outdoors as you can plant beans in the fall and winter and harvest them during the dry weeks of winter. I did have luck in North Florida growing black-eyed peas and mung beans to the dry stage. They seem to resist the rain better than the other varieties I tried, like the classic "Jacob's Cattle" soup bean. That said, I have since done an experiment with picking an entire bean plant when the pods are filled out and getting rubbery, then taking it inside and hanging up the entire plant by the roots to dry. This gives me decent dry beans, though younger green pods on uprooted plants will not amount to anything.

Runner beans refused to set more than a few pods, so I gave up on them. Limas also failed regularly on me. So, though I am listing beans here as a caloric staple, not all beans are created equal and not all will make good dry beans for you. In the green stage, however, most beans are a reliable and easy-to-grow vegetable.

Beans come in a wide range of varieties and types, ranging from annuals to perennials, bush to pole, soup beans, green beans, long beans and more. Bush types support themselves on short vines and bear quicker than pole types but they are less productive (some estimates say pole beans produce twice as much as bush types) and a little touchier, though they're still one of the easiest vegetables to grow. If you can manage to get dry beans, they are quite valuable as a staple due to their high starch and protein content. Green beans, unfortunately, are quite low in calories, so they don't make the "calorie crop" cut.

Beans are a warm-season crop and should go in the garden after all danger of frost, but not once things have gotten super-hot (except for yard-long beans and black-eyed peas, which grow no matter what the heat is outside). To grow bush varieties, plant in rows 16" apart with your beans about 6" apart in the rows. That gives you three rows in one of your 4' wide beds. Beans can take crowding a lot better than some other crops. Mung and some black-eyed peas are bush types, as are most black beans. "Contender" beans are a good green bean as well as a decent soup bean. It's become a favorite on our homestead, with better flavor than Tendergreen and Kentucky Wonder.

Beans need little or no fertilization unless the soil is really dead. They benefit from moderately fertile soil and regular water. The beans I planted by my grey water drain make a lot more pods than the ones out in the field that only get watered once or twice a week.

Pole beans need support to grow, as they'll vine to a height of 10' or so if you let them. Without support, they scramble on the ground and produce poorly. My favorite method for trellising is to cut pieces of 5/8" rebar to 8' in length, then hammer them 2' deep into the ground, placing them up to 16' or so apart. I then tie a piece of paracord or other rope from the top of one to the top of the other, getting it tight but not so tight it pulls them down. I tie another piece of paracord at about 1' over the ground from one piece of rebar to the other. Then I tied strings from the top piece of paracord to the bottom at regular intervals and plant beans beneath them. Alternately, cattle panels make very good bean trellises. Or you can make bean teepees with three long sticks tied at the top. Plant 3 or 4 beans at the base of each pole and let the beans climb to the middle. In a pinch, you can just ram individual sticks into the ground for each bean. Or let them grow on your chainlink fence, so long as the neighbor is okay with that.

Green beans are a very nice addition to your daily meals and are quite good when raw from the garden, dipped in homemade dressing or eaten right off the bush. To grow bush varieties, plant in rows 16" apart with your beans about 6" apart in the rows. Beans can take crowding a lot better than some other crops. The first variety of bean I ever grew was Burpee's "Golden Wax" bean, which has bright yellow pods. It's not a particularly tasty variety but I still grow it for nostalgia's sake.

As for pole types, Kentucky Wonder beans are easy to grow and produce well, though the best green bean I have grown in Florida is the "yard-long bean," also known as the "snake bean." They are a very productive and heat tolerant bean when picked green, though the dry beans are thin and not good for much other than planting. The hyacinth bean (also known as the lablab bean) can be cooked green as a shell bean but I have only grown them once. Another round is coming up in my gardens right now. The yields are high, but the beans must be boiled when green as they are toxic raw. When fully ripe—that is, hard and dry—Green Deane recommends soaking them overnight, then boiling them, throwing out the water, then boiling them again to remove toxic glucosides. I have not tried this but it is a staple crop in Asia so I will try them that way this year. The green beans we shelled from the pods when they filled out and boiled for a long time we ate with no ill effects. However, the foliage on the vines is scratchy and may sting you if your skin is sensitive. The leaves are edible boiled, and the root can be dug, boiled and eaten as a starch. Lablab beans are very vigorous and easy to grow with high yields and lots of beautiful purple flowers. Give them a good trellis, as they are monster vines. If you cannot find seeds for sale in packets, try looking in the dry bean section of an Indian or Asian market and planting what you find. Often, dry beans will germinate from the store. That is how I am growing mung, black beans and limas (trying again—I love limas) right now.

Black Pepper (S)

Latin name: *Piper nigrum*
Cold-hardiness: 32 degrees
Mature height if unpruned: Unknown
Propagation: Cuttings, seed

Black pepper likes lots of sun and starts readily from cuttings. I was not able to get it to fruit in North Florida but you should have luck in South Florida. Plant it in decent soil and keep it watered, but not flooded. Its cousin *Piper lolot* has a wonderful flavor and grows similarly. Plant cuttings with a couple of nodes and they will root.

Chayote (S, C, N)

Latin name: *Sechium edule*
Cold-hardiness: 32 degrees
Mature height if unpruned: At least 40'
Propagation: Planting the fruit

Chayote is a bizarre perennial squash that tastes like a cross between cucumbers and a mild pear. It is sometimes called the "vegetable pear." I like growing them, but my family is not particularly fond of the flavor or texture. It is edible raw or cooked and is a tropical vegetable so it cannot take frosts. You can find chayote for sale in many supermarkets. Buy one or ten, take them home, then put them on your counter or someplace warm to sprout.

The entire fruit is the seed, so do not cut it open. Just let it sit until a vine starts emerging from the crevice at one end. Then, provided the danger of frost has passed, you can plant it out in your yard or garden by something it can climb. Bury them on their sides about 2/3 deep in the soil and the vine will grow out and start climbing. About half the ones I plant in Florida just rot in the ground, but the ones that catch grow vigorously. Chayote do not set fruit until late summer or fall, and then they'll

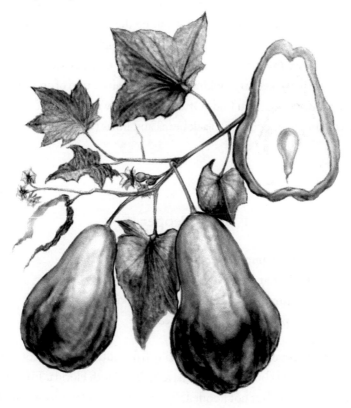

make an abundance of chayote squash, often high up into the trees if they can get there. Freezes will take the vines to the ground, but they often grow back again the next spring. I mulched mine and they would re-sprout as soon as things warmed up again, then travel back up the pomegranate tree I had supporting them. Save some fruit before your first frost if you are in the northern part of the state so you can plant more in the spring.

Dragonfruit (S)

Latin name: Hylocereus spp.
Cold-hardiness: 32 degrees
Mature height if unpruned: It just keeps
climbing forever and ever
Propagation: Cuttings, seeds

Dragonfruit thrives in hot, dry places and doesn't mind Florida sand. It loves full sun and cannot take freezing weather.

Dragonfruit will happily climb into trees but be careful—it'll climb way higher than you can reach. The Chinese in the Caribbean used a style of welded support column with a ring at the top that allows dragon fruit to scramble up through the middle then tumble over.

There is also a method of running two parallel bars along a row of dragon fruit. The Chinese call this style a bow support.

The idea is simply to keep the dragon fruit plants accessible for care, pollination and harvesting.

Also, according to UF:

Pitayas are fast growing and produce extensive growth. If no pruning is done, eventually there will be a very dense mass of stems that will reduce light penetration to the stems and interfere with harvesting the fruits. Furthermore, a dense tangle of stems may result in increased incidence of insect and disease problems. Production pruning involves the removal of damaged, diseased, or dead stems and those that reach the soil. Also remove stems that interfere with cultural practices and harvesting. Selectively remove some stems and train and tie remaining stems to the trellis to prevent stem breakage and crowding. Try to select healthy, strong stems. Pitaya plants are vigorous and may require pruning one to three times per year.

Dragon fruit flower all year around in the tropics. Their flowers are very large, beautiful and fragrant. The blooms only open at night from 9:00 P.M to 6:00 A.M.

They fruit better and make larger fruit if they are hand-pollinated. All you need to do this is a paint brush or a Q-tip.

Any time after 9:00 P.M, go out to your dragon fruit plant. Hold the bloom carefully and take the pollen off of the flower's anthers with your Q-tip or paintbrush. Then put the pollen onto the stigma. Hand-pollinating dragon fruit is very simple and worthwhile, as it takes the risk out of the process and ensures good fruit set. It takes a little more than a month for the fruit to be ready after pollination.

Dragon fruit is ready when it is bright red and shiny. To eat, simply pick it, cut it in half, and eat the inside with a spoon.

Dragonfruit can be started either by cuttings or by seed. Cuttings grow and fruit faster than seedlings. According to UF "Pitaya may be propagated from seed, but fruit and stem characteristics are variable, and the time from planting to fruit production may be up to 7 years." (https://edis.ifas.ufl.edu/hs303). To take dragon fruit cuttings, cut a piece of dragonfruit stem at about six to eight inches long. Newer growth is better. At the bottom inch of the cutting, cut all three ridges off to expose the fibrous middle.

Leave the cutting to air-dry for seven days. Do not put it in water or water it at all during that time. When seven days is over, plant your dragon fruit cutting into a pot or directly into the ground. It will root in a couple of weeks. When grown from cuttings, dragonfruit takes fourteen months to fruit in tropical climates. In South Florida it's likely to take longer unless you have great growing conditions.

Grapes (S, C, N)

Latin name: *Vitis (spp.)*
Cold-hardiness: Far beyond Florida
Mature height if unpruned: 60'
Propagation: Cuttings, ground-layering

If you want to grow grapes in Florida, stick with muscadine varieties.

Other grape varieties, such as "champagne," "Concord" and other popular varieties, just won't live long-term in the south. Eventually they succumb to disease except for the hearty and easy to grow muscadine varieties.

Muscadine grapes are improved varieties of one species of wild grape native to the New World: *Vitis rotundifolia*. They have that wild vigor in them still and their growth is a marvelous thing to behold.

Most of the grape-growing problems I've encountered with my gardening clients is related to having non-muscadine grapes on their homestead. The classic French/Californian/Greek grapes will die here. It's a matter of when, not if. You'll see them sold in the garden centers in later winter and early spring. Resist the temptation.

Remember this helpful, incredibly forced rhyme: "It won't do fine unless it's muscadine!"

Muscadines come in all types. There are a few seedless cultivars being experimented with, but all the ones I've seen for sale are seeded. My favorites are the big gold varieties; however, there are also nice black and bronze muscadine varieties you can grow. The old cultivars like Carlos and Fry are still great, or you can try newer patented varieties.

Whatever you do, just make sure you plant at least two different vines. Muscadine grapes usually need to be pollinated by a different cultivar. Just grab at least two types with two different names.

When I have grown grapes alone, I've run them on wires as commercial operations do. A good commercial spacing on muscadines is 16'-20' apart. I've planted them as close as 6', but they became a big mess. The vines are terrifyingly vigorous and will run a good 20 or more feet down the wires in a season and tangle all together in a profusion. I'd go at least 10' apart—you really don't need to overplant. Plant your grapes and keep them mulched, weeded and watered carefully until they're growing happily. The first year is key. After that, I found they do fine just on rainfall.

But this is a food forest book, not a "growing grapes on wires" book. In the food forest, I recommend planting some muscadines on trees that you'll be pollarding. Try growing them up a nitrogen-fixer, then chopping the tree and the vines down to 6' in height every winter. Or let a vine climb into a pruned fruit tree. The big problem with muscadines and trees is that they'll run far away from you and fruit where you can't reach the grapes. I had a bunch (no pun intended) of wild muscadine grapes growing in my North Florida food forest over the neighbor's fence and up into some water oaks. We'd get a decent amount of fruit, but we had to use a pole to pick most of it.

Muscadine grapes like a hit or three of fertilizer during the spring and summer. 10-10-10 with minor nutrients is what the commercial growers I've met used, but I fed mine on compost, rabbit manure and compost tea and had them do wonderfully without any chemical fertilizer. You can feed with slow-release organic matter like manure/compost any time. If you want to use something strong like blood meal or 10-10-10, feed them at the beginning of the year as they're waking up, then give them another hit or two into the summer, not later in the year when they're moving towards going dormant for the winter. Still, even without feeding, they'll produce. They were made for Florida.

Pruning increases the amount of fruit you harvest. If you're not chopping them like mad, they won't hit their full potential. You won't kill them. Just cut off most of the vines, leaving 2–3 recent buds on strong vines. Those will shoot out and bloom in spring.

Do this during the winter or very early spring before the grapes wake up and start budding and blooming. In North Florida I pruned them in early February. The growth they'll put on after pruning is a marvelous thing.

Muscadine grapes start easily from vine cuttings. They also root when ground layered. Many times, I got extra grapes on accident, as wayward vines rooted themselves into the mulch around my plants. I have tried sprouting the seeds without luck, though I only tried once as they are easy to grow from cuttings.

Ivy Gourd (S, C, N)

Latin name: *Coccinea grandis*
Cold-hardiness: 32 degrees
Mature height if unpruned: 20'
Propagation: Cuttings

Coccinea grandis is super easy to grow and produces continuously for years. It's also known as the "ivy gourd" or sometimes "tindoora" if you are talking with Indians

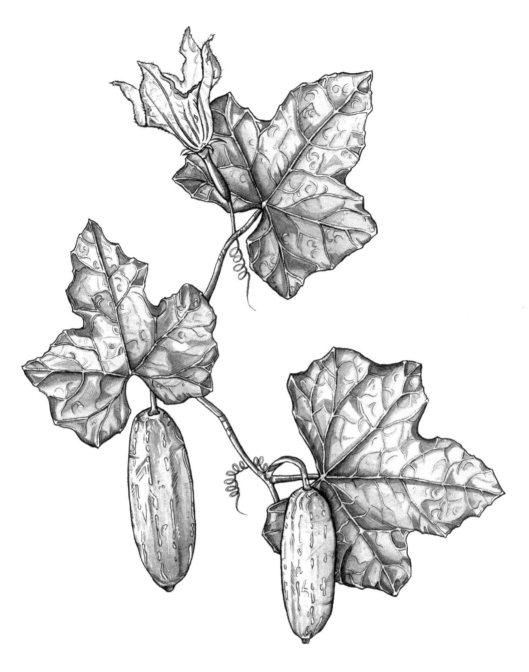

(from India). They can be found occasionally in the wild and come both male and female. Only the latter fruits and it does not require a mate to make cucumbers. The resultant seeds will be sterile as well, which is good. Florida has enough invasive plants creeping around already.

The plants have little or no pest issues and produce in dry or wet conditions, producing large white blooms that give way to small mottled green cucumbers. If the cucumbers sit on the vine too long, they turn into an inedible sour, red mush. This vegetable is usually cooked but I also like them raw or pickled.

An isolated female ivy gourd in your garden, if kept from wandering off, can be controlled and generally won't be too invasive, but be very careful planting these things in a food forest. You will fight it forever! Every joint of the plant can root in the ground and it doesn't care about drought, bad soil, or property lines. They'll choke out trees and nothing seems to eat them.

Don't say I didn't warn you.

If you have a male and a female, the seeds will be viable and are likely to get spread all over the place. I would not grow male plants as I do not want this species to invade all of Florida. Female plants are propagated easily via cuttings, which root readily in moist soil in a shady spot.

Jicama/Yam Bean (S, C, N)

Latin name: *Pachyrrhizus erosus*
Cold-hardiness: 32 degrees
Mature height if unpruned: 20'
Propagation: Seed, tubers

Jicama is a multi-purpose perennial. Every part of the plant is poisonous except for the root, which is a pleasant-flavored tuber. It is a nitrogen-fixing plant and the vines make a good green chop-and-drop, though you'll lose your root harvest that way. The seeds contain rotenone, which is a natural pesticide. I have not tried to extract and use it, however.

The first time I grew jicama it was on accident. A good friend gave me seedlings which were allegedly from some seeds I had previously given him. I thought they were yard-long beans until they grew a little and I realized the leaves weren't right. The vines grew like crazy, covering the trellises I made and running off everywhere. Then they bloomed, and when I saw the flowers I started to worry about them possibly being kudzu, which looked quite similar. Eventually I identified them as jicama and to this day I have no idea how we ended up mixing up jicama and yard-long beans. The seeds do not look similar, though the plants are both members of the *Fabaceae* family.

If you can't find jicama seeds, you can buy a root from the store and plant the whole thing in the spring (or any time, if you live in South Florida). It will grow vines which will then bloom and set pods, giving you plenty of seeds to plant the next year.

From seed, jicama roots take quite a while to develop. Mine made roots in the fall after being planted in the spring. Though the above-ground vines will die in a frost, plants regrow from the roots in the spring. Older roots can get huge and become inedible. Harvest roots for the table when they are less than one year old.

The roots are edible raw or cooked. Plant jicama in a sunny part of your food forest or near something it can climb to reach the light.

Malabar Spinach (S, C, N)

Latin name: Basella alba
Cold-hardiness: 32 degrees
Mature height if unpruned: 20'+
Propagation: Seeds, cuttings

Malabar spinach is an exotic tropical green that does well in Florida. Its large leaves are fleshy and mucilaginous. Some eat them raw but I find they make my throat feel scratchy unless they are cooked. On Caribbean islands, Malabar spinach can be seen rambling over fences and rum shacks, down the sides of houses and on stick trellises in garden beds. It's a perennial with tender climbing vines that comes in two main varieties, green and red. Both taste the same to me, but the green type usually has larger leaves.

Malabar spinach likes sun, water and decent soil. At various times of the year it will bloom and drop small purple fruit to the ground which later sprout to make new vines. It's easy to grow from transplants but seed germination isn't as easy. For some reason, they seem to grow better when they plant themselves than when planted on purpose.

Cut pieces of stem and stick them in moist soil and they root readily. Give Malabar spinach a place to climb and it will ramble all over. In North Florida it will usually get killed in the winter by cold, as it's a truly tropical plant. However, the seeds that fell in summer often sprout again and give you vines the next year. In South Florida, Malabar spinach is a year-round crop.

Add leaves to stews and stir-fries. Young leaves can be eaten raw but I have found they make my throat scratchy so I no longer do so. You can make Malabar spinach really unhealthy and much more delicious by taking an egg, a few cups of flour and water, plus some salt and garlic powder, and smashing the leaves in it to make a dough. Fry the patties in oil to make delicious fried Malabar spinach cakes.

Passionfruit—and Kin! (S, C, N)

Latin name: *Passiflora spp.*
Cold-hardiness: Varies
Mature height if unpruned: Varies
Propagation: Cuttings, seeds

Florida's native *Passiflora incarnata*, often called the "maypop," is a common native wildflower and, according to *Birds and Blooms*, "Four butterflies use Maypop for their caterpillars: Variegated Fritillary, Gulf Fritillary, Zebra Longwing, and Julia Longwing." *(https://www.birdsandblooms.com/gardening/flower-gardening/maypop-passion-vine-butterflies/)*

In our backyard in North Florida we regularly found both gulf fritillary and zebra longwing caterpillars on our maypops. The fruit of the maypop contains mostly air inside, with maybe a teaspoon of delicious pulp that tastes like tropical fruit punch, much like its better-known culinary cousin the passionfruit, AKA *Passiflora edulis*. The latter, however, is much more productive and a better edible. Another common passionfruit relative is the giant grenadilla (*Passiflora quadrangularis*), which makes almost football-sized fruits that are filled with sweet pulp. My favorite of the family is the delicious *Passiflora laurifolia,* which is the most delicious fruit of the whole bunch, with a marvelous explode-in-your-mouth tropical flavor that you would not believe. Also known as the "water lemon," it is a very common wild food in the Caribbean and is quite refreshing on a hot day. Another popular member of the passionfruit family is the "banana passionfruit," which is actually any of a number of species. I have not grown any of this type.

The most cold tolerant of the passionfruit in Florida is the native maypop, which grows much farther north than our state. The least cold tolerant I have seen growing is probably the giant grenadilla which is a very tropical plant and likely won't grow too far out of South Florida. I saw a nice specimen at the Rare Fruit and Vegetable Council of Broward County and was able to obtain seeds which germinated readily.

The "normal" passionfruit which is a much-beloved addition to tropical drinks and punches, *P. edulis*, comes in both purple and yellow forms. They failed to fruit, then froze to death in my North Florida food forest and did not come back. After losing two plants, I gave up on them and just grew maypops instead.

However, I recently had a conversation with Mark Bailey at the Marion County Extension Office and he shared stories of successful plantings in North Florida producing hundreds of fruit. To keep them through winter, the lowest couple of feet of the stem are protected with mulch or wrapped in insulation. In spring, they resprout and grow vigorously, producing lots of fruit again. As passionfruit sets fruit on new growth, the winter acts as a rejuvenating period for them by freezing back lots of old growth and resetting the plant to produce again.

In South Florida, passionfruit and their kin are beautiful and easy-to-grow additions to a food forest and will happily grow into the trees and drop an abundance of ripe fruit. Maypops can be found growing wild in awful sandy soil in the scrubland as well as in good hardwood forests.

Seeds germinate readily and usually take a few weeks to come up. Cuttings are also easy to start.

Smilax (S, C, N)

Latin name: *Smilax spp.*
Cold-hardiness: Far beyond Florida
Mature height if unpruned: Varies
Propagation: Seeds, root division

Smilax, also known as briars or greenbriars, is much despised by homeowners for its rampant thorny vines which do a number on your arms and legs.

In my humble—and dare I say gracious and merciful—opinion, their nasty nature is more than redeemed by the delicious shoots which pop up in spring from the large starchy roots.

In late winter and early spring they're everywhere in Central and North Florida. Some of the shoots are tiny but some rival asparagus in both their girth and flavor.

Go hunting and break off the shoots about 6–12" back from the tip. Just snap them where they break easily. Then saute them in butter and garlic with some salt... delicious. I used to hate smilax until I found out how delicious it was, now I actually let it grow in my food forest—though I still don't plant it on purpose. The roots are also edible, though fibrous. Note that some species have bitter shoots, so be sure to nibble a bit first to see if you're getting a good variety before you cook up a huge batch. I actively kill off and remove bitter varieties that appear in my food forests.

As for propagation—don't bother. The birds will do it for you.

Vanilla (S)

> **Latin name:** *Vanilla planifolia*
> **Cold-hardiness:** Probably above 32 degrees
> **Mature height if unpruned:** 40'+
> **Propagation:** Cuttings

Vanilla is a vining orchid which takes some work to grow, especially if you want it to fruit. I grew vanilla vines fairly easily in the tropics but have not yet tried growing them in South Florida.

One of the reasons I love the University of Florida is that they cover all kinds of weird plants, including this one. I like to imagine plant scientists being handed lists of plants and asked to write about how they can be grown in Florida. I found their write-up on vanilla amusing:

According to IFAS:

The best way to bring vanilla home is to buy a potted plant or cutting of V. planifolia. Large cuttings (24 to 36 inches) can root and flower in just 2 to 3 years. Smaller cuttings will take longer, likely 3 to 4 years. In general, vanilla begins to flower when the vine diameter reaches 0.25 to 0.5 inches.

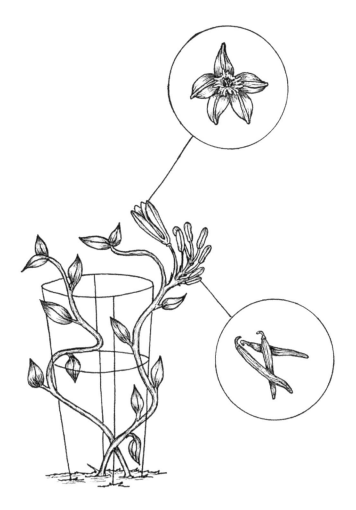

Plant the vines at the base of some support structure. They prefer areas with good air flow and bright, mottled shade. A garden tree or shaded trellis will work well. Once rooted, these lovely orchids require little. In the home garden they do not require frequent watering, pruning, or fertilizing.

Vanilla orchid flowers are large and fragrant. Each flower lasts for only one day but V. planifolia will go on flowering for about 2 months. Some species can flower for even longer periods of time. And once flowering is over, the plant begins producing its famous fruits: vanilla beans.

Vanilla bean production is certainly not for the impatient. Once the plants flower, they must be hand pollinated. Successfully pollinated flowers will produce a bean that takes about 9 months to mature. The four-step curing process takes another few months. It is a long process but for the dedicated gardener it can be a rewarding one.

Someone who really loves plants wrote that. It's not easy, but at least UF believes in you, oh dedicated gardener!

Vanilla likes some shade and is quite happy hugging the side of a tree in your food forest; however, if you plant it next to a tall tree you'll have a hard time pollinating the flowers when they appear up in the branches. Better to keep it on something shorter. I saw orchids growing well at the Belmont Estate in Grenada on pollarded *Gliricidia sepium* trees. As they outgrow the tree they are on, you can wrap them around themselves again.

To propagate vanilla, I took cuttings and put them against the trunks of trees with the bottom few inches laid in a bed of mulch—not in the soil. I learned this from watching videos of farmers on vanilla farms in Central and South America. The plant is semi-epiphytic but likes that bit of moist mulch to get going and start climbing.

Yams (S, C, N)

Latin name: *Dioscorea (spp.)*
Cold-hardiness: 32 degrees (aboveground)
Mature height if unpruned: 40'
Propagation: Bulbils, roots

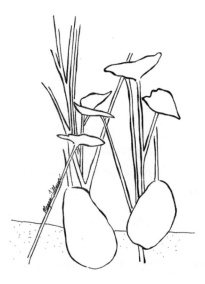

As everyone knows by this point, I am a huge fan of true yams, also known as "name" yams (said "nay-may"). They are not related even distantly to sweet potatoes despite sharing the name "yam." Yams are a climbing vine that can make huge roots beneath the ground. So far, I have grown purple, white and yellow greater yams (*Dioscorea alata*), potato yams (*Dioscorea escuelenta*), Chinese yams, also known as cinnamon vine (*Dioscorea polystachya*), the edible variety of *D. bulbifera*, which bears potato-sized roots on hanging vines and is quite rare, Lisbon yams (an improved *D. alata* cultivar) and a few other types I can't find the names for. My favorite producers are the white/yellow *D. alata* types, also known as the "greater yam" or the "winged yam." It's on the Florida invasive species list which tells you just how easy a crop it is to grow.

In the Caribbean and tropical portions of Asia, Central America and Africa, yams are staple crops that feed everyone through the fall and winter months and on into spring. On some islands, they grow rampantly in the wild and are dug with machetes by the poor during the winter dry season. In Florida, finding propagative material can be a wild goose chase but it is by no means impossible. I have seen "name" yams for sale at Publix and if you buy one of them, you can divide it and plant multiple hills of yams.

There are also quite a few edible yams growing wild in the state; however, make sure you do not mistake the common air potato (*Dioscorea bulbifera*) for the edible *Dioscorea alata*. The wild specimens of *D. bulbifera* in Florida are not edible and are poisonous. *D. alata*, however, can be found in the wild and propagated provided you can tell it apart from its poisonous cousin. You can also look up my yam/air potato identification video on YouTube to see the difference in growth and leaves and you'll be an expert in no time.

Yams can be propagated by a variety of means. You can take existing roots, like the one you found at a produce market, and cut it into pieces about half the size of your fist, making sure you keep as much of the skin intact on each piece as possible, then dust the cut portions of the individual pieces with ashes to prevent rot and fungi, then plant them in the ground or in a pot to sprout, then transplant those sprouted pieces into the ground later.

I have also started *D. alata* from cuttings but did not get to compare the yields to tuber-grown and I am sure they will not produce as large a root in the first year. One of the best ways to grow most yams is from the small, bulbous, aerial roots that grow on the vines in fall. These are called bulbils. As the yam vines die back in fall and winter, they fall to the ground and sprout in the spring.

Yams can be planted from fall through spring no matter where you are in the state. They have a pronounced dormancy period that lasts from November until sometime in the spring, earlier or later depending on the species and rainfall. Yams like compost and mulch at planting but don't seem to need much else. And they don't even need that.

Plant your yams about 2–3' apart in rows 4' apart or make individual hills a few feet apart. Plant cut pieces, bulbils or sprouted pieces 2–4" inches deep so they don't dry out in the ground. It's important to make sure you plant in a spot with loose soil so the roots can expand down. Hills aren't a bad idea because they're easier to dig later, though they dry out faster than flat-planting. Make sure you have a trellis or a tree in mind before the vines start growing out of control. When they come up, they shoot up very fast, probably growing a foot a day or more, and will turn into a tangled mess if you aren't ready for them. I have had good luck letting them climb along fences and up into trees. It may be shady under a tree but they'll climb up into the canopy quickly and unfurl an abundance of leaves at the top, capturing the sunlight they need to grow their tubers.

I once pollarded a sweetgum sapling at about 7' tall and planted a few yams around the base every year to climb it, throwing the cut sweetgum leaves and branches on the ground as mulch for the yams. At the end of the year when we dug yams, I cut off the top of the tree again. This worked well for years.

If you have a wide-spreading tree, you can plant yams under it and run strings down from the branches and let them climb up into it. I do not recommend covering all your favorite fruit trees with yams but I view all magnolias, oaks, dogwoods and other non-food trees to be fair game as living yam trellises. I had a black cherry tree in the North Florida Food Forest with multiple yams planted at its base. Over the summer the vines would climb at least 40' to the top of the tree.

When the vines die back in fall and winter, you can dig yams or leave them in the ground until you want them. They usually run from 3–10lbs in size the first year, depending on how well they were treated, how much rain they got and how fertile the soil is. If you wait too long to dig them, they'll start sprouting again in the spring. You can dig them when the vines first appear but don't wait more than a couple weeks as the roots start deteriorating as they feed the growing vines. If you want to grow really big yams or don't need the food at the time of resprouting, just let the vines go. They'll suck the energy out of the yam in the ground and it will shrink and rot away as it feeds the new aboveground growth.

The second-year growth on well-rooted yams is incredible. I've seen a fat vine shoot up eight feet from a large root without putting out a single leaf, reaching for the sky and sunlight as fast as it could grow. These vines will be bigger and make more leaves than they did in the first year. Over summer and fall they'll build a new and larger root beneath the ground. Second-year yam tubers can easily surpass 20lbs.

Once you have yams, it's easy to grow more. You'll get a few bulbils for planting from first-year yams and a bunch from second-year ones. So long as you don't dig them they just keep growing every year, though parts of the roots will get gnarled and woody. One really cool thing about yams is that you can harvest them in fall, then cut off the top couple of inches of the root where the vine had been, then plant it back into the hole where you dug the yam. This top part is called the "head" and can be planted over and over again and it will grow new vines and a root beneath it.

If you want to keep already dug yams over the winter, just put a bunch in a bucket somewhere and throw some leaves or sawdust or a bit of soil over them until you want to plant them again in spring. Freezing weather kills the above-ground growth of yams but that happens late enough in the year that it won't affect your yields. Furthermore, new growth on yams invariably shows up after the last frost date in Florida so you do not have to worry about them getting frozen.

Most yams contain oxalate acid crystals in the roots so they cannot be eaten raw, with the exception of Chinese yam. Some people's skin is irritated by peeling yams so wear gloves when you process them. Just cut off the top couple of woody inches— the head—and then peel the rest of the yam. It's slippery and slimy when raw so be careful not to slip and cut yourself as you peel. Then chop the peeled roots into pieces and use them as you would white potatoes, cooking until they are fork tender. This usually takes about twenty minutes of boiling. They are good in stews or boiled and mashed. Yams also cook quite well in a crockpot. Mashed yams with cheese, butter and salt are excellent. If you cut yams into smaller pieces and boil them until they are soft, you can then pour off the water and fry them into yam fries.

The flavor of most yams is similar to a white potato, starchy and not sweet. If you make beef stew and substitute yams for potatoes your guests won't even know the difference. Though slimy when raw, they are not at all slimy when cooked, so fear not. This is just a great staple carbohydrate crop. I am eternally grateful to my friend Craig Hepworth for sharing his love of yams with me years ago, when he told me how he thought it was the top survival staple crop to grow in Florida. After my first year of growing them, I found myself in complete agreement.

If I had to pick one staple survival crop for Florida, yams would be it. They are a must-add carbohydrate crop for any food forest, and once established will usually keep planting themselves without any help from you.

HERBACEOUS PLANTS AND GROUND-COVERS

Gingers and Turmeric (S, C, N)

Latin name: *Zingiberaceae* family
Cold-hardiness: 32 degrees (aboveground)
Mature height if unpruned: 3–4'
Propagation: Root division

All you need to grow ginger and turmeric are some fresh roots with living "eyes" on them. The eyes are growth buds from which the green shoots grow. Chances are, you won't even have to buy roots or starts from a seed company, as many grocery stores—particularly organic markets—stock fresh roots right in the produce section. Just watch to make sure the eyes aren't cut off, as I've seen done on some imported Chinese ginger roots.

If you're interested in growing ginger to sell, you'll likely be better off buying clean seed roots from someone, though I've never had trouble with any of the plants I've started from grocery store or farmer's market roots.

Ginger roots are quite a bit larger than turmeric roots so I break them up into a few pieces that each have at least 3 or 4 eyes on them. Turmeric roots I usually plant entire unless they're in a clump, then I break them up. Don't let the roots sit around on your counter and dry out for too long or they won't grow. Just take them and plant them right into the soil if you live in a warm area or into a big pot if you don't. Then wait—it sometimes takes a long time for ginger to send up shoots. Plant fall through spring. I plant mine at about 3–4" depth in loosened soil.

Ginger and turmeric are perennials with a growing season and a dormant season. In spring, shoots emerge from the ground when the weather is nice and warm. Ginger pops up faster than turmeric. Turmeric is a slowpoke. The plants wait until a couple of warm months pass then really get started in summer. If you plant roots and they don't come up right away, don't worry—as I said, they have a dormancy period. When their internal timers say "sprout!", they'll sprout.

Ginger and turmeric do not like high temperatures or harsh sunlight. They sunburned badly in my North Florida garden if I didn't plant them in the shade.

Instead, I grew them beneath the fruit trees in my food forest where they produced quite happily, though I didn't really follow the rules on feeding and watering. They can take a lot of neglect and not die, but they'll produce much better—and faster—if you feed and water them regularly.

Ginger and turmeric burn if you give them too much fertilizer and grow more leaves than roots if they get too much nitrogen. My advice is to plant them in good soil and load the plants up with compost. Mulching is great.

Commercial growers hill up ginger (much as you would potatoes) a few times over the growing season to ensure well-shaped roots and plenty of growth; however, I haven't done this and it hasn't been necessary. Maybe one day I'll do so as an experiment and see if the yields improve.

Ginger and turmeric like regular watering but do not like to sit in water or constantly wet soil. When the weather is cool (say, below around 70F), the plants just sit around without doing much. When it gets hot outside (say, around 90F+), they also slow down. I had both conditions in North Florida but keeping them in the shade moderated things quite a bit and kept them going.

Ginger and turmeric never had any real pest or disease problems in my Florida gardens. A few leaves may get gnawed now and again, but the plants usually take care of themselves.

In November ginger and turmeric leaves yellow and die back to the ground whether it freezes or not. If it freezes all the aboveground growth is knocked down faster but even if it doesn't they will go dormant. This is the time to harvest roots. A lot of the root development takes place in the last little bit before the plants die down so don't be too eager to harvest. I allowed my plants to form clumps and didn't harvest until the second year. When I did harvest, I got plenty of roots from each clump and would just leave a few pieces in the hole after harvesting so they'd come back again in the spring. Ginger is more productive for me than turmeric with much larger roots. Sometimes I would just dig out a chunk of ginger root from one of my clumps—any time in the year—when we needed some for a recipe or an upset stomach. Turmeric I usually harvested in one fell scoop after letting it grow for a couple of years into a respectable clump.

When you harvest, try to be gentle with the roots. Earlier in the season they are more delicate due to the new growth. This is sometimes called "baby ginger." If you pull them later after the tops die in the fall/winter, ginger and turmeric have tougher roots.

If you want to skip all that work of growing in the ground, just grow ginger or turmeric in a large pot. It's quite forgiving. Just don't overwater or let it dry all the way out.

Give ginger and turmeric a try and you'll be growing them for life. As a bonus, you can use the leaves for tea or added to soup like bay leaves for a little tropical zip.

Ginger and Turmeric

Pineapples (S, C, N)

Latin name: *Ananas comosus*
Cold-hardiness: 32 degrees
Mature height if unpruned: 3'
Propagation: Slips, tops, division

Pineapples grow easily in South Florida but growing them becomes progressively harder as you move north in the state due to their intolerance for freezing weather.

There was an Ocala farmer named Adam Eichelberger who launched a commercial pineapple venture over a century ago, as recorded by local historian David Cook:

> *After the war [of Northern Aggression], Adam returned to Ocala to try to regain his fortune. It was a difficult time for everyone, but he found a solution in what he now called his Banana Hill Nursery. He would sell trees and plants to others, and also would sell planted orange groves. He also took a gamble in growing pineapple plants and was wildly successful until the first time the winter temperature fell below freezing. At one time in the 1870s, the Banner said he had shipped more than 500 barrels of pineapples north aboard the Ocklawaha River steamboats. Expectations were high—but soon dashed.*

You may do well growing unsheltered pineapples in North Florida for a few years, then BAM!, you get a 20-something degree night and your pineapples are dead. However, if you plant pineapples around the base of larger trees they'll often do just fine through winter and will eventually give you fruit. I think the canopy of a food forest system will help immensely in keeping them alive. Though pineapples like full sun, they still fruit in some shade.

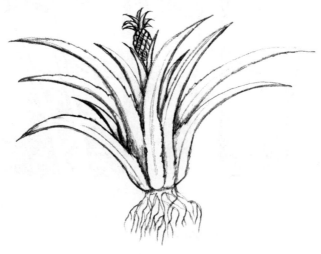

Pineapples have shallow root systems and can take a couple years to produce from a top or a slip, yet you can start them any time you want, put them aside, start more, put them aside, and eventually, you'll have tons of pineapples. Just do it in between taking care of your faster-producing plants and you'll get there.

In South Florida, pineapples can be tucked into any empty space as you have planting material. The thorny types are particularly good for boundary lines and places where you don't want traffic.

Pineapples like mulch and compost. If the leaves start to get very yellow or reddish, it often means they're starving. A light fertilizer solution or some compost is usually good enough to make them happy again.

As your plants grow, they often make side shoots which you can separate and plant. Some pineapple varieties make a bunch of small shoots on the base of the fruits which work as planting material.

When planting pineapple tops, peel off the remaining fruit and the bottom few leaves of the top until you see some little root nubs beneath, then plant the top in the soil. This helps the plants get established faster. I do not recommend rooting tops in water as they'll often rot. Plus, it's easy to just stick them in the ground to root.

Rootbeer Plant (S, C, N)

Latin name: *Piper auritum*
Cold-hardiness: Around 32, but regrows
       after frost
Mature height if unpruned: 10'+
Propagation: Division

This attractive plant has a tropical look and large, aromatic, velvety leaves. It smells and tastes just like root beer, thanks to the presence of safrole, which is the same compound found in sassafras. We've made a great tea from the leaves and used them in cooking.

According to CABI, "It is very popular in Guatemala and is widely used for seasoning snail soup."

Fascinating. Have you tried it yet? Feel free to share your root beer plant snail soup recipes with me at:

David The Good
c/o EWE GROSS
1234 Heckno Road,
Nowumgonnabeesik, FL 33843

Root Beer Plant

Though it has invasive potential, rootbeer plant can be kept under control. Just yank it up where you don't want it. This is easier in the northern part of the state where it slows down in the cold and freezes back in the winter. It will be harder to keep under control in the southern half of Florida. Rootbeer plant likes full shade to part sun and thrives in the dappled light of a food forest understory. North of Ocala it never set seeds for me but propagates easily if you divide off suckers and transplant them.

Seminole Pumpkins (S, C, N)

Latin name: *Curcurbita moschata*
Cold-hardiness: 32 degrees
Mature height if unpruned: N/A
Propagation: Seed

When a gardener thinks of pumpkins, he probably pictures Halloween decoration rather than a staple food crop. Yet pumpkins and winter squash are quite decent crops in their own right and often taste much better than the flavorless orange pumpkins on sale in October. In Florida, the winning survival staple pumpkin is the native Seminole Pumpkin. Though its origins are murky, it was reported as a native crop by the Spanish back in the 1500s, so if any of us can be called natives, the Seminole pumpkin surely can. The Seminole pumpkin comes in a wide range of varieties, likely due to crosses. Some years ago I set up an online gallery of Seminole pumpkins to catalog strains and growing locations sent to me by readers. There are some that ripen green, though most ripen tan. There are varieties clocking in at 12lbs or more and others that are only a couple of pounds. What connects them is their rampant growth and reliability, their resistance to diseases and vine borers and their rich orange sweet-flavored flesh and long storage time. Chances are the variety has drifted and crossed with other *C. moschata* species, as it's more of a land race than a true variety, but boy oh boy, it's a good grower and a top-notch survival crop.

It isn't the only pumpkin/winter squash that thrives in Florida, however. There are many varieties of "calabaza" from Central America and Mexico that will take the heat and produce well. There are also varieties from farther north, such as the "Tan Cheese" pumpkin, which produced outrageously well for my friend Rick a little south of Ocala, Florida. Most northern varieties of pumpkin suffer in Florida due to powdery mildew, vine borers and the heat, so don't get carried away looking at the gorgeous varieties from cooler climes. Hubbards failed for me in Florida, even though they loved my garden in Tennessee. Boston Marrow is probably a no-go, as are most of the *C. pepo* and *C. maxima* varieties I tried. Butternut, being a *C. moschata*, can do well in Florida but is regularly eclipsed in production and disease resistance by

Seminole Pumpkins. Seminoles just don't quit. If you plant one pumpkin/winter squash, make it Seminole. Many gardeners in the state save and share seeds. It's good to have friends. If you don't, you might have luck finding Seminole pumpkins in some seed catalogs. Baker Creek Heirloom Seeds has a variety they grow and sell. I usually avoid ebay as a seed source as there are too many scammers on there, but there are some newer seed shops on Etsy that carry good varieties, including my daughter's "Good Gardens" store.

In South Florida, you can plant pumpkins and winter squash year-round. In Central and North Florida, start them after the danger of frost has passed. Direct seeding is better than transplanting for vigorous plants.

Pumpkins and winter squash need lots of room to roam. They can be trellised but that is a risky business as they like to root at the nodes of the vines and gain more strength that way. If they climb, they cannot root all over the place, which also makes them more likely to be murdered by Pumpkin Public Enemy #1, the vine borer. A vine that gets drilled by vine borers but has a lot of rooted sections will shrug off the

damage and keep going. Sometimes the damaged vines will even end up divided into two separate plants that will both go on to produce pumpkins. The modular nature of *C. moschata* pumpkins really helps it cope with the stress of Florida growing.

Plant pumpkins and winter squash on mounds that are 8' apart in all directions. You can probably push them as close as 5', but don't go any closer than that as crowding reduces yields. Put them in full sun. They'll take half but tend to run for the light if they get the chance and will be weak in shade. The vines can grow a surprisingly long distance and will fight for space and reduce yields if you crowd them. I grew pumpkins along the edge of my tropical garden where they could ramble down into the drainage ditch and around the back of my compost pile and under my starfruit tree, which kept them from running wild all over my tomatoes and pak choi. At my current location I grow them in their own patch of dirt well away from the main gardens.

I grow pumpkins on mounds, like most everyone, because that's just the way everybody does it. Where I change the game is by burying a bunch of nitrogenous material under the mound. I call it the "Melon Pit" method, because it's also great for growing melons.

To make melon pits, dig a hole that's at least 2' deep. 3' is better. This is easy in sand but hard in clay or on lime rock soils. Do your best. Now throw in some kitchen scraps and other horrid stinky things. Meat or fish scraps are great. Dog droppings are fine. Humanure, goat organs, an old lasagna, raw chicken manure, hair, a shovel of compost, a dead pet, your enemies, whatever. We grew a great Seminole pumpkin over a dead rat once. The idea is to put some super rich food underneath the vines that the roots will find and kick-start the plant's growth. This will not hurt you— no one will know what you did and it won't make you sick. Once you've thrown a horrifying thing or three into your melon pit, cover it over and make a mound on top. Make sure your loathsome, wretched, vomit-inducing, nasty, horrible material is a solid 2–3' down if you can, as that usually keeps roving critters from digging it up again. Now plant 3–5 pumpkin seeds in the mound around an inch deep and water deeply. In 4–8 days, they should pop up. Within a week or two, their roots will go deep enough to hit the scary stuff and they'll turn deep green. In a couple more weeks they start running and you are off to the races.

Keep the weeds and grass down at first so your pumpkins can conquer the space without competition. Once they really get rolling, you won't have to worry about weeding as the vines will cover everything. Water as needed. It's normal for pumpkins to wilt in the mid-day heat, so don't worry too much about that, but if you get up early in the morning and your pumpkins are wilting, you either need to water or look for vine borer damage. Vine borers are nasty insects that lay their eggs in the stem of pumpkin vines. The eggs hatch and turn into worms that chew their way along inside the stems, causing your plants to lose their connection to water. As I mentioned above, Seminole pumpkins can often shrug off the damage due to their ability to root at the nodes, but I've still lost them on occasion. When I attempted to grow the much more susceptible Hubbard squash, I dusted the vine bases every week with Sevin dust or sprayed them with neem to keep the borers out. With Seminole pumpkins, however, I skip the evil pesticides and just let them root everywhere.

If you move the end of pumpkin vines that are more than a few days old, you'll see that the nodes on the new growth are already starting to put out roots. I encourage this by throwing handfuls of sand and mulch over nodes in the vines, figuring that more roots equal a much higher chance for the plant to survive the inevitable borer attacks.

If white mildew shows up on your pumpkin leaves, try treating it with a few tablespoons of plain yogurt shaken up into a spray bottle of rain or well water (chlorinated water kills the bacteria in yogurt!) and sprayed on the leaves in the evening. The beneficial bacteria in the yogurt seem to beat the infection down. Generally, I only have mildew appearing on my vines late in the season when they're about to die anyhow so I don't worry about it.

Many people have written me with variations of "Help! My pumpkins are blooming but they aren't setting fruit!" This is normal for members of the squash family. First, you'll get a bunch of blooms that are just males, producing pollen but lacking an ovary. Later, as the plant matures, it will start producing the occasional female bloom. These are identifiable by looking at the base of the flower. It will have what looks like a small pumpkin beneath the bloom—the ovary—unlike the male blooms which are just a yellow funnel with no bulge at the bottom. If female flowers are fertilized by a bee or other insect, or by the gardener, the nascent pumpkin at the bottom will usually start to grow into an actual pumpkin. If you aren't seeing a lot of bee activity, just go out with a paintbrush and dust the brush around on the anthers (the part where you see the pollen grains) of a male flower, then dust it on the stigma (it's the center piece coming up from inside the bloom) of a female flower. Good job—you are now a human bee-ing. Buzz buzz.

Sometimes pollination doesn't take and the bloom will drop off. This may be because the vine is young or because weather conditions were not right or because the female bloom failed to meet the male bloom of her dreams. Don't worry about it. The plant will make more blooms. If your vines grow smaller and weaker as they move away from the melon pit, I recommend watering them with a foliar fertilizer. Diluted urine works really well on them, as does Dave's Fetid Swamp Water, as do various commercial fertilizers. Make sure they get some water now and again so they can maintain their rampant growth.

Pumpkin vines will climb over anything and everything, often growing a foot or more in a day. I've seen pumpkins hanging out of trees before. If they start to invade your garden beds, gently pick up the new vines and turn them in another direction.

Sometimes I turn them in a curving 90 degrees and stick a stick in the ground next to the vine to keep it there. Steve Solomon sometimes chops the ends off but he's ornerier than I am, so I stick to being a namby-pamby vine whisperer just in case I cut down on their potential yields.

Once you have fertilized flowers, the pumpkins drop their yellow bloom and begin to swell. They start out a pale green color and mature to their final colors over a month or so. A pumpkin or winter squash is ready to harvest when the stem yellows or browns or the main vine dies. You'll be tempted to cook one right away, but the flavor of a newly harvested pumpkin pales in comparison to one allowed to sit on the shelf and cure for a month or more. That develops the sweetness and flavor. It's also wonderful to see a row of pumpkins sitting on a shelf. (As I type this, there is a row of them on the office bookshelf behind me.)

Seminoles can keep for quite a long time. The smaller ones with the darker tan skin seem to keep longer than the larger ones with paler tan skin, but I have had both sitting at room temperature inside for over a year without spoiling. One small one I was given by Jacksonville Permaculture Guru Alex Ojeda kept for two years before we opened it up and ate it. It was rather dry inside but still sweet and edible. What a great survival crop! My guess is that the Indians inadvertently bred this variety for storage by eating their pumpkins through the year and saving the last ones for seed, though that's just conjecture on my part.

Pumpkins can be added to soups, cut in half with the seed mass scooped out and roasted in the oven or baked into delicious pies. The taste of a Seminole pumpkin is much like that of a good orange sweet potato, rich and buttery. The seeds can also be roasted or fried in oil for a delicious snack. Just be sure to save some for next year.

Seed saving is simple. Just scoop some out and dry them on paper towels for a week or so, then pop them into a sealed baggie or jar to store in the fridge until you need them. They'll still germinate after a couple of years if kept this way. They do not store as well at room temperature, lasting perhaps a year before losing viability. Just be sure to label what you have. I currently have a mess of unlabeled baggies of seeds that I thought I would remember but don't. *C. moschata* types regularly cross with others inside the species, which means if you grow a long-necked Central American pumpkin next to your Seminoles, then save seed, you may end up with weird, long-necked Seminole types the next year.

As a final note on pumpkins and squash—they do not like the high heat and bugs of midsummer in Florida. Get them in early. One year I had them pop up in my compost heap and run rampant, then die back in July and August, then somewhat recover in the fall and bear me a second crop. This is not common, however, so plant accordingly.

In a food forest, I find pumpkins and winter squash to be best utilized in the early phases when you have lots of open space. They make a great ground cover in sunny spots but do not like much shade. If you just cleared ground and started a food forest, consider putting in some pumpkin hills in between your newly planted trees so you can get yields while you're waiting. As the food forest matures, pumpkins must be relegated to the edges where they can get the sun they need to thrive.

Save seeds from fully ripe pumpkins by washing them and drying them out well, then storing in the fridge in a sealed bag or jar until needed.

Sweet Potatoes (S, C, N)

Latin name: *Ipomoea batatas*
Cold-hardiness: 32 degrees (aboveground)
Mature height if unpruned: 1'
Propagation: Slips, roots

Sweet potatoes are a top-notch staple calorie crop in the Sunshine State. Sweet potatoes are planted by cutting vines from existing sweet potatoes and planting them out. These are called "slips." In my garden I plant sweet potato slips about 12–16" apart in rows 3' apart. Loosen the ground before you plant them to ensure they can make decent roots. In the food forest, I tuck them here and there around trees and perennials in places where I have at least half sun. Slips do not need to be rooted before you plant them. Just cut pieces of sweet potato stem, remove all the leaves except for one or just the little ones, then plant them on their sides a couple inches deep with one end of the slip sticking out of the ground, then water them. For a few days, they'll wilt and look awful, but they root readily and start running quickly. At the base of each planted slip, potatoes will form in a few months.

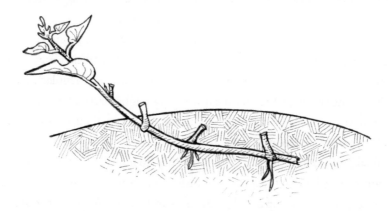

If you do not have slips to plant, it is easy to start your own from begged, borrowed or purchased sweet potato roots. I once bought an assortment of different sweet potatoes in varying colors from an organic market, started slips, then planted them willy-nilly in my garden. That year we had a lot of fun digging potatoes that ranged from white to yellow to orange and deep purple. To start slips from sweet potato roots, lay them on their sides in soil just beneath the surface. Water regularly but don't make them sopping wet. Keep this flat in half-sun. In a few weeks, shoots will start emerging from the roots. As they grow to 12" long, you can carefully trim or break them off to plant out. Planting season for sweet potatoes is year-round in South Florida and after all danger of frost in Central and North Florida. You can keep planting there until June or so. Sweet potatoes will grow in mulch or bare ground but they do not like full shade. Dappled shade will still get you some potatoes and I had good luck planting them in mulched areas of my food forest in North Florida, where they bore quite well. It's best to plant in different areas from year to year, but you might get away with growing them a couple of years in the same spot. My potato yields decreased greatly when I just let the vines keep running and running for a couple of years.

Sweet potatoes like organic matter in the ground and really appreciate potassium (wood ashes are a good source) but do not feed them much—if any—nitrogen or they will produce abundant vines and few roots. I have made this mistake before. The plants looked amazing but made almost no roots whatsoever.

Sweet potato leaves are edible raw or cooked but are reportedly much better for you cooked as they contain some anti-nutrients when raw.

After a few months in the ground, you can do some digging to see if your plants are making roots. The boniato types I have grown—that is, mostly red types with white flesh from Latin America and the Caribbean—took much longer to produce than the traditional American orange types. White varieties are starchier and drier and not as sweet but make a nice change from the very sweet orange types. I usually just plant sweet potato slips in the spring, then let them grow all the way into November when the weather gets too cool for much more growth, then I dig up the roots.

Sweet potato roots can be boiled or fried and, like the leaves, are not good to eat raw.

When you harvest your sweet potatoes, give them a week or two to lay out and cure in a shady, dry location or they will not taste as nice and sweet as the ones you buy from the store. Do not wash them before curing and be careful not to damage roots when you dig them or they won't keep as long. Once they are mature in the ground, you can dig them as you like over the course of some months or just harvest them all, cure them, and let them sit in a cool, dry location in cardboard boxes or baskets. They keep in my air-conditioned pantry for months. Remove any potatoes that go bad and eat damaged ones first.

Sweet potatoes make a very good ground cover for new food forest projects as they'll run rampant and suppress weeds while still getting you a harvest.

Feather Cockscomb/Lagos Spinach (S, C, N)

Latin name: *Celosia argentea*
Cold-hardiness: 32 degrees
Mature height if unpruned: 2–3'
Propagation: Seeds

Celosia argentea is a common ornamental flower which comes in a variety of beautiful forms. A cousin of amaranth and spinach, it has leaves that are a good, hearty green when cooked. I do not recommend eating them completely raw due to the oxalic acid content, but they are fine sauteed.

Seeds can be harvested when the flower heads get long and white. You can tip the points downwards and roll the bloom between your fingers to get the seeds to release. They are tiny, deep black and shiny. Plant after all danger of frost in spring. They can be direct seeded or transplanted.

Longevity Spinach (S, C, N)

Latin name: *Gynura procumbens*
Cold-hardiness: 32 degrees
Mature height if unpruned: 3'
Propagation: Cuttings

Longevity spinach (*Gynura procumbens*) was made for Florida. It's so easy to grow and healthy that you'll wonder how you went without it. The leaves have an interesting fresh flavor that I immediately liked. It's a good salad stuffer or a cooked green.

Longevity spinach is a half-vining herbaceous perennial that tolerates poor soil, drought and heat but benefits from water and compost. Propagation is by stem cuttings. Just break off a piece of stem, stick it in the ground, water it and it will root. Longevity spinach takes sun and shade well. Its pretty purple-and-green cousin Okinawa spinach has a milder flavor but was much less hardy in my North Florida garden, wilting in the heat and dying in the winters.

Longevity spinach does not like frost and often dies if it freezes to the ground. If a frost is coming, take a few cuttings from your plants in fall and put them in a pot to root, then plant them out again in spring.

Finding longevity spinach may not be easy. Ask around and make friends. People are often trading plants in the comments of my YouTube videos, so be friendly and you'll soon find yourself with some cuttings—and once you have them, you're off to the longevity spinach races.

Okinawa Spinach (S, C, N)

Latin name: *Gynura bicolor*
Cold-hardiness: 32 degrees
Mature height if unpruned: Up to 2'
Propagation: Cuttings

Okinawa spinach is a perennial vining ground cover, usually less than 16" tall. It's in the same genus as longevity spinach but has not grown as vigorously for me and did worse in full sun. The leaves are edible raw or cooked and make an excellent mild salad green. If your area freezes and your Okinawa spinach is out in the open, it will likely melt and die during a frost. It's a good idea to take cuttings and pot them up to plant again in the spring or plant this species in a sheltered area. Down in South Florida, Okinawa spinach is a great year-round salad stuffer. It's also prettier than longevity spinach. Its deep green leaves with purple undersides and its rambling nature make it a great ground cover for edible landscaping as well as a great addition to a food forest project. Okinawa spinach responds well to regular harvesting. Cuttings root easily in soil or in water.

Surinam Spinach/Waterleaf/Surinam Purslane (S, C, N)

Latin name: *Talinum fruticosum*
Cold-hardiness: 32 degrees
Mature height if unpruned: 2'
Propagation: Seed, cuttings

Surinam purslane is a perennial herb with small, attractive pink flowers. They are ridiculously easy to grow and can take drought and poor soil, though they make thicker and better leaves with regular rain and good soil. The leaves are edible raw or cooked, though sometimes can be a bit high in oxalic acid and will make your mouth feel scratchy when eaten raw. It likes full sun but can handle a little shade. Freezes may kill unsheltered plants to the ground in North Florida. Surinam purslane stems root readily— I often just stick them in the ground during the rainy summer months and they root. The plant also self-seeds prolifically and will show up all over the place, which I don't mind a bit.

African Blue Basil

NITROGEN-FIXERS AND SUPPORT SPECIES

In this chapter we'll run over some of my favorite nitrogen-fixing trees, plus a few other useful and pleasant species that may be worth adding to your Florida food forest system. The world of plants is so vast that I could make lists for years and not reach the end. These are just some good ones for starters. In a food forest your range of species is only limited by your climate and your imagination. Add whatever you like! These will just give you a head start. In the case of nitrogen-fixers and biomass/chop-and-drop species, add plenty of individuals so you will have something to feed your forest floor. Note that some of these trees are invasive species, which means you will have to decide if you really want to introduce them to your area or not. If they're already in your yard, though, use the heck out of them. I rarely kill invasive trees. Instead, I chop them down repeatedly to feed to the trees I want to keep. This has the dual benefit of giving me free mulch and keeping the invasives from setting seed.

African Blue Basil (N, C, S)

Latin name: *Ocimum kilimandscharicum x basilicum "Dark Opal"*
Cold-hardiness: 32 degrees
Mature height if unpruned: 3'
Propagation: Cuttings
Uses: Edible, pollinator attractor

If you can remember the Latin name for African blue basil, you are a better man than I. Come on! Latin is hard enough without all that craziness!

African blue basil is a sterile cross between African camphor basil and a purple sweet basil cultivar developed in the 50s. It's also a perennial, which is uncommon for basils. Though the leaves are edible and some people love them, they taste a bit like Vick's VapoRub smells. Where this plant really shines is as a pollinator attractor. If you plant one, it will be constantly abuzz with insect activity. They are lovely in a food forest and really feed the bees.

African blue basil does not set seed but starts easily from cuttings. Frosts may kill them so it's not a bad idea to start a few cuttings in fall and protect them through the winter if you live in North Florida.

Aralia (S)

Latin name: *Aralia spp.*
Cold-hardiness: 32 degrees
Mature height if unpruned: 3'
Propagation: Large cuttings
Uses: Hedging

When I was a kid my dad and my grandfather used aralia extensively for creating hedges in their South Florida yards. The common, broad-leafed type grows almost vertically and makes an attractive, tropical boundary for tropical climates.

You can take 5' stem cuttings, strip off most of the leaves, then bury the bottom of the cutting a foot or so in the ground and they will root. Just water them occasionally to get them started. Plant them a foot or two apart and you have a quick screen. Aralia takes sun or shade and there are a lot of quite ornamental cultivars with great variation in the leaf shapes and the size of the shrub. Though it's not a particularly good multipurpose plant, I am fond of it for sentimental reasons as they remind me of being a kid and helping dad plant them in our side yard. They do one thing and they do it well: hedging!

Australian Pine (S, C)

Latin name: *Casuarina spp.*
Cold-hardiness: Teens
Mature height if unpruned: 100+'
Propagation: Seed, cuttings
Uses: Nitrogen-fixer, timber, firewood

The tall, willowy growth of Australian pines is a common sight in South Florida. As a kid I remember stepping on their sharp seed "cones" while running down John U. Lloyd beach. According to the Florida Fish and Wildlife Conservation Commission:

Australian pine now occurs throughout South and Central Florida, the West Indies, Mexico, and elsewhere in tropical regions outside its native range.

Because of its aggressive growth rate, never plant Australian pine trees. There are native trees that provide shade and do not harm the environment. Possession of Australian pine with the intent to sell or plant is illegal in Florida without a special permit.

Several species of Casuarina were introduced from Australia to Florida during the 1890s. Although commonly called pines, these plants are angiosperms, not conifers. Australian pines were widely planted in Florida to form windbreaks around canals, agricultural fields, roads and houses. Habitats disturbed by both human activities and natural events seem particularly prone to invasions by Australian pine. Because Australian pine trees are resistant to salt spray, and can grow close to sea water, they have invaded thousands of acres of southeastern and southwestern coastal areas of Florida.

Hey—it's a pioneer species! It's just doing the jobs native plants won't do!

Seriously, though, it's highly invasive. Its "needles" drop on the ground and are allelopathic, suppressing the growth of other plants in the area. But it does have some great uses. First of all, the tree is a nitrogen-fixer which can be used to repair terrible ground by adding nitrogen. Second, it's got great timber. A reader once sent me a picture of a beautiful table his father made from Australian pine wood. Third, it's an amazing firewood.

Though we are not allowed by state law to plant them, I would definitely harvest existing ones for their wood, both for building projects and for fuel. According to Perdue University, "the wood, burning with immense heat, even when green, has been called the best firewood in the world."

If you have it, use it.

Bougainvillea (S, C)

Latin name: *Bougainvillea spp.*
Cold-hardiness: 32 degrees
Mature height if unpruned: 10–20'
Propagation: Cuttings
Uses: Death Hedge

One of my favorite sights in Key West are the sprays of bougainvillea blooms spilling over fences in the bright tropical sun. This plant is a tropical treasure that thrives on neglect. That said, the only use I have for them in a food forest is for hedging. They are a fantastic death hedge plant that tears up potential intruders while presenting a bright and cheery face to neighbors. Think of them as a gorgeous redhead in a green dress—with a Tommy gun. Cuttings root easily in mini-greenhouses. Just be careful as the roots break off very easily during transplanting.

Shepherd's Needle (N, C, S)

Latin name: *Bidens alba*
Cold-hardiness: 32 degrees
Mature height if unpruned: 4'
Propagation: Seed
Uses: Edible, Pollinator attractor

Though a much-hated weed in some yards, this is a wonderful plant. It's a no-care bee attractor that feeds hives across the state. The leaves are also edible and we enjoy their green, earthy flavor sauteed with our scrambled eggs in the morning. The small, daisy-like blooms turn into small, spiky heads of seeds with hooks on them that love to grab clothing and animal fur. If you want lots of pollinators in your yard, let some shepherd's needle grow. You almost certainly won't have to plant it, but if you want to propagate shepherd's

Bougainvillea

needle, just bury your prickly socks in the garden after walking through a patch of the stuff.

Black Locust (N, C)

Latin name: *Robinia pseudoacacia*
Cold-hardiness: Far beyond Florida
Mature height if unpruned: 4'
Propagation: Seed, cuttings
Uses: Nitrogen-fixer, timber

Black locust is another hated "invasive" in Florida. It appears here and there in North Florida and I've had friends complain about how much they hate this hard, thorny tree. It's got some great uses, though, and I would happily include a few in my food forest.

Steve Gabriel at Cornell University lists some of its benefits:

- Because it (black locust) fixes nitrogen from the atmosphere, the trees grow incredibly fast (3–4 feet in a season) and can quickly become windbreaks, shelterbelts, and shade and shelter for animals in silvopasture grazing systems.
- The nutritional value of the leaves is similar to alfalfa, making it a valuable feed for ruminant livestock. Some sources claim excessive consumption can lead to toxicity, but many farmers have found their animals naturally limit their intake. (horses excepted)
- The tree has been used to support nutrition in other crops, from grains to other trees. Research has shown increases in nitrogen in barley grain crops interplanted with locust, and black walnuts interplanted with locust as "nurse" trees were shown to rapidly increase their growth.
- The flowers are important sources of food for honeybees. In Hungary, Black Locust is the basis of commercial honey production.
- The high-density wood is the most rot resistant wood we can grow in our climate, making it an ideal material for fenceposts, hope poles, outdoor furniture, decks, and other projects that require weatherproof materials.
- Its BTU rating is among the highest, making it an excellent firewood in both heat value and coaling ability. At our last house, we actually ruined a woodstove by burning *too much* locust, which gets extremely hot.

There are plenty of reasons to grow this tree. Just put it someplace where the thorns won't be a problem. I think it would make a great chop-and-drop tree if you're not going to walk around barefoot. It will also grow readily from damaged roots and suckers whenever it likes, so keep that in mind. To grow your own black locust, nick and soak seeds in water overnight, then plant. Or transplant suckers.

Bottlebrush Tree (N, C, S)

Latin name: *Callistemon spp.*
Cold-hardiness: Far beyond Florida
Mature height if unpruned: 4'
Propagation: Seed
Uses: Pollinator attractor, hedging

This species is excellent for attracting bees to your food forest. It's also pretty and makes a nice boundary hedge. Bottlebrush likes full sun. Plant them here and there between your fruit trees for maximum pollinator action. I planted my first food forest bottlebrush after visiting Taylor Gardens Nursery and seeing one covered with buzzing honeybees. Sold!

Cassia (various) (N, C, S)

Latin name: *Cassia spp.*
Cold-hardiness: Varies
Mature height if unpruned: 4'
Propagation: Seed
Uses: Nitrogen-fixer

There are many cassia varieties that grow in Florida, most of which are nitrogen-fixing species with beautiful yellow flowers. Some are shrubs, some are trees. In both the North and South Florida food forest projects, I planted Christmas cassia for nitrogen-fixation. Though it may actually be a senna. Cassia is one of those plant genera where a bunch of stuff got dumped over the years. As IFAS notes:

Starting as early as 1912, the USDA Office of Foreign Seed and Plant Introduction made repeated imports of the plant we now know as Christmas cassia. Most of the introductions were under the name Cassia bicapsularis—now known as Senna bicapsularis—and that name has stuck with the plant for decades. Subsequent research has shown that almost all of the plant material cultivated under the name Senna bicapsularis is in fact Senna pendula. An examination of herbarium specimens from the University of Florida, University of South Florida, and Fairchild Tropical Botanic Garden suggests that true Senna bicapsularis is quite rare in cultivation in Florida, while Senna pendula is common and widespread.

TL;DR summary: cassias are a taxonomic dumpster fire.

If it's any kind of nitrogen-fixing bean and pea family thing, I usually plant it. Cassia trees usually start easily from seed that has been nicked and soaked in water overnight.

Cecropia (S)

Latin name: *Cecropia spp.*
Cold-hardiness: 32 degrees
Mature height if unpruned: 60'+
Propagation: Seed, Cuttings
Uses: Chop and drop, biomass, edible

Cecropia trees are a common sight in the West Indies and Central America, especially in disturbed areas. This fast-growing tropical pioneer species has a distinct spreading umbrella shape that makes it a beautiful addition to a food forest. It can be chopped repeatedly and used for animal fodder or compost or it can be allowed to become a canopy species. Because of its open growth pattern, it does not cast much shade on trees below.

The first time I saw one in person was at ECHO in Ft. Myers. Our guide mentioned how many large leaves the tree dropped and how useful they were for compost. When I moved to the Caribbean a few months later we had the tree everywhere and I got to know it much better. The leaves break down very fast and do make great compost, whether cut green or raked up after falling from the tree.

The fruit of this tree is also edible and reportedly sweet; however, the height of the tree makes harvest difficult. Leaves make a good tea and are a good smoke when used as tobacco substitute. Sadly, they do not contain nicotine so I don't get the point, but I did try them and they are a decent smoke.

Cecropia can be grown from seeds or cuttings.

Chaste Tree (S, C, N)

Latin name: *Vitex agnus-castus*
Cold-hardiness: Beyond Florida
Mature height if unpruned: 16'
Propagation: Seed, Cuttings
Uses: Pollinator attractor, medicinal

Chaste tree is a lovely, purple-flowered shrub or small tree that really brings in the butterflies. The hard little fruits are supposed to be good for balancing hormonal issues in women and easing the symptoms of menopause. The foliage has a pleasant earth aroma as well and is good for tea. Semi-hardwood cuttings are easy to root in mini-greenhouses. I planted a whole flat of cuttings a few months ago and put the planting flat inside a sealed white trash bag underneath a magnolia tree for a couple of months. When I opened up the bag, I had lots of rooted cuttings. I do not know how they start from seeds, as I haven't tried.

Comfrey (N, C, S)

Latin name: *Symphytum officinale*
Cold-hardiness: Far beyond Florida
Mature height if unpruned: 5'
Propagation: Seed, Division
Uses: Chop and drop, medicinal,
        pollinator attractor

There are some reports of comfrey being "dangerous" to consume, but I think these reports are overstated. That said, I am not a doctor and all that nonsense, so use comfrey leaves at your own risk. I had a bad cut on my finger once and a nurse friend recommended putting crushed comfrey on the wound as well as drinking a tea of the leaves. I did both and it healed remarkably fast. I have since used it to heal the wounds of friends and family. We smash the leaves into a paste with some rosemary and raw honey, then put it on skin irritations and cuts that aren't healing well.

Comfrey did poorly for me in my North Florida garden. It disliked the heat and needed more water than I wanted to give it, so for multiple years I quit recommending it to gardeners. Then in 2019, an attendee of one of my gardening events showed up with a bunch of huge, healthy comfrey which they had grown in South Florida. The variety I had been growing was "Bocking 14," and this was another, wilder type, so if you want happy comfrey, skip the Bocking stuff and get the toughest, wildest strains you can find.

Comfrey is beloved by permaculturalists due to its excellent fertilizing potential. It is an excellent nutrient accumulator and can be cut repeatedly and will grow back just fine. Comfrey handles shade in Florida and is excellent when planted around the base of fruit trees. Just chop down now and again and let the leaves rot in place to feed the tree—or plant a big comfrey patch somewhere and cut the leaves and throw them around anything you want to feed.

Roots can be divided and planted. Even small roots will often make new plants—just keep them moist until they get established. You can dig up a comfrey plant and cut up some of the roots, then bury them lightly in pots to grow. Shoots usually come up in a few weeks.

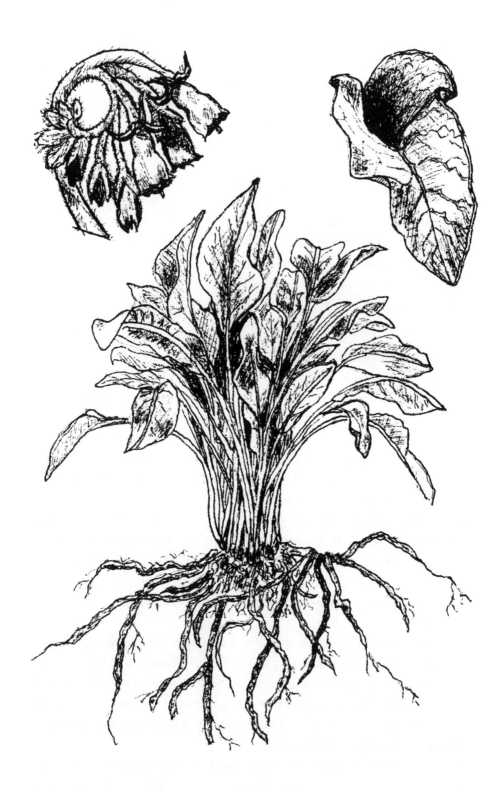

Comfrey

Coral Bean (S, C, N)

Latin name: *Erythrina herbacea*
Cold-hardiness: Beyond Florida
Mature height if unpruned: 3–5'
Propagation: Seed
Uses: Nitrogen-fixer, pollinator attractor

Coral bean is a Florida native that is somewhat common in the northern half of the state. It's a small perennial shrub that produces beautiful tubular blooms that hummingbirds love to visit. The resulting bean pods split open, displaying brilliant red beans inside. Do not make chili from them as they are poisonous. Also, baked beans are out. And definitely no coral beans and rice. Just enjoy how ornamental they are without putting them in your mouth.

Coral beans are good nitrogen-fixers and add beauty to the food forest, growing and blooming in partial shade or full sun. To grow your own coral bean plants, nick and soak the beans in water until they swell, then plant them.

Coral Honeysuckle (N, C)

Latin name: *Lonicera sempervirens*
Cold-hardiness: Far beyond Florida
Mature height if unpruned: 20'+
Propagation: Seed
Uses: Pollinator attractor

Coral honeysuckle is an attractive flowering vine that looks great climbing into your food forest trees. It's visited by hummingbirds and butterflies and is good for your soul. We grew one up into a pear tree in North Florida where it provided a popular rest stop for zebra longwings. They are

not reported to grow in the Southern half of the state. Coral honeysuckle can be grown from cuttings.

Dwarf Poinciana (N, C, S)

Latin name: *Caesalpinia pulcherrima*
Cold-hardiness: 32 degrees
Mature height if unpruned: 16'
Propagation: Seed
Uses: Nitrogen-fixer

When I was a kid there was one of these trees growing in my grandparents' side yard. They called it a "dwarf poinciana," which is just one of many common names for this lovely ornamental. It's also called Pride of Barbados and Peacock Flower, among other names. It's not really a dwarf form of the Royal Poinciana (*Delonix regia*) but it has similar blooms and leaves. Both are in the Fabaceae family and fix nitrogen.

This tree would sometimes freeze to the ground in my North Florida food forest and then grow back in the spring. We also used it as a chop and drop, though the branches can be spiny. To grow your own, nick seeds and soak them overnight, then plant.

Ear-pod Tree (N, C, S)

Latin name: *Enterolobium spp.*
Cold-hardiness: 32 degrees (young growth)
Mature height if unpruned: 80'
Propagation: Seed
Uses: Nitrogen-fixing, edible seeds

In March of 2015 I visited A Natural Farm in Howey-in-The-Hills with my friend Curtiss and bought a nice Cherry of the Rio Grande shrub for my North Florida food forest. On the way home to the Ocala area, I spotted a massive *Enterolobium contortisiliquum* (dare you to say it three times fast!) tree by the side of the road in Fruitland Park and Curtiss stopped so we could look at it. The tree was incredible—at least 60' tall with a spread of more than 100'.

Obviously, that sized tree would be a bit big for the average food forest, but before you get scared and decide not to plant one, remember that you can chop and drop almost anything. *Enterolobium* trees excel in Florida as fast-growing, nitrogen-fixing chop-and-drop trees for the food forest. If you have space in your yard to let one grow large they are magnificent—and if you ever get the chance to run one through a sawmill, the lumber is a lovely red-brown with white sapwood.

Its fellow genus-sharer *Enterolobium cyclocarpum* is the national tree of Costa Rica, where it is called "Guanacaste." That tree is known for its fast growth rate and massive trunk which is often used to make gigantic slab tables. The only variety I've seen in Florida is *Enterolobium contortisiliquum*, though *E. cyclocarpum* is certainly here as well. The two species are regularly mixed up. *E. cyclocarpum* has seeds that are edible when roasted. I found big stands of it in Indonesia and imported seeds to Grenada where it grew well in my tropical food forest. One day they may hate me for that, but hey—whatcha gonna do? The seeds cried out to be planted! It can't be as bad as Bill Mollison's ill-fated plantings of honey locust.

I saw multiple individuals of *Enterolobium* in Craig Hepworth's food forest in Citra which had frozen back partially and regrown larger for multiple years. The deep green of the growth even in poor sand attested to their usefulness as a nitrogen-fixer. This tree has great potential for repairing poor soil, regular chop-and-drop, charcoal making and for building a forest floor quickly.

If you find the "earpods" and want to plant your own *Enterolobium* trees, bust the pods open and remove the seeds inside. Then saw into the hard seeds and soak them overnight. They should swell up in the water. If not, nick them deeper and soak again until they do. Plant in the location you want them to grow or put them in pots to plant later. Seedlings emerge within three weeks.

Lead Tree (N, C, S)

Latin name: *Leucaena leucocephala*
Cold-hardiness: 32 degrees
Mature height if unpruned: 16'
Propagation: Seed
Uses: Firewood, nitrogen-fixing, animal fodder, chop-and-drop

Lead tree is very common across the Caribbean and can be seen here and there growing wild in Florida as an invasive species.

The UF Center for Aquatic and Invasive Plants notes:

Lead tree was most likely distributed by man because of its many uses. This multipurpose tree is used for fuel wood, lumber, animal fodder, and green manure. Ornamental uses include windbreaks, shade trees, and erosion control. Lead tree may have been introduced into Florida for cattle fodder and controlling erosion. Found in Southern Florida, including the Florida Keys, lead tree can be seen along roadsides and hammock margins in Miami-Dade and Monroe counties. Lead tree is a Category II invasive species.

I have also seen this tree father north in the state, particularly closer to the shore where overnight lows are not as harsh. I grew it North of Ocala and it would suffer some frost damage and come back. Lead trees are small but grow very fast and can be cut again and again for nitrogen-rich chop and drop. The long branches and trunks can be cut for decent rocket stove fuel.

To grow your own, nick the seeds and soak them in water overnight, then plant. Trees grow quite quickly and are an excellent feed for goats and other ruminants.

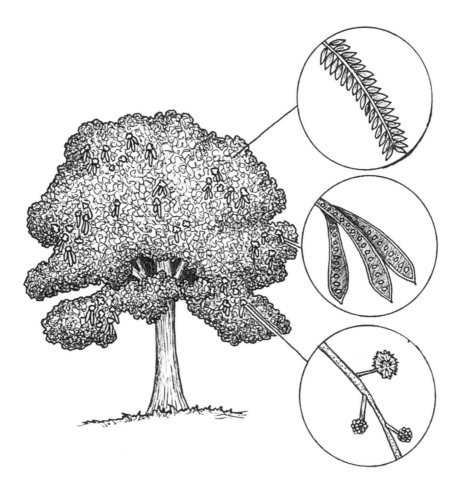

Mahogany (S)

Latin name: *Swietenia mahagoni*
Cold-hardiness: 32 degrees
Mature height if unpruned: 50'+
Propagation: Seed
Uses: Timber

When I was a kid my Grandfather was always growing mahogany trees from seed. He was a skilled carpenter and boatbuilder and got a kick out of the fact that he could grow mahogany in his yard down in South Florida. We children found the tree fascinating. It had these incredible rock-hard seed pods that would occasionally explode and release a burst of good-sized helicopter seeds that looked like something designed by Leonardo da Vinci. Grandpa never harvested any of the wood from the tree to the best of my knowledge, but it was right there shading the open side of the carport where he did his carpentry. Since then I have always had a fond place in my heart for the tree, as it reminds me of him.

There are multiple species of trees in the *Swietenia* genus that are called "ma-hogany," but *Swietenia mahagoni* is the one native to Florida. Though they aren't edible, I believe they're worth planting just for their beauty. They won't grow much north of South Florida, but in my hometown of Ft. Lauderdale I've occasionally seen them used as shade trees in the landscape.

My grandpa started seeds by sticking them in a potting soil full of dirt and letting the rain water them. He'd get seedlings, though I'm not sure how long they took to sprout.

I have read that the genetics of this species have degraded significantly due to the largest specimens being cut for timber, leaving less desirable and shorter trees behind. If you grow them from seed, I recommend planting seeds from the biggest, straightest and healthiest-looking tree you can find.

Mimosa Tree (N, C)

Latin name: *Albizia julibrissin*
Cold-hardiness: Far beyond Florida
Mature height if unpruned: 25'
Propagation: Seed
Uses: Nitrogen-fixer, chop and drop

Mimosa is a beautiful tree that, once invited into your area, never wants to leave. As the UF Center for Invasive and Aquatic Plants writes:

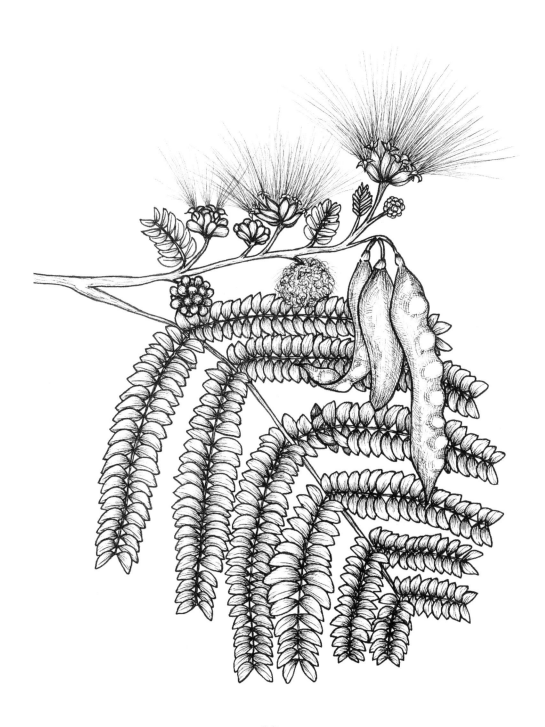

Mimosa

Mimosa is a strong competitor in open areas or forest edges. It can grow in various soil types, produces large amounts of seed, and resprouts when cut back or damaged. Mimosa reduces sunlight and nutrients available to desired species because of the denseness of the stand. An opportunist, mimosa will take advantage of disturbed areas, either spreading by seed or germinating in contaminated soil. Mimosa is often seen along roadsides and open vacant lots in urban/suburban areas and can become a problem along banks of waterways, where its seeds are easily transported in water.

Mimosa is not recommended by UF/IFAS. It is listed as invasive/no use in all parts of the state by UF/IFAS Assessment and as a Category 1 invasive by FLEPPC.

In North Florida the mimosa tree has become an ineradicable part of the forests. It's everywhere on roadsides and in abandoned lots, where it fills in open spaces and grows even on terrible soil.

If you have them in your yard, they are a good chop-and-drop species. I used their ability to fix nitrogen and regrow after pruning as a way to feed my fruit trees in my North Florida food forest. If you keep them from setting seed, they won't become invasive and are a useful species for building the forest floor fast. If they're not already in your area, you probably shouldn't add them.

To start seedlings, nick and soak the seeds in water overnight, then plant. Of course, this propagation note is for educational purposes only.

Empress Tree (N, C)

Latin name: *Paulownia spp.*
Cold-hardiness: Far beyond Florida
Mature height if unpruned: 40–50'
Propagation: Seed
Uses: Nitrogen-fixer, chop and drop, timber

Paulownia trees are known as the world's fastest growing hardwood. Like many fast-growing trees, they are also known to be invasive. The light, strong wood is used for musical instruments and other woodworking projects. I once owned a bass guitar with a Paulownia body and it was amazingly light, though solid, with a good punchy tone. If you want to make bass guitars in your food forest, I can recommend this tree. Besides its sweet, funky tones, the tree has huge leaves when young and creates a lot of biomass.

Though I had some Paulownias in my previous food forest project they were only a couple feet tall when I left and I did not get to give them a proper test as a chop and drop. They meet all the requirements for a great one, however, and I will be experimenting with them on my new property. This tree likes full sun.

P. tomentosa seems to be the most invasive member of this family. If you are concerned about causing ecological destruction but still want to try a Paulownia, grow one of the less aggressive members of the genus. In the Florida panhandle and across Alabama, Paulownias have become a troublesome invasive species.

Seeds are tiny and germinate readily when sprinkled on top of a flat of soil and kept moist. I recommend watering them, then putting some plastic wrap over the top until they germinate. When the seedlings are a few inches tall, pot them up or plant directly in the ground.

Pentas (N, C, S)

Latin name: *Pentas lanceolata*
Cold-hardiness: 32 degrees
Mature height if unpruned: 4'
Propagation: Seed, softwood cuttings
Uses: Pollinator attractor

Pentas are a cheery easy-to-grow flower in sun or half-shade. In the Southern half of the state they bloom year-round but will freeze back and re-grow in the Northern half.

If you want lots and lots of pollinators along with splashes of brilliant red, pink and white color, plant a few cultivars of Pentas in the food forest. They are lovely and will bring cheer to your yard.

Cuttings root easily.

Red Cedar (N, C)

Latin name: *Juniperus virginiana*
Cold-hardiness: Far beyond Florida
Mature height if unpruned: Varies from
shrub-size to large tree
Propagation: Seed, Cuttings
Uses: Timber, gin, hedge

Like its cousin *Juniperus communis,* this Florida native tree also produces berries you can use to flavor homemade gin. It's also great for rot-resistant timber, though its growth rate is slow. Propagation from both seeds and cuttings is a little difficult, making it worth buying from nurseries where it is commonly available. The tree is sometimes dioecious, sometimes monoecious, so plant a few if you wish to get berries.

Royal Poinciana (S)

Latin name: *Delonix regia*
Cold-hardiness: 32 degrees
Mature height if unpruned: 40'
Propagation: Seed
Uses: Nitrogen-fixer, chop and drop

The Royal Poinciana, also known as the Flamboyant Tree, is a classic ornamental tree in South Florida and through the Caribbean islands. Its nitrogen-fixing ability is in some doubt due to the lack of nodulation on the roots; however, its rich green color even in poor soil indicates that like many other members of the *Fabaceae* family, it's almost certainly making its own nitrogen. The tree grows quite fast into a large, dropping umbrella shape. I planted one

Red Cedar

in North Florida despite its tropical pedigree and though it has not grown into a full tree, it regrows regularly after frosty winters. Chopped branches and leaves rot down quickly and are useful for building a forest floor.

To germinate royal poinciana seeds, break open the giant pod and remove the seeds, then nick the hard seed coats and soak them overnight. Plant seeds in pots. Germination usually takes place in about two weeks.

Shampoo Ginger (N, C, S)

Latin name: *Zingiber zerumbet*
Cold-hardiness: 32 degrees
Mature height if unpruned: 4'
Propagation: Roots, division
Uses: Lotion

This ginger is all over the place. Though the roots are technically edible, they taste like bitter dirt. The long-lasting flower cones can be squeezed and the juice that emerges is useful for your hair and skin. The plants die back in winter and remerge in spring. Frosts won't kill them as they come back just fine from the roots.

Shampoo ginger grows best with some shade. Divide clumps and plant the roots to get more shampoo ginger than you would ever want or need.

Silverthorn (N, C, S)

Latin name: *Eleagnus pungens*
Cold-hardiness: Varies
Mature height if unpruned: 16'
Propagation: Layering
Uses: Death Hedge, nitrogen-fixer, edible

Silverthorn is a common hedge plant with attractive dark-green and silver growth on rich brown stems. It bears small edible fruits in late winter which are good when eaten fully ripe. The sharp branches and massive mounding growth habit of silverthorn makes it a very good privacy screen and barrier to both man and beast. They are impenetrable! I planted silverthorn along the edge of my nursery in North Florida to keep the

neighbors from having to look at my piles of potting soil and pots. Right next to the

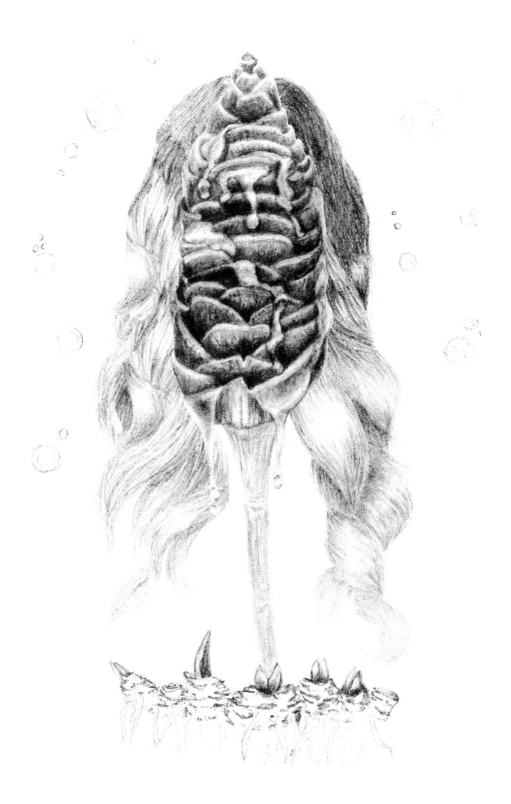

Shampoo Ginger

hedge I also planted three citrus trees, which I regularly fed by chopping and dropping silverthorn prunings around them. Those trees grew like gangbusters. It loves full sun but also grows in partial shade.

I have not attempted to grow silverthorn from seed but I have had luck burying a portion of a living branch and letting it root in the ground. We also successfully rooted cuttings under mist, though it took some time for them to take and the strike rate was poor.

Tree Marigold/Mexican Sunflower (S, C, N)

Latin name: *Tithonia diversifolia*
Cold-hardiness: 32 degrees
Mature height if unpruned: 20'
Propagation: Cuttings
Uses: Pollinator attractor, nutrient accumulator,
biomass producer, chop and drop

When I found out about these guys years ago, I was hooked. Known as "Mexican sunflowers" or "tree marigolds," these knock-out flowers are 15–20' tall. They're massive and excellent for serious chop-and-drop, as a gardener can cut them 3–4 times a year and throw the stems and leaves around plants and trees that need feeding.

The abstract of one study I found on the use of *T. diversifolia* reports:

Green leaf biomass of tithonia is high in nutrients, averaging about 3.5% N, 0.37% P and 4.1% K on a dry matter basis.... Tithonia biomass decomposes rapidly after application to soil, and incorporated biomass can be an effective source of N, P and K for crops. In some cases, maize yields were even higher with incorporation of tithonia biomass than with commercial mineral fertilizer at equivalent rates of N, P and K. In addition to providing nutrients, tithonia ... can reduce P sorption and increase soil microbial biomass.

I had a more in-depth study on their potential posted to my website but the link to the original is now gone. Suffice it to know that this plant has been Scientifically Approved (TM) for fertilizing your Florida food forest.

In the northern half of the state *T. diversifolia* freezes in the winter and comes back from the roots in spring.

The only time of year my Mexican sunflowers bloomed in my North Florida food forest was in November, but they bloom much longer in the Great South Florida Food Forest Project. The butterflies and bees love the flowers and the blooms make

great cut flowers, with a rich honeyed aroma. When one of my children was born I remember cutting a bunch of the blooms and putting them next to the bed where Rachel was recuperating with our newborn.

Cuttings root very easily. Just pop pieces of woodier stem pieces into a pot or the ground and they'll be growing in no time. Plant them out after the last frost and you'll have your own forest of giant flowers by next fall.

Plant them everywhere. Cut again and again and feed that food forest!

One final note: there is a cousin of *T. diversifolia* which is also called "Mexican sunflower." It's Latin name is *T. rotundifolia*. Don't mix them up, as *T. rotundifolia* is an annual, is much smaller, and does not work well as a chop and drop.

Water Hyacinth (N, C, S)

Latin name: *Eichhornia crassipes*
Cold-hardiness: Far beyond Florida
Mature height if unpruned: 1'
Propagation: Seed, division
Uses: Nutrient accumulator, biomass producer

Water hyacinth is a prolific invasive aquatic plant that costs the state of Florida millions every year. It's a biomass machine, reproducing at an incredible rate and choking up waterways. It's also a great fertilizer for your gardens.

Once removed from the water, the plant dies and rapidly rots down into the ground, releasing water and a range of nutrients. It's worth growing in ponds (kept far from any waterways!) just to add to your gardens and compost piles.

A gardener could throw one plant in a pond and it would quickly turn into many plants, which could then be harvested for compost. Actually, don't do that. Please forget I ever said it was possible.

CONCLUSION

There are a bazillion good reasons to get started with a food forest here in Florida.

If you're worried about neighbors thinking you're nuts, do a little extra planting and mulching so your forest looks like landscaping. Get going!

If you're not sure what to plant, plant a bunch of everything and then give away the fruit you don't like to the poor. Pop trees in the ground!

If you're worried about moving one day, don't. Just add lots of fruit trees and perhaps someone else will enjoy them. You've made the world a better place. Get outside and get planting!

If you're worried about an uncertain future, having a lot of food planted in the ground will be a weight off your shoulders. Go plant!

I hope to see lots of food forests pop up across our state.

Please visit me on the web at www.thesurvivalgardener.com for more inspiration and thank you for reading.

May God bless your efforts.

David The Good

APPENDIX : NORTH/CENTRAL FLORIDA GARDENING CHEATSHEET

Though South Florida is incredible for growing a wide range of tropical species, the rest of the state doesn't have it so easy. To help those of you in USDA zones 8 and 9 decide how hard you want to work at gardening, I present the following list of plants according to how easy or difficult they are to grow in Florida north of Orlando.

Totally Stupid Easy:

Amaranth, Boniato, Canna lilies (edible flowers/roots), Chaya, Collards, Loquat, Mulberries, Mung beans, Mustard, Perennial cucumber (ivy gourd), Persimmon *(native and Japanese),* Southern peas, Spanish needle *(Bidens alba),* Sugar cane, Sweet potatoes, Water Spinach, Wild Plums, Yams *(Dioscorea spp.),* Yard-long beans (snake beans), Yaupon holly (for tea)

Still Pretty Easy:

Basil, Cassava, Chinese water chestnuts, Dill, Everglades Tomato, Fig, Florida cranberry (Jamaican sorrel or "roselle"), Green beans (bush), Hot peppers, Kale, Lettuce, Loofah gourd, Malabar spinach, Malanga, Moringa, Mysore raspberry, Nopale cactus, Okra, Peanuts, Pears, Peas, Radishes, Seminole/Tan cheese pumpkin, Simpson stopper, Turnips, Wormwood

Takes Some Work:

Apples, Avocados (cold-hardy types), Banana (Raja puri, Orinoco, finger types), Banana (Cavendish, Gros Michel, grocery types), Beets, Bell Peppers, Bitter melon, Blueberries, Broccoli, Cabbage, Cantaloupe, Carrots, Cattley guava, Cauliflower,

Chard, Chestnut, Cucumbers, Eggplant, Elderberry, Garlic, Grapes (muscadine), Grain corn, Jujube, Kohlrabi, Longevity Spinach, Muscadine grapes, Naranjilla, Nasturtium, Okinawa spinach, Olive, Onions, Oregano, PawPaw, Peaches, Pecans, Pineapple, Pomegranates, Rosemary, Strawberries, Summer squash/Zucchini, Sunflowers, Surinam cherry, Surinam purslane, Tea *(Camellia sinensis)*, Thornless blackberries, Tobacco, Tomatoes (cherry), Watermelon, Wheat, White potatoes, Winter squash (most types)

Getting Danged Hard:

Asparagus, Brussels Sprouts, Carob, Cherries (except black cherry), Cinnamon, Citrus *(Citrus spp.),* Coffee, Comfrey (Bocking 14), Hops, Jabuticaba, Jerusalem artichokes, Katuk, Key Lime, Kiwi, Mangos, Papaya, Pigeon pea, Plantains, Raspberry (except Caroline and Mysore), Rhubarb, Runner bean, Tomatoes (non-cherry types)

Forget It:

Betel nut, Black sapote, Brazil nut, Breadfruit, Cacao, Coca, Coconut Palms, Cranberries, Gooseberries, Head lettuce, Horseradish, Jackfruit, Longan, Lychee, Macadamia nut, Plantain, Tamarind, Vanilla

THE ARTISTS

Bloom, Andrea Kay: Andrea is passionate about growing happy, edible plants and happy people. She devotes herself to learning all she can and then taking action to better her life and the lives of others, especially her husband and her three living littles. Andrea has suffered many catastrophes in her life, from being hit by a car, to losing her first child, to losing her home and town to wildfire. Yet through it all, she keeps going, and she keeps growing. Andrea's latest project is creating Food Forest Rows. Last spring she planted 450' worth of 6-foot-wide mounded rows on a quarter-acre suburban lot. She has studied Environmental Horticulture, Restoration Ecology, Urban Forestry, Regenerative Agriculture and Permaculture, Experiential Education, Soil Science, Biology, and Chemistry at UC Davis, CSU, Sacramento, and Sacramento City College. However, she has studied so much more through reading, observing, and experimenting outside of college! (p. 298)

Coggins, Colleen: Just your garden-variety bear who loves to draw. (p. 125, 181)

Craighead, Michael: Michael owns and operates Nero digital design studio based in Roanoke, Virginia. Nero specializes in Brand Identity, Brand Development, Web Design, Graphic Design, and Video Marketing. (p. 102, 200, 231, 272)

Darasart, Sayamol (Saya): Sayamol is a Branding Designer, Event Designer, Artist, and Florist from Thailand. She is passionate about flowers, nature, and wedding events. Her dream is to have her art exhibited in another country. (p. 137, 233, 262)

Davis, Marissa: Marissa decided to learn to draw while on bedrest during her second pregnancy. Every day she drew her mom's tabby cat, Clarence, plus anything else she could see from her spot on the recliner. A month after her son was born (full-term, thank you God!), she saw a post from her favorite gardening YouTuber asking for volunteers to illustrate a food forest book. Marissa decided this would be the perfect challenge to test her new skills and cap off an unexpected yet rewarding era of her life. (p. 284, 286, 287)

Dolomore, Kate: Kate is a self-taught artist who grew up in the woods of Central Florida. When not creating art, Kate is outside birding, botanizing, and reveling in the abundance of inspiration provided by nature. (p. 167, 199, 250)

Evans, Kayla: Kayla is a true daughter of the South, raised in Texas with arts and crafts in hand since as early as she can remember; she was always a creator at heart.

When not at her desk, you can typically find her knee-deep in the garden watching things grow. (p. 6, 150, 299)

Fairchild, Lacey: Based in British Columbia, Lacey is an illustrator and cartoonist. After doing freelance character design work for many years, Lacey has recently branched into book covers and interiors. She has created illustrations for Castalia House's *Junior Classics*, *Heidi*, and *The Jungle Books*. She also illustrates and writes for Arkhaven Comics's *Hypergamouse* comic strip. (p. 145, 149)

Feng, Lejia: Lejia is an illustration student and is happy to be part of this project. She hopes this book inspires you to grow your own food forest! (p. 151, 165)

Gallo, Sophie: Sophie Gallo is a self-taught painter, born and raised in the beautiful state of Michigan. When she isn't busy creating paintings for commissions and her Etsy business, NewShirePenAndBrush, she spends her time writing and working in her garden. (p. 22, 83, 84, 155, 215, 245, 283)

Gebeline, Monique Monique has been married 23 years, has four children (three sons, one daughter), three dogs, two cats, and over 300 plants/trees/shrubs/vines and nine garden beds on two acres. Originally from Philadelphia, PA, she moved to coastal Mississippi eight years ago. It was the best thing she ever did. She has been a stay-at-home mother most of her life but is now working as a shipping coordinator at the logistics company her husband works for. Her oldest son passed away from a rare spinal/nerve cancer at age eight (diagnosed at age four) in 2007 (he would be 22 now). In Philadelphia, Monique's family was active in the childhood cancer community and local children's hospitals and operated a 501c3 in her son's name, helping families with housing and medical expenses/needs. She has had medical issues and challenges for the last ten or more years and finally was diagnosed with autoimmune inflammatory arthritis. Gardening has helped her through all of it, and the community holds the greatest people on the planet. (p. 147, 168, 170)

Giroux, Jessica-Lynn: Jessie is a wife and mother of three currently living in Rhode Island. She is a self-taught artist specializing in pen-and-ink drawings, watercolor, paper-craft, and graphic design. She has been creating primarily with watercolor and micron pens for the last three years. In the last year, her greeting card business has grown substantially with custom handmade greeting cards available in various designs and media. Gardening has always been a passion that she now shares with her family and sees as a way for her to connect with God. She and her husband have dreams of a homestead but for now, are blooming where they're planted. Follow her on Instagram @jessie_g_art_ or email her at jessie.giroux.art@gmail.com. (p. 59, 110, 115, 116, 159, 184, 293)

Guidry, Bambi Sue Pitre: Bambi currently resides in Thibodaux, Louisiana, with her husband, Gus. Raised between her two homes in Naples, Florida, and Golden

Meadow, Louisiana, her art mimics the surroundings and culture of her two beloved states. She is self-taught, dabbling throughout life but taking a more serious path in the last five years. Her initial studies were in oil but have expanded to acrylics, watercolors and ink. (p. 183, 185)

Hale, "Buddy" Lonnie: Buddy Hale has practiced the craft since he was a young man. He enjoys sculpting, painting, and drawing images inspired by the loving forces of nature. He loves to teach the next generations what awesomeness lies all around them. Buddy believes there is never truly a dull moment. He loves to capture the beautiful design that flows through us all. It is an eternal job to do so. (p. 107, 240)

Handrich, Loren: Loren is a wife and stay-at-home mother to four in Northwest Montana. (p. 127, 129, 130, 155, 209, 216)

Hay, Jennifer: Jennifer is a homeschooling mom of two boys who occasionally dabbles with drawing, chalk, and watercolor; she is often found singing praises to God; slowly becoming a journeyman blacksmith, and channeling her inner hobbit through a love for plants and food. (p. 191, 256, 288)

Holcombe, Hollie: Hollie lives east of Portland, OR with her husband Chris, their spirited seven-year-old kid, and a dog. She has a Permaculture Design Certificate from Oregon State University, a Master's of Architecture from the University of Pennsylvania, and a B.S. in Architecture from the University of Minnesota. She currently chairs the planning commission of her small city when she's not helping with plants or keeping her CAD landscape plan up to date. (p. 17, 70, 111, 112, 154, 163, 236)

Howard, Rebecca: Follower of Jesus, saved only by His Grace, wife of a great man, veteran homeschool mom, grandmother, musician, artist, and backyard subtropical gardener. Her long-term goal is to own a golden retriever therapy dog to cheer and encourage those who need cheer and encouragement. (p. 178, 182, 203, 246)

Humphries, Jeremiah: Jeremiah is an illustrator from Minnesota. He writes: "Please hire me so I can buy more motorcycles, kettlebells, and beef." Jeremiah was also the inspiration behind the Jack Broccoli novel series, as well as the illustrator of the latest entry, *Garden Heat: A Jack Broccoli Novel*. (p. 2, 4, 12, 61, 74, 88, 89, 93, 94, 95, 96, 97, 201, 201, 292, 282)

Jacob, Carolyn: A native Floridian, Carolyn is "livin' the dream" with her husband Matt, children Timothy and Toriana, and an assortment of furry, feathered, and shelled critters. Her interests include herbal and natural health, growing a food forest, and trying to learn old-timey, self-sufficiency skills. She enjoys going on drawing dates with her kids and carves out time for art, coffee, and relaxing in the AC! She hopes to eventually grow and harvest her own coffee. She has one plant—so far. (p. 210, 301)

Kersh, Katie: Katie lives in Louisiana, where she likes to drink coffee, draw, and hang out with her family and friends. (p. 36, 48, 190)

Krieser, Elan: Elan is a self-taught artist whose abilities have been present since early childhood. She was born and raised in Regina Saskatchewan, CA, and has shown her original artworks with the Regina Federation of Artists (RFA) in their bi-annual spring and fall art shows. Elan works with several mediums, but her favorite and original love is for pencil mediums, including chalk pastels. Elan has donated prints of her work to Habitat for Humanity, Breast Cancer Action Saskatchewan, and the Regina "Curling Classic" for Parkinson's Research. (p. 114, 108)

Land, Amanda: Amanda is a Florida native designer and illustrator with a gardening obsession. You can find her on Instagram @landofamanda for commissions, collaborations, or to check out her humbling ventures in organic Florida gardening. (p. 81, 157)

Laughlin, Hanna: Hanna is a middle-grade art teacher in central Florida. She enjoys gardening and working towards establishing a homestead. She absolutely loves her life as a mommy to Eoin (6) and wife to her husband, Hoss. Her family's dream is to move somewhere cold and open a Christmas tree and reindeer farm under the name Off Kilter Holiday Farms, with the intent of hosting a one-stop holiday destination. (p. 173, 198, 205, 226, 251, 291)

Mills, Tom: Tom is a mission and sustainability-focused video producer as well as a content creator on YouTube (GreenShortz and GreenShortz DIY channels). He is an Eagle Scout and loves mountain biking and being outdoors. (p. 280, 281)

Mosley, Colton: Colton is a young artist who was one of the very first to submit a piece for this book. (p. 218)

Mize, Ruth: Ruth is a recent high school graduate entering into art school with a plant-passionate dad. (p. 188, 189)

Neimes, Michael "Nemo": Michael is a born-and-raised Floridian. He got his love of nature from his grandparents. His grandpa had his own garden and many fruit trees in his yard. His maternal grandmother always had a garden and would take him foraging for mushrooms and blackberries. Michael planted his first tree from seed (orange tree) at seven and recently started gardening after purchasing his first house. Michael is thankful to David for so much guidance via his books and videos! (p. 119)

Pappas, Oliver Sage: Oliver Sage Pappas grew up on the foggy coast of central California, the middle son of two working artists. He was encouraged early on by his mother to pursue his talent in art and later attended the San Francisco Art Institute and the Academy of Art in San Francisco, where he studied Illustration, Fine Art, and Painting. Most recently, Oliver has been working primarily with digital illustration but still draws much of his inspiration from nature. He now lives with his family in Florida, where he enjoys the colorful abundance of subtropical gardening. (p. 132, 134, 156, 196, 242)

Price, Laura: Laura is an artist and professional violinist who tried to draw a mango for this book, only to find out that she was violently allergic to mangos. Her arms and hands became so swollen after handling the fruit that she was unable to play her violin. She was not able to finish her drawing, but we are glad she tried—and that she lived through the ordeal. My apologies, Laura!

Rafalski, Wendy: Wendy likes to grow stuff and paint stuff. Zone 5b sandy loam is what she has to work with. (p. 117, 135, 227, 228, 229)

Sacred Visions Studio – Arianna, Kai, & Avery Nakashima: Three siblings living in Florida, passionate about art, gardening, and making a positive difference in the world. Together they create eBooks, animation, music, and more. Additionally, they have worked on two murals at the Wakulla County Ext, in Crawfordville, FL. You can find them at www.SacredVisionsStudio.com or www.AwakenTheWildSoul.com. (p. 140, 146, 161, 187, 193, 195, 217, 260)

Schallert, Nicole: Nicole Schallert is a student at Dr. Phillips Elementary School in Orlando, FL. She enjoys gardening and art. Her artwork is often inspired by Pablo Picasso and Romero Britto and takes on a rainbow of colors. She has won multiple art contests, and her work was displayed at the district office. This book was Nicole's first experiment with drawing and shading all in pencil. She enjoyed the challenge and did much research with her dad to make sure the illustration was accurate. Her father, Greg Schallert, aided by cleaning up the digital artwork after it was scanned. He also digitally drew an up-close leaf and fruit to accompany Nicole's work. When not creating, the family enjoys exploring all that Florida has to offer, including trails, forests, gardens, beaches, and of course, theme parks. (p. 106)

Sensible, Tom: Tom likes to build things from wood. He also enjoys drawing, piddling around in the garden, and playing the banjo. (Please note that "piddling around in the garden" is not to be confused with some of David The Good's watering/fertilizing techniques. It simply means "having fun.") When writing bios, Tom speaks about himself in the third person. He feels that if he does this, it will sound as if some profoundly wise art-scholar was writing the words instead of him. (p. 25, 33, 67, 73, 76, 86, 104, 105, 166, 176, 212, 259)

Skoglund, Anders: Anders' two biggest passions in life are drawing and gardening. You can find his art on deviantart.com/paranoidanders or swedishdadbear on Instagram. (p. 72)

Stroup, Jeremy: Jeremy Stroup is an artist based in Fort Wayne, IN. He currently works in fine art and illustration, often focusing on local flora and fauna. He has a passion for gardening, video games, and martial arts movies. (p. 138, 152, 153, 153, 175, 186, 220, 221, 222, 269)

Suarez, Lydia Jane: Lydia Suarez has a B.S. in Biology from James Madison University and has a passion for homesteading. Growing up in the suburbs of Virginia Beach, Lydia always knew she had a calling to live the farm life and has worked on horse farms in her hometown and central Virginia, training horses and fox hunting. While living on a horse farm, Lydia took advantage of empty space to grow food. Lydia's current endeavor involves her new business, Teacup Greens LLC, growing and selling microgreens and nursery stock at the local Farmers Markets in Hampton Roads, Virginia. (p. 163, 274, 279, 295, 296)

Sujay, C.S: Sujay is not a professional but enjoys sketching as a hobby. (p. 214)

Sumasky, Jesse: Jesse is a 25-year-old Southwest Florida native, who loves growing tropical fruit trees and vegetable gardening. (p. 106, 172, 174, 219)

Tahiri, Michelle: Michelle is inspired by her love of Mother Earth. Her creative designs are infused with trees, plants, water, and wildlife. She uses a variety of media to express her passions, including painting, sketching, wood burning, and photography. She often utilizes natural materials of seashells, rocks, and wood as backdrops. Currently, she spends her time transforming her property in central Florida into a permaculture food and medicinal forest using many native edible plants. She plans to open her property to the public by 2025. (p. 143)

Tillman, Meggie: Meggie is an artist who lives in Monterey, California. She works with oil and acrylic paints, colored pencils, and alcohol markers. She lives with Steve, the Musical Gardener, and Jack, the Playful Dog Who Loves to Take Walks. (Note: never let your dog have access to your keyboard!!) (p. 50, 252, 287)

Trotter, Aaron Voronoff: A world-traveling sketch artist, Aaron has visited many cities to draw his Illustrated Playing Cards. During the pandemic, he rediscovered a love for gardening and found David The Good a great inspiration. (p. 136, 161, 238)

Werth, Lori: Raised in Kansas, Lori Werth now resides in sunny Florida. Lori draws from a successful career as a graphic designer and photographer, having spent 30 years with the U.S. Air Force as a graphic designer and photographer. Having been an artist all of her life, she now enjoys pulling from her favorite turquoise color of the emerald coastal waters. Her favorite medium in this season of life is designing fluid art on canvas with acrylics, epoxy, and glass. For more about Lori and her artwork, email her at lawerth@gmail.com (p. 277)

West, Kevin: Kevin is a founding partner and Executive VP of Full Media, a healthcare digital marketing agency. He lives with his wife, Stephanie, and children: Rowen, Kainen, and Kade, in Chattanooga, TN. (p. 248, 297)

Whitley, Kindell: Kindell is an artist with a passion for gardening. She has been growing her own food for the last 20 years, from desert areas to swamps, and she is always learning. She works mainly in graphite, acrylic, and digital graphics. (p. 271, 38)

Thanks also to these artists, whose illustrations we didn't manage to fit in the text.

Black Pepper, by Laryssa Herbert   *Nitrogen Fixing Pods, by Cat Owens*

Black Sapote, by Gregory Schallert

ABOUT THE AUTHOR

Growing food is an obsession for David The Good. Every year he tests crops, experiments with fertilizers, analyzes yields and writes extensively on his results. Along the way, he's planted a wide variety of international root crops, created three food forests in three separate climates, pored over thousands of pages of esoteric gardening texts, and become a sought-after expert in gardening and preparedness circles. His popular YouTube channel is one of the top resources for Florida gardeners and his books are regular bestsellers in their categories on Amazon.

Thanks to great parents who encouraged his writing and gardening skills, he latched onto the concept of organic food production at a young age, planting his first garden at age six. Since then he's spent almost four more decades in the garden and shared his knowledge with many thousands of readers in publications ranging from *Mother Earth News* to *Natural Awakenings* to *Backwoods Home*.

David currently has a quarter acre experimental garden, a tropical food forest at the southern tip of Florida, a plant nursery and a plant collection which includes a baffling array of edible and useful perennials.

He is the author of ten gardening books and two gardening thrillers.

David has also invested many hours testing low-tech gardening tools and solutions for grid-down situations.

He is also the husband of the lovely Rachel Goodman, who homeschools their many children while attempting to feed them all on the strange and experimental crops constantly making their way into the kitchen.

Ingram Content Group UK Ltd.
Milton Keynes UK
UKHW051713150523
421750UK00014B/105